DEVELOPMENTAL COGNITIVE NEUROSCIENCE

Library

To my parents, Krystyna Dobraczynska and James Johnson, who provided both my nature and my nurture.

DEVELOPMENTAL COGNITIVE NEUROSCIENCE

An Introduction

MARK H. JOHNSON

SECOND EDITION

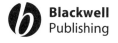

BLACKWELL PUBLISHING
350 Main Street, Malden, MA 02148-5020, USA
9600 Garsington Road, Oxford OX4 2DQ, UK
550 Swanston Street, Carlton, Victoria 3053, Australia

First published 1997
Second edition published 2005 by Blackwell Publishing Ltd

2   2005

Library of Congress Cataloging-in-Publication Data

Johnson, Mark H. (Mark Henry), 1960–
    Developmental cognitive neuroscience / Mark H. Johnson. – 2nd ed.
        p.   cm.
    Includes bibliographical references and index.
    ISBN 1-4051-2629-9 (pbk. : alk. paper)
    1. Cognitive neuroscience.   2. Developmental psychology.   I. Title.

    QP360.5.J64   2005
    612.8′2 – dc22

                                                                2004009017

ISBN-13: 978-1-4051-2629-8 (pbk. : alk. paper)

A catalogue record for this title is available from the British Library.

Set in 10/12.5 pt Rotis Serif
by Graphicraft Ltd, Hong Kong
Printed and bound in the United Kingdom
by TJ International, Padstow, Cornwall

The publisher's policy is to use permanent paper from mills that operate a sustainable forestry policy, and which has been manufactured from pulp processed using acid-free and elementary chlorine-free practices. Furthermore, the publisher ensures that the text paper and cover board used have met acceptable environmental accreditation standards.

For further information on
Blackwell Publishing, visit our website:
www.blackwellpublishing.com

⟐ CONTENTS

List of Figures   vii
List of Tables   x
Preface to the Second Edition   xi
Preface to the First Edition   xiii
Acknowledgements   xv
List of Abbreviations   xix

1   The Biology of Change   1

2   Building a Brain   19

3   Vision, Orienting, and Attention   53

4   Perceiving and Acting on the Physical World:
        Objects and Number   78

5   Perceiving and Acting on the Social World   92

6   Memory and Learning   119

7   Language   130

8   Frontal Cortex, Object Permanence, and Planning   146

9   Cerebral Lateralization   158

10 Interactive Specialization   164

11 Toward an Integrated Developmental Cognitive Neuroscience   178

Appendix: Atypically Developing Brains   185
References   189
Index   219

⟲ FIGURES

1.1   Seventeenth-century "spermist" drawing   4
1.2   Simple three-layered connectionist neural network   8
1.3   The epigenetic landscape of Waddington (1975)   15
2.1   Embryonic and fetal development of the human brain   21
2.2   Simplified schematic diagram showing cerebral cortex as
      a thin sheet composed of six layers   24
2.3   A typical cortical pyramidal cell   25
2.4   Cellular structure of the human visual cortex based
      on Golgi stain preparations   28
2.5   The development of density of synapses in human primary
      visual cortex   31
2.6   Cytoarchitectural map of the cerebral cortex   33
2.7   The radial unit model of Rakic (1987)   35
2.8   Patterning of areal units in somatosensory cortex   39
2.9   Schematic representation and summary of projections from
      the sensory receptor surface through the thalamus to the cortex
      in the normal visual system, the normal auditory system,
      and lesioned ferrets   43
2.10 PET images illustrating developmental changes in local cerebral
      metabolic rates for glucose (ICMRGlc) in the normal human infant
      with increasing age   47
3.1   Diagram of the developmental sequence of visual behavior and
      ventral- and dorsal-stream neural systems contributing to this   55
3.2   Simplified schematic diagram illustrating how projections from
      the two eyes form ocular dominance columns in the visual
      cortex   56
3.3   (A) Afferents from both eyes synapse on the same cells in layer 4
      (B) Afferents are segregated on the basis of eye origin   58
3.4   Typical development of ocular dominance patches of cortex   59

3.5   Diagram representing some of the main neural pathways
       and structures involved in visual orienting and attention   61
3.6   The oculomotor delayed response task as designed for use
       with infants   68
3.7   Grand-average saccade-locked potentials at Pz
       in 6-month-old infants, 12-month-old infants, and adults   69
3.8   Three types of saccades made by young infants in response to
       two targets briefly flashed as shown   71
3.9   Heart-rate-defined phases of sustained attention   74
4.1   Major routes whereby retinal input reaches the dorsal and
       ventral streams   79
4.2   A diagram showing the object processing model of Mareschal
       et al. (1999)   84
4.3   Gamma-band EEG activity recorded from infants in the Kaufman
       et al. (2003) experiment   86
5.1   Some of the regions involved in the human social brain network   93
5.2   Data showing the extent of newborns' head and eye turns
       in following a schematic face, a scrambled face, and a blank
       (unpatterned) stimulus   96
5.3   Human newborn and model response to schematic images   98
5.4   Outline sagittal view of the chick brain showing the main
       visual pathway to IMHV   100
5.5   The detailed architecture of the model is designed around
       the anatomical connectivity of IMHV and its primary input area,
       the hyperstriatum accessorium (HA)   101
5.6   Face-matching task   108
5.7   Example of the edited video image illustrating the stimulus for
       Experiment 1 in Farroni et al. (2000)   110
5.8   Results of the preferential looking study with newborns   111
6.1   Some of the key brain structures involved in memory,
       in particular the dorsolateral prefrontal cortex and
       orbitoprefrontal cortex   121
7.1   Some of the key structures involved in language processing   131
7.2   Cortical areas showing increases in blood oxygenation on fMRI
       when normal hearing adults read English sentences, when
       congenitally deaf native signers read English sentences,
       and when congenitally deaf native signers view sentences
       in their native sign language (American Sign Language)   136
7.3   Covert language task: group average fMRI activation in the
       unaffected and affected members of the KE family   143
8.1   Interaction between wakefulness and the linguistic nature of
       the stimuli   153
8.2   Summary of the sequence and anatomical distribution of
       the coherence patterns reported by Thatcher (1992)   154

8.3   (A) Rate of growth of EEG coherence between frontal and
      posterior lobes during middle childhood (F 7–P 3)
      (Thatcher, 1992); (B) Rate of growth of working memory
      (counting span and spatial span) during the same age range   155
9.1   A summary diagram of the model proposed by Geschwind,
      Behan, and Galaburda   161
10.1 The formation of representations in the cortical matrix model
      under two different architectural conditions   177

⬓ TABLES

1.1   Levels of interaction between genes and their environment   7
3.1   Summary of the relation between developing oculomotor pathways
      and behavior   65
3.2   Marker tasks for the development of visual orienting and attention   66
5.1   Stimulus-dependent effects of neurophysiological manipulations   102
6.1   The major memory systems and developmental tasks   122
10.1 Three viewpoints on human functional brain development   165

⬚ PREFACE TO THE SECOND EDITION

In the eight years since publication of the first edition of this book, developmental cognitive neuroscience has grown from newborn to toddler: still uncertain on its feet, but just beginning to put together fragments of knowledge. While the first edition was described by one leading figure as "a clarion call for a new way of doing both developmental psychology and cognitive neuroscience," the present edition puts more emphasis on making sense of the data already in hand.

Since the last edition a number of trends have become apparent in the field. First, the field has actually settled on the phrase "developmental cognitive neuroscience" as the name that best describes it. While it could be said that the first edition was the book that gave the field its name, it is my hope that its most important contribution was in attracting new researchers to the topic. Another trend of note is that some of the more heated debates about both behavioral and neuroscience evidence are becoming resolved as more evidence from different sources and methods becomes available. A surprising amount of agreement is breaking out in the field, with many issues turning out to be not black or white, but a subtle and interesting shade of grey. A third trend in the field is the recent flurry of books and review chapters. This made me question whether or not there was still a need for this book. On reflection, however, I have convinced myself that a basic introduction that serves as a "feeder" into more detailed and comprehensive edited volumes is still valuable. In fact, teachers should note that this second edition is specifically designed to be used with one or more of three current edited volumes (Nelson & Luciana, 2001; Johnson, Munakata, & Gilmore, 2002; de Haan & Johnson, 2003), and specific recommendations for further reading from these volumes are highlighted throughout the text. Since our young field can often feel somewhat fragmented to the student, I continue to believe that the single voice and unified perspective presented in this book are important.

Because this book is intended as an introduction, its coverage is necessarily selective. While this was challenging for the first edition, the massive increase in data over the past years made the prospect of choosing what to exclude even more daunting. As in the first edition, my choices were guided by focusing on areas where the developmental cognitive neuroscience approach has been most avidly pursued, rather than topics dominated by a developmental psychology or an adult cognitive neuroscience approach. Needless to say, my own particular interests and biases are evident throughout.

As with the first edition, I am indebted to colleagues and collaborators for educating and informing me on a variety of topics. I was privileged to chair a panel to review the current state of our knowledge on the development of Perception, Attention, and Memory (funded by the McDonnell and Sackler foundations). The discussions and presentations at these meetings brought me up to date, and particularly helped with the new chapter on Objects and Number. My colleagues at the Centre for Brain & Cognitive Development, particularly Gergely Csibra and Denis Mareschal, kept me abreast of current developments in a variety of fields. Rick Gilmore, Gaia Scerif, and Gert Westermann kindly provided their comments on a draft of the revisions to the book. Michelle de Haan, Brian Hopkins, and Annette Karmiloff-Smith gave me comments on specific chapters. From Blackwell, Sarah Bird persuaded me to undertake the second edition, and Jennie Brown, Justin Dyer, Roberta Herrick, Katie Menssen, Leslie Tucker, and Agnes Volein all contributed invaluably to the production.

Teachers may wish to note that a website accompanies this book with teaching aids: www.blackwellpublishing.com/dcn

PREFACE TO THE FIRST EDITION

In the first chapter of this book I describe some of the factors responsible for the recent emergence of a subdiscipline at the interface between developmental psychology and cognitive neuroscience. I have chosen to refer to this new field as "developmental cognitive neuroscience," though it has been known under a number of other terms such as "developmental neuro-cognition" (de Boysson-Bardies, de Schonen, Jusczyck, McNeilage, & Morton, 1993). Though a series of edited volumes on the topic has recently appeared, like most newly emerging disciplines there is a time lag before the first books suitable for teaching appear. This book and the Reader which I edited in 1993 (Johnson, 1993) are initial attempts to fill the gap. While some may believe these efforts to be premature, my own view is that the lifeblood of any new discipline is in the students and postdocs recruited to the cause. And the sooner they are recruited, the better.

Is developmental cognitive neuroscience really significantly different from other fields that have a more extended history, such as developmental neuropsychology or cognitive development? Clearly, it would be unwise to rigidly demarcate developmental cognitive neuroscience from related, and mutually informative, fields. However, it is my belief that the emerging field has a number of characteristics that makes it distinctive. First, while there is some disagreement about exact definitions, the fields of developmental neuropsychology and developmental psychopathology focus on atypical development, while commonly comparing them to normal developmental trajectories. In contrast, cognitive neuroscience (including the developmental variant outlined in this book) focuses on normal cognitive functioning, but uses information from deviant functioning and development as "nature's experiments" which can shed light on the neural basis of normal cognition. This book is therefore not intended as an introduction to the neuropsychology of developmental disorders. For such information the reader is referred to the excellent introductions by Cicchetti and Cohen (1995) and Spreen, Risser, and Edgell (1995).

Second, unlike many in cognitive development, this book adopts the premise that information from brain development is more than just a useful additional source of evidence for supporting particular cognitive theories. Rather, information about brain development is viewed as both changing and originating theories at the cognitive level. Third, developmental cognitive neuroscience restricts itself to issues at the neural, cognitive, and immediate environmental levels. In my view it is a hazard of some interdisciplinary fields that the focus of interest is diffused across many different levels of explanation. This is not to deny the importance of these other levels, but a mechanistic interdisciplinary science needs to restrict both the domains (in this case aspects of cognitive processing) and levels of explanation with which it is concerned. Finally, developmental cognitive neuroscience is specifically concerned with understanding the relation between neural and cognitive phenomena. For this reason, I have not discussed evidence from the related field of developmental behavior genetics. In general, developmental behavior genetics tends to be concerned with correlations between the molecular level (genetics) and gross behavioral measures such as IQ. With some notable exceptions, little effort is made to specifically relate these two levels of explanation via the intermediate neural and cognitive levels. Having pointed out the different focus of developmental cognitive neuroscience, my hope is that this book is written to be both accessible and informative to those in related and overlapping disciplines.

The above comments go some way to explaining the choice of material that I have presented in the book. However, I have no doubt that there is a substantive amount of excellent experimentation and theorizing that could have been included but was not. Since this is intended as a brief introduction to the field, I have chosen to focus on a few particular issues in some detail. Of course, the choice of material also reflects my own biases and knowledge since the book is intended as an introductory survey of the field as viewed from my own perspective. I apologize in advance for the inevitable omissions and errors.

The book is aimed at the advanced-level student and assumes some introductory knowledge of both neuroscience and cognitive development. Students without this background will probably need to refer to more introductory textbooks in the appropriate areas. I also hope that the book will attract developmentalists with an interest in learning more about the brain, and cognitive neuroscientists curious as to how developmental data can help constrain their theories about adult functioning. But most of all I hope that the book inspires readers to find out more about the field, and to consider a developmental cognitive neuroscience approach to their own topic.

⬚ ACKNOWLEDGEMENTS

The author and publishers gratefully acknowledge the following for permission to reproduce copyright material:

Figure 1.3 from C. H. Waddington (1975), *The Evolution of an Evolutionist*, Edinburgh University Press. Reproduced by permission of Edinburgh University Press. www.eup.ed.ac.uk

Figure 2.1 from W. Maxwell Cowan (1979), *The Development of the Brain*. Copyright 1979 by Scientific American, Inc. Reproduced by permission of Mr Nelson H. Prentiss.

Figure 2.6 from K. Brodmann in A. Brodal (ed.) (1981), *Neurological Anatomy in Relation to Clinical Medicine*, Oxford University Press, figure 12.2. Figure 12.2 from Chapter 12: The Cerebral Cortex, p. 791, from *Neurological Anatomy in Relation to Clinical Medicine*, 3/E, by Alf Brodal, copyright © 1969, 1981 by Oxford University Press, Inc. Used by permission of Oxford University Press, Inc.

Figure 2.7 from P. Rakic (1987), "Intrinsic and extrinsic determinants of neocortical parcellation: a radial unit model", in P. Rakic and W. Singer (eds), *Neurobiology of Neocortex*. Report of the Dahlem Workshop on Neurobiology of Neocortex, Berlin, 17–22 May, 1987, John Wiley and Sons. Copyright © 1987 John Wiley & Sons Limited. Reproduced with permission.

Figure 2.8 from D. D. M. O'Leary (1989), "Do cortical areas emerge from a protocortex?", *Trends in the Neurosciences*, vol. 12, pp. 400–406, Elsevier Trends Journals, Cambridge, UK. Copyright © 1989, with permission from Elsevier.

Figure 2.9 from A. W. Roe, S. L. Pallas, J. O. Hahm and M. Sur (1990), "A map of visual space induced in primary auditory cortex", *Science*, vol. 250, pp. 818–820, American Association for the Advancement of Science. Copyright © 1990 AAAS. Reproduced with permission of the AAAS and the authors.

Figure 2.10 from H. T. Chungani, M. E. Phelps and J. C. Mazziotta (1987), "Positron emission tomography study of human brain functional development", *Annals of Neurology,* vol. 22, pp. 487–497. Copyright © 1987. Reproduced by permission of John Wiley & Sons Limited.

Figure 3.1 from J. Atkinson and O. Braddick (2003), "Neurological models of normal and abnormal visual development", in M. de Haan and M. H. Johnson (eds), *The Cognitive Neuroscience of Development,* Hove: Psychology Press, figure 3.2, p. 50. Reproduced by permission of Thomson Publishing Services.

Figures 3.2 and 3.4 from K. D. Miller, J. B. Keller and M. P. Stryker (1989), "Ocular dominance column development: analysis and simulation", *Science,* vol. 245, pp. 605–615, American Association for the Advancement of Science. Copyright © 1989 AAAS. Reproduced with permission of the AAAS and the authors.

Figure 3.3 from R. Held (1985), "Binocular vision: behavioral and neuronal development", in J. Mehler and R. Fox (eds), *Neonate Cognition: Beyond the Blooming, Buzzing Confusion,* chapter 3. Copyright Lawrence Erlbaum Associates, Inc., Mahwah, New Jersey.

Figure 3.5 from P. H. Schiller (1998), "The neural control of visually guided eye movements", in J. E. Richards (ed.), *Cognitive Neuroscience of Attention,* Mahwah: Lawrence Erlbaum Associates, Inc., figure 1.20, p. 34.

Figure 3.7 from G. Csibra, L. A. Tucker, A. Volein and M. H. Johnson (2000), "Cortical development and saccade planning: The ontogeny of the spike potential", *Neuroreport,* vol. 11, 1069–1073, figure 1. Reproduced by permission of Lippincott Williams & Wilkins and the authors.

Figure 3.9 from J. E. Richards and B. J. Casey (1991), "Heart rate variability during attention phases in young infants", *Psychophysiology,* vol. 28, Cambridge University Press. Reproduced by permission of the publisher.

Figure 4.1 from M. A. Goodale, L. S. Jacobson, A. D. Milner and D. I. Perrett (1994), "The nature and limits of orientation and pattern processing supporting visuomotor control in a visual form agnosi", *Journal of Cognitive Neuroscience,* vol. 6, no. 1, 43–56. Copyright © 1994 by the Massachusetts Institute of Technology.

Figure 4.2 from D. Mareschal, K. Plunkett and P. Harris (1999), "A computational and neuropsychological account of object-oriented behaviours in infancy", *Developmental Science,* vol. 2, 306–317. Reproduced by permission of Blackwell Publishing.

Figure 4.3 from J. Kaufman, G. Csibra and M. H. Johnson (2003), "Representing occluded objects in the human infant brain", *Proceedings of the Royal Society B: Biology Letters, DOI 10.1098/rsbl.2003.0067,* figure 2. Reproduced by permission of The Royal Society and the authors.

Figure 5.3 from C. C. Goren, M. Sarty and P. Y. K. Wu (1975), "Visual following and pattern discrimination of face-like stimuli by newborn infants", *Pediatrics,* vol. 56, 544–549 and M. H. Johnson and J. Morton (1991), *Biology and Cognitive Development: The Case of Face Recognition,* Oxford: Blackwell Publishing, figure 4, p. 23. Reproduced by permission of Blackwell Publishing. (additional credit)

From James A. Bednar and Risto Miikkulainen, "Learning Innate Face Preferences", Neural Computation, 15:7 (July, 2003), pp. 1525–1557. © 2003 by the Massachusetts Institute of Technology.

Figure 5.6 from A. M. Passarotti, B. M. Paul, J. R. Bussiere, R. B. Buxton, E. C. Wong and J. Stiles (2003), "The development of face and location processing: an fMRI study", *Developmental Science*, vol. 6, no. 1, pp. 100–117, figure 2. Reproduced by permission of Blackwell Publishing.

Figure 5.7 from T. Farroni, M. H. Johnson, M. Brockbank and F. Simion (2000), "Infant's use of gaze direction to cue attention: the importance of perceived motion", *Visual Cognition*, vol. 7, no. 6, pp. 705–718, figure 4, p. 32. Reproduced by permission of Taylor and Francis Ltd. http://www.tandf.co.uk/journals

Figure 6.1 from F. Bloom, C. A. Nelson and A. Lazerson (2001), *Brain, Mind and Behaviour*; © 1985, 1988, 2001 by Educational Broadcasting Corporation with permission of Worth Publishers. From *Brain, Mind, and Behavior*, 3/e by Floyd Bloom, et al. © 1985, 1988, 2001 by Educational Broadcasting Corporation. With permission of Worth Publishers.

Table 6.1 from M. de Haan and M. H. Johnson (2003), *The Cognitive Neuroscience of Development*, Hove: Psychology Press, table 5.1, p. 103. Reproduced by permission of Thomson Publishing Services.

Figure 7.1 from C. M. Leonard (2003), "Neural substrate of speech and language development", *The Cognitive Neuroscience of Development*, Hove: Psychology Press, figure 6.3. Reproduced by permission of Thomson Publishing Services.

Figure 7.2 from H. Neville and D. Bavelier (2002), "Specificity and plasticity in neurocognitive development in humans", Brain Development and Cognition: A Reader, Oxford: Blackwell, pp. 251–270, figure 14.7. Reproduced by permission of the publisher.

Figure 7.3 from F. Liégeois, T. Baldeweg, A. Connelly, D. G. Gadian, M. Mishkin and F. Varga-Khadem (2003), "Language fMRI abnormalities associated with FOXP2 gene mutation", *Nature Neuroscience*, vol. 6, no. 11, pp. 1230–1237, figure 1. Reproduced by permission of the journal and the authors.

Figure 8.2 from G. Dehaene-Lambertz, S. Dehaene and L. Hertz-Pannier (2002), "Functional neuroimaging of speech perception in infants", *Science*, vol. 298, p. 2015, figure 3. Copyright © 2002 AAAS. Reproduced with permission of the AAAS and the authors.

Figure 8.3 from R. W. Thatcher (1992), "Cyclic cortical reorganization during early childhood. Special Issue: The role of frontal lobe maturation in cognitive and social development", *Brain and Cognition*, vol. 20, no. 1, p. 31, figure 2. Copyright © 1992, with permission from Elsevier.

Figure 8.4 from R. Case (1992), "The role of the frontal lobes in the regulation of cognitive development", *Brain and Cognition*, vol. 20, no. 1, p. 55, reprinted with the kind permission of Academic Press, Inc., Florida. Copyright © 1992, with permission from Elsevier.

Figure 9.1 from I. C. McManus and M. P. Bryden (1991), "Geschwind's theory of cerebral lateralization: developing a formal, causal model", *Psychological Bulletin*, vol. 110, pp. 237–253. Copyright © 1991 by the American Psychological Association. Reprinted with permission.

The publishers apologize for any errors or omissions in the above list and would be grateful to be notified of any corrections that should be incorporated in the next edition or reprint of this book.

ABBREVIATIONS

ADHD	attention deficit/hyperactivity disorder
ASL	American Sign Language
CANTAB	Cambridge Neuropsychological Testing Automated Battery
DLPC	dorsolateral prefrontal cortex
DNMS	delayed non-match to sample
EEG	electroencephalography
ERP	event-related potential
FEF	frontal eye fields
FFA	fusiform face area
fMRI	functional magnetic resonance imaging
GABA	Gamma-aminobutyric acid
HD-ERPs	high-density event-related potentials
IMHV	intermediate and medial part of the hyperstriatum ventrale
IS	interactive specialization
ISI	inter-stimulus interval
LGN	lateral geniculate nucleus
MGN	medial geniculate nucleus
MRI	magnetic resonance imaging
Nc	negative component
NIRS	near infra-red spectroscopy
PET	positron emission tomography
PKU	phenylketonuria
PN	projection neuron
SLI	specific language impairment
SOA	stimulus onset asynchrony
SP	spike potential
STS	superior temporal sulcus
WS	Williams syndrome

1 THE BIOLOGY OF CHANGE

In this introductory chapter I discuss a number of background issues for developmental cognitive neuroscience, beginning with historical approaches to the nature–nurture debate. Constructivism, in which biological forms are an emergent product of complex dynamic interactions between genes and environment, is presented as an approach to development that is superior to accounts that seek to identify pre-existing information in the genes or external environment. However, if we are to abandon existing ways of analyzing development in terms of "innate" and "acquired" components, this raises the question of how we should best understand developmental processes. One scheme is proposed for taking account of the various levels of interaction between genes and environment. In addition, a dissociation is introduced between innate representations and architectural constraints on the emergence of representations within neural networks. Following this, a number of factors are discussed that demonstrate the importance of the cognitive neuroscience approach to development, including the increasing availability of brain imaging and molecular approaches. Conversely, the importance of development for analyzing the relation between brain structure and cognition is reviewed. In examining ways in which development and cognitive neuroscience can be combined, three different perspectives on human functional brain development are discussed: a maturational view, a skill learning view, and an "interactive specialization" framework. Finally, the contents of the rest of the book are outlined.

1.1 VIEWPOINTS ON DEVELOPMENT

As every parent knows, the changes involved in the growth of children from birth to adolescence are truly amazing. Perhaps the most remarkable aspects of this growth involve the brain and mind. Accompanying the four-fold increase in the volume of the brain during this time are numerous and sometimes surprising changes in behavior, thought, and emotion. An understanding of how the developments in brain and mind relate to each other could potentially revolutionize our thinking about education, social policy, and disorders of mental development. It is no surprise, therefore, that there is increasing interest in this new branch of science from grant funding agencies, medical charities, and even Presidential summits. Since the publication of the first edition of this book in 1997, this field has become known as *developmental cognitive neuroscience.*

Developmental cognitive neuroscience has emerged at the interface between two of the most fundamental questions that challenge humankind. The first of these questions concerns the relation between mind and body, and specifically between the physical substance of the brain and the mental processes it supports. This issue is fundamental to the scientific discipline of cognitive neuroscience. The second question concerns the origin of organized biological structures, such as the highly complex structure of the adult human brain. This issue is fundamental to the study of development. In this book I will show that light can be shed on these two fundamental questions by tackling them both simultaneously, and specifically by focusing on the relation between the postnatal development of the human brain and the cognitive processes it supports.

The second of the two questions above, that of the origins of organized biological structure, can be posed in terms of *phylogeny* or *ontogeny*. The phylogenetic (evolutionary) version of this question concerns the origin of species, and has been addressed by Charles Darwin and many others since. The ontogenetic version of this question concerns individual development within a life span. The ontogenetic question has been somewhat neglected relative to phylogeny, since some influential scientists have held the view that once a particular set of genes have been selected by evolution, ontogeny is simply a process of executing the "instructions" coded for by those genes. By this view, the ontogenetic question essentially reduces to phylogeny. In contrast to this view, in this book I argue that ontogenetic development is an active process through which biological structure is constructed afresh in each individual by means of complex and variable interactions between genes and their environments. The information is not in the genes, but emerges from the constructive interaction between genes and their environment (see also Oyama, 2000). However, since both ontogeny and phylogeny concern the emergence of biological structure, some of the same mechanisms of change have been invoked in the two cases.

FURTHER READING: OYAMA, 2000

The debate about the extent to which the ontogenetic question (individual development) is subsidiary to the phylogenetic question (evolution) is otherwise known as the nature–nurture issue, and has been central in developmental psychology, philosophy, and neuroscience. Broadly speaking, at one extreme the belief is that most of the information necessary to build a human brain, and the mind it supports, is latent within the genes of the individual. While most of this information is common to the species, each individual has some specific information that will make them differ from others. By this view, development is a process of unfolding or triggering the expression of information within the genes.

At the opposing extreme, others believe that most of the information that shapes the human mind comes from the structure of the external world. Some facets of the environment, such as gravity, patterned light, and so on, will be common throughout the species, while other aspects of the environment will be specific to the individual. It will become clear in this book that both of these extreme views are ill conceived, since they assume that the information for the structure of an organism exists (either in the genes or in the external world) prior to its construction. In contrast to this, it appears that biological structure emerges anew within each individual's development from constrained dynamic interactions between genes and various levels of environment, and is not easily reducible to simple genetic and experiential components.

It is more commonly accepted these days that the mental abilities of adults are the result of complex interactions between genes and environment. However, the nature of this interaction remains controversial and poorly understood, although, as we shall see, light may be shed on it by simultaneously considering brain and psychological development. Before going further, however, it is useful briefly to review some historical perspectives on the nature–nurture debate. This journey into history may help us avoid slipping back into ways of thinking that are deeply embedded in the Western intellectual tradition.

Throughout the seventeenth century there was an ongoing debate in biology between the so-called "vitalists," on the one hand, and the "preformationists," on the other. The vitalists believed that ontogenetic change was driven by "vital" life forces. Belief in this somewhat mystical and ill-defined force was widespread and actively encouraged by some members of the clergy. Following the invention of the microscope, however, some of those who viewed themselves as being of a more rigorous scientific mind championed the preformationist viewpoint. This view argued that a complete human being was contained in either the male sperm ("spermists") or the female egg ("ovists"). In order to support their claim, spermists produced drawings of a tiny, but perfect, human form enclosed within the head of sperm (see figure 1.1). They argued that there was a simple and direct mapping between the seed of the organism and its end state: simultaneous growth of all the body parts. Indeed, preformationists of a religious conviction argued that God, on the sixth day of his work, placed about two hundred thousand million fully formed human miniatures into the ovaries of Eve or sperm of Adam (Gottlieb 1992)!

Of course, we now know that such drawings were the result of overactive imagination, and that no such perfectly formed miniature human forms exist in the sperm or ovaries. However, as we shall see, the general idea behind preformationism, that there is a pre-existing blueprint or plan of the final state, remained a pervasive one for many decades in biological and psychological development. In

Figure 1.1 Drawings such as this influenced a seventeenth-century school of thought, the "spermists," who believed that there was a complete preformed person in each male sperm and that development merely consisted in increasing size.

fact, Oyama (2000) suggests that the same notion of a "plan" or "blueprint" that exists prior to the development process has persisted to the present day, with genes replacing the little man inside the sperm. As it became clear that genes do not contain a simple "code" for body parts, in more recent years, "regulator" and "switching" genes have been invoked to orchestrate the expression of the other genes. Common to all of these versions of the nativist viewpoint is the belief that there is a fixed mapping between a pre-existing set of coded instructions and the final form.

On the other side of the nature–nurture dichotomy, those who believe in the structuring role of experience also view the information as existing prior to the end state, only the source of that information is different. This argument has been applied to psychological development, since it is obviously less plausible for physical growth. An example of this approach came from some of the more extreme members of the behaviorist school of psychology who believed that a child's psychological abilities could be entirely shaped by its early environment. More recently some developmental psychologists who work with computer models of the brain have suggested that the infant's mind is shaped largely by the statistical regularities latent in the external environment. While such efforts can reveal hitherto unrecognized contributions from the environment, it will become evident in this book that these computer models can also be an excellent method for exploring types of interaction between intrinsic and extrinsic structure.

FURTHER READING: BATES & ELMAN, 2002

The viewpoints discussed above share the common assumption that the information necessary for constructing the final state (in this case, the adult mind) is present prior to the developmental process. While vitalists' beliefs were sometimes more dynamic in character than preformationists', the forces that guided development were still assumed to originate with an external creator. Preformationism in historical or modern guises involves the execution of plans or codes (from genes) or the incorporation of information from the structure of the environment. Oyama (2000) argues that these views on ontogenetic development resemble pre-Darwinian theories of evolution in which a creator was deemed to have planned all the species in existence. In both the ontogenetic and phylogenetic theories of this kind a plan for the final form of the species or individual exists prior to its emergence.

A more recent trend in thinking about ontogenetic development is constructivism. Constructivism differs from preformationist views in that biological structures are viewed as an emergent property of complex interactions between genes and environment. Perhaps the most famous proponent of such a view with regard to cognitive development was the Swiss epistemologist Jean Piaget. The essence of constructivism is that the relationship between the initial state and the final product can only be understood by considering the progressive construction of information. This construction is a dynamic process to which multiple factors contribute. There is no simple sense in which information either exclusively in the genes or in the environment can specify the end product. Rather, these two factors combine in a constructive manner such that each developmental step will be greater than the sum of the factors that contributed to it. The upshot of this viewpoint is not that we can never understand the mapping between genetic (or environmental) information and the final product, but rather that this mapping can only be understood once we have unravelled some of the key interactions that occur between genetic and environmental factors during ontogeny. Unfortunately, this means that there are unlikely to be quick breakthroughs in understanding the functions of regions of the human genome for psychological development.

FURTHER READING: PIAGET, 2002

Until recently the constructivist view suffered from the same problem as vitalism, in that the mechanisms of change were poorly specified and the emergence of new structures from old resembled the conjuror's trick of making a rabbit appear from a hat. Even the "mechanisms" proposed by Piaget appeared somewhat elusive on closer inspection. Another problem with the constructivist approach was that, despite its emphasis on interaction, it was unclear how to analyze development in the absence of the traditional dichotomy between innate and environmental factors. By taking a cognitive neuroscience approach to psychological development, in conjunction with a number of new theoretical approaches, we will see that it is now possible to flesh out the constructivist approach to development and to provide new ways to analyze cognitive and brain development.

1.2 ANALYZING DEVELOPMENT

Viewpoints on cognitive development that involve reducing behavior to information derived from genes, on the one hand, and/or information derived from the external environment, on the other, have commonly used the distinction between "innate" and "acquired" components. The term "innate" has rarely been explicitly defined, and has a somewhat chequered history in developmental science. Indeed, it has been dropped from use, and even actively banned, in many areas of developmental biology. The main reason for the term having been dropped from use in fields of biology such as ethology and genetics is because it is simply no longer useful since it has become evident that genes interact with their environment at many levels, including the molecular. One compelling example of this point, discussed by Gottlieb (1992), concerns the formation of the beak in the chick embryo.

The production of the (toothless) beak in the chick embryo results from the coaction of two types of tissue. However, if, in an experimental situation, one of these types of tissue (mesenchyme) is replaced with the same tissue from a mouse, then teeth will form instead of a beak! Thus, as Gottlieb (1992) points out, the genetic component that is necessary for the chick to produce teeth has been retained from the reptilian ancestry of birds. More generally, the phenotype that emerges from these chick genes can vary dramatically according to the molecular and cellular context in which they are located.

Thus, there is no aspect of development that can be said to be strictly "genetic," that is, exclusively a product of information contained within particular genes. If the term "innate" is taken to refer to structure that is specified exclusively by genetic information, it refers to nothing that exists in the natural world, except for genes themselves. In cognitive science, however, use of the term "innate" has persisted despite repeated calls for it to be dropped from use (e.g. Hinde, 1974; Johnston, 1988; Gottlieb, 1992; Oyama, 2000). Presumably its persistent usage reflects the need for a term to describe the interaction between factors intrinsic to the developing child and features of the external environment. In considering this issue, Johnson and Morton (1991) suggested that it is useful to distinguish between the various levels of interaction between genes and their environment. Some of these are shown in table 1.1. Within this analysis, the term "innate" refers only to changes that arise as a result of interactions that occur within the organism, and does not equate with "genetic." That is, it refers to the *level of the interaction between genes and environment, and not to the source of the information.* I will adopt this working definition of the term in this book. Interactions between the organism and aspects of the external environment that are common to all members of the species, the species-typical environment (such as patterned light, gravity, etc.), were referred to as "primal" by Johnson and Morton. Interactions between the organism and aspects of the environment unique to an individual, or subset of member of a species, were referred to as "learning."

Based on a series of experiments on the effects on brain structure of rearing rats in impoverished or comparatively enriched early environments, Greenough, Black, and Wallace (2002) proposed a similar distinction between two types of information storage induced by the environment. Changes induced by aspects of the environment that are common to all members of a species were classified as "experience-expectant" information storage (= "species-typical"), and are associated with selective synaptic loss. The second type of information incorporated by the brain through interaction with the environment was referred to as "experience-dependent" (= "individual-specific"). This referred to interactions with the environment that are, or can be, specific to an individual and are associated with the generation of new synaptic connections. Clearly, the boundary between these types of experience is often difficult to ascertain, and there have been many instances from ethological studies where behaviors thought to be innate turn out to be primal on closer study.

FURTHER READING: GREENOUGH ET AL., 2002

Using this framework it is possible to analyze aspects of development into underlying components. Normally in developmental psychology this is done in terms of components of cognition or behavior. In a cognitive neuroscience approach, by contrast, we can use evidence from different components of brain structure to constrain our thinking about cognitive development. Specifically, we can inquire

Table 1.1   Levels of interaction between genes and their environment

Levels of interaction	Term
Molecular	Internal environment
Cellular	Internal environment (innate)
Organism–external environment	Species-typical environment (primal)
	Individual-specific environment (learning)

into the extent to which aspects of a given neural circuit are innate (defined above as the product of interactions within the organism, and not sensitive to experience). Different aspects of brain structure and function are probably differentially sensitive to the effects of postnatal experience. The following analysis, which for simplicity I apply to the example of a simple abstract neural network, will assist in the later discussion of brain development and plasticity. A similar, but more detailed, analysis is presented in Elman et al. (1996).

The human brain is composed of very complex neural circuits bathed in a variety of chemicals that can regulate and modulate function. Therefore, when considering ways to analyze plasticity in such circuits it is useful to start with a simpler system that shares the same general properties. Connectionist neural network models involve nodes (simplified neurons) and links that can vary in strength (simplified synapses and dendrites). Learning in such networks takes place by varying the strength or extent of connections between nodes according to learning rules, some of which approximate those thought to be used in real brains (such as "Hebbian" learning rules).

FURTHER READING: MUNAKATA & STEDRON, 2001; BATES & ELMAN, 2002

Figure 1.2 shows a simple connectionist neural network. There are a number of ways it could be sensitive to training. First, the basic architecture of the network could alter as a result of experience. This could involve a change in the number of nodes, the learning rule, or the extent to which the nodes are interconnected. There are, in fact, a few neural network models that change in this way. Another possibility is that while the basic architecture of the network is fixed, the strength of the connections between the nodes varies according to a weight-adjustment

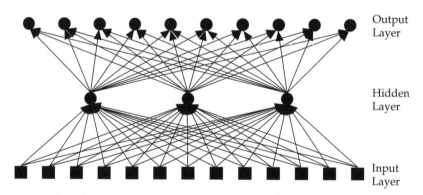

Output
Layer

Hidden
Layer

Input
Layer

Figure 1.2 A simple three-layered connectionist neural network in which groups of nodes are joined by links. Changes in the strength of links as a result of training are determined by a learning rule.

learning rule. This is the way that most connectionist neural networks encode information. Since representations in artificial connectionist networks are dependent on the particular pattern of link strengths between nodes, allowing these to vary with the input means that different representations may emerge as a result of experience. In terms of the brain, we can think of these changes as residing in the details of microcircuits and synaptic efficacy. When the basic architecture of the network is fixed but the link strengths vary, we may say that the network shows an *innate architecture. More specifically, the representations that emerge as a result of training are constrained by the architecture of the network.* In chapter 2 we will review evidence consistent with the view that the primate cerebral cortex imposes architectural constraints on the development of representations.

Within this framework, there are, however, also two other possibilities. The first of these is that both the basic architecture of the network and the patterns and strengths of links between nodes are innate (as defined in table 1.1), and thus insensitive to external input. I will refer to this as the network possessing *innate representations.* In later chapters we will see that there is little evidence that the human neocortex possesses innate representations. The second alternative possibility is that both the architecture and the detailed pattern and strength of links are malleable as a result of training. In the next chapter we will see that only under extremely atypical environmental conditions, or in cases of genetic atypicality, do we see changes in the basic architecture of the primate brain.

1.3 WHY TAKE A COGNITIVE NEUROSCIENCE APPROACH TO DEVELOPMENT?

Until the past decade, the majority of theories of perceptual and cognitive development were generated without recourse to evidence from the brain. Indeed, some authors argued strongly for the independence of cognitive-level theorizing from considerations of the neural substrate (e.g. Morton, Mehler, & Jusczyk, 1984). Evidence from the brain was thought to be either distracting, irrelevant, or hopelessly complex. However, our understanding of brain function has improved significantly over the past twenty years or so. Accordingly, many believe that the time is now ripe for exploring the interface between cognitive development and brain development, and a spate of books on the topic have appeared (e.g. Nelson & Luciana 2001; Johnson, Munakata, & Gilmore, 2002; de Haan & Johnson, 2003). Further, the integration of information from biology and cognitive development sets the stage for a more comprehensive psychology and biology of change than was previously thought possible: a developmental cognitive neuroscience. By the term "cognitive neuroscience" I include not only evidence about brain development, such as that from neuroanatomy, brain imaging, and the behavioral or cognitive effects of brain lesions, but also evidence from ethology. Ethology, a science pioneered by Tinbergen, Lorenz, and others in the 1940s and 1950s, concerns the study of a whole organism within its natural environment (see Tinbergen, 1951; Lorenz, 1965; Hinde, 1974). We shall see that ethology is a powerful complement to neuroscience, and that the two fields combined can change the way we think about critical issues in perceptual and cognitive development.

In general, insights from biology have begun to play a more central role in informing thinking about perceptual and cognitive development, for a number of reasons. First, a range of powerful new methods and tools have become available to cognitive neuroscientists. These techniques permit questions to be asked more directly than before about the biological basis of cognitive and perceptual development. One set of tools relate to neuroimaging – the generation of "functional" maps of brain activity based on changes in either cerebral metabolism, blood flow, or electrical activity. Some of these imaging methods, such as positron emission tomography (PET), are of limited utility for studying transitions in cognitive development in normal infants due to their invasive nature (requiring the intravenous injection of radioactivity-labeled substances) and their relatively coarse temporal resolution (on the order of tens of seconds). In contrast, two current techniques are readily applied to development in normal children – high-density event-related potentials (HD-ERPs) and functional magnetic resonance imaging (fMRI).

FURTHER READING: CASEY, THOMAS, & McCANDLISS, 2001; NELSON & MONK, 2001

HD-ERP is a method of recording the electrical activity of the brain by means of sensitive electrodes that rest on the surface of the scalp. These recordings can either be of the spontaneous natural rhythms of the brain (electroencephalography – EEG), or the electrical activity time-locked to a stimulus presentation or action (ERPs). Since the ERP from many trials is averaged, the spontaneous natural rhythms of the brain that are unrelated to the stimulus presentation average to zero. However, there has also been recent interest in rapid bursts of high-frequency EEG that appear to be related to stages of information processing in the brain (event-related oscillations) (Csibra, Davis, Spratling, & Johnson, 2000). With a high density of electrodes on the scalp, algorithms can be employed which infer the position and orientation of the brain sources of electrical activity (dipoles) for the particular pattern of scalp surface electrical activity. Some of the assumptions necessary for the successful use of these algorithms are actually more likely to be true of infants than adults. For example, lower levels of skull conductance and fewer cortical convolutions may improve the accuracy and interpretability of HD-ERP results in infants relative to adult subjects (but see Nelson, 1994, and Johnson et al., 2001, for discussion of this methodology as applied to infants).

Functional-MRI allows the non-invasive measurement of cerebral blood oxygen levels with the prospect of spatial resolution on the order of millimeters and temporal resolution of several seconds, using MRI machines commonly available in modern medical facilities. This technique is being applied to children in several laboratories, though factors such as noise, vibration levels, and enclosure still make it difficult to use with healthy infants (see Casey et al., 2001, for details).

In addition to this armory, a technique that holds promise for the future is near infra-red spectroscopy (NIRS). This is a form of optical imaging, meaning that it depends on measuring tiny changes in the scatter or bending of weak light beams as they pass through the skull and brain (see Meek 2002). Changes in blood oxygenation can be detected with this method, and therefore it could provide an excellent alternative to fMRI for use with young infants. At the time of writing, however, the technique is still being developed in several laboratories.

Another useful tool for linking brain development to behavior is the "marker task." This method involves the use of specific behavioral tasks which have been related to one or more brain regions in adult humans and non-human primates by neurophysiological and/or brain imaging studies, and preferably by more than one method. By studying the development of performance on the task at different ages and in different contexts, the researcher can gather evidence about how the observed behavioral change is accounted for by known patterns of brain development.

In this book, I will survey several lines of inquiry which illustrate the marker task approach. There are also weaknesses of the marker task approach, such as that findings from one task sometimes don't generalize to others, and it can be difficult to compare results from pools of participants that differ significantly. Another challenge stems from the design of a task that is sufficiently limited in its demands as to give interpretable results with infants or young children, and yet sufficiently demanding to call upon "interesting" cognitive capacities. Moreover, since different brain regions may be critical for the same task at different ages (Goldman-Rakic, 1971), the interpretation of results is made more complex. Nevertheless, the marker task approach is a useful methodology that promises to provide insight into the development of neurocognitive systems.

Marker tasks need to be based on the cognitive abilities of young infants. Obviously, behavioral tasks involving verbal instruction or output are not feasible. Further, young infants only have a short attention span in terms of the length of time they are prepared to cooperate with the experimenter. Consequently, studies involving extensive training are not feasible either. Fortunately, however, a number of methods have been developed for testing infants that utilize their natural tendencies to look at conspicuous and novel visual stimuli. One of these pro-cedures, called "preferential looking," involves presenting paired visual stimuli, and recording the time that the infants choose to look at each. Another procedure, called "habituation," involves showing the same stimulus repeatedly until the infant shows a clear decrease in the time she spends looking at it. When a certain criterion for the looking decrement is reached, a novel stimulus is presented and the increase or recovery in looking time is recorded. If there is significant recovery of looking time, we may infer that the infant can discriminate between the two stimuli. If there is little or no recovery, we may infer that the infant is unable to discriminate between them. Other techniques for eliciting discriminative responses from young infants include using rate of sucking to measure habituation, the use of an eye-tracker to determine exact patterns of looking, and the use of heart rate measures.

Beyond neuroimaging and the marker task, techniques exist in molecular genetics which allow the lesioning of particular genes from the genome of an animal. An example of this is the deletion of the alpha-calcium calmodulin kinase II gene which results in so-called "knockout" mice being unable to perform certain learning tasks when adults (Silva, Paylor, Wehner, & Tonegawa, 1992; Silva, Stevens, Tonegawa, & Wang, 1992). This method opens new vistas in the analysis of genetic contributions to cognitive and perceptual change in animals, and may be particularly fruitful when applied to well-studied animal models of development such as visual imprinting in chicks and song learning in passerine birds. These animal models may also be useful when investigating the role of genetic deletions/atypicalities for neurocognitive development in disorders of known genetic origin.

FURTHER READING: PENNINGTON, 2001, 2002; TAGER-FLUSBERG, 2003

Animal models are another way that the cognitive neuroscience approach can contribute to the study of development. A number of animal models of behavioral development have reached a stage where some of the principles discovered may be applicable to aspects of human development (see Blass, 1992). One example discussed later in this book is work on the neural basis of visual imprinting in the chick (see Horn, 1985; Johnson, 1991, for reviews). This line of research has implicated particular regions of the chick brain in visual imprinting, and has identified electrophysiological, neuroanatomical, and molecular correlates of this process. A neuronal network model of one of these brain regions has been developed, allowing the computational analysis of such phenomena as sensitive periods for learning (O'Reilly & Johnson, 2002). Further, the dissociation of neural systems underlying components of filial preference behavior in the chick has been used to argue for a similar dissociation in the development of face recognition in human infants (see chapter 5). In another example of the application of animal data to human development, comparisons between the behavioral development of humans and other primates can illuminate the importance of language to changes in other domains of cognition (see chapter 7). Consequently, while homologies between species must be made with great care, well-studied animal models increasingly provide useful theoretical and empirical insights into cognitive development in humans.

FURTHER READING: OVERMAN & BACHEVALIER, 2001; O'REILLY & JOHNSON, 2002

Importantly, theories which incorporate and reveal relationships between brain structures and cognitive functions will be useful in understanding the effects of early brain injury or genetic disorder on cognitive development. Evidence derived from infants with congenital and acquired brain damage will be discussed throughout later chapters. Beyond its clinical utility, this line of evidence can also contribute to the development of theories about functional specification, critical periods, and plasticity in the brain. Thus, there is a two-way interaction between clinical evidence and basic research in developmental cognitive neuroscience.

1.4 WHY TAKE A DEVELOPMENTAL APPROACH TO COGNITIVE NEUROSCIENCE?

Ontogenetic development is the constructive process by which genes interact with their environment at various levels to yield complex organic structures such as the brain and the cognitive processes it supports. The study of development is necessarily multi-disciplinary since new levels of structure that emerge as a result of this process (such as particular neural systems) often require different levels and methods of analysis from those that preceded them. The flip side of this is that development can be used as a tool for unraveling the interaction between seemingly disparate levels of organization, such as that between the molecular biology of gene expression and the development of cognitive abilities such as object recognition. Further, the human adult brain, and the mind it sustains, is composed of a complex series of hierarchical and parallel systems which has proven very difficult to analyze in an exclusively "top-down" manner. Brain damage induced by surgical lesions, or by accident or stroke, is unlikely to cleanly dissociate different levels of hierarchical organization. The developmental approach may allow different levels of hierarchical control to be observed independently. Specifically, it presents the opportunity to observe how various neurocognitive systems emerge and become integrated during development. For example, in chapter 3 we will see how different brain pathways underlying eye movement control emerge and become integrated during development.

1.5 THE CAUSE OF DEVELOPMENTAL CHANGE

Those inclined to see development as the unfolding of pre-existing information in the genes tend to adopt a maturational view of developmental psychology in which infants have reduced versions of the adult mind which increase by steps as particular brain pathways or structures mature. In contrast, taking a constructivist view of development involves attempting to unravel the dynamic relations between intrinsic and extrinsic structure which progressively restrict the phenotypes that can emerge. The distinction between these two approaches has also been noted by Gottlieb (1992), who refers to them as "predetermined epigenesis" and "probabilistic epigenesist." Predetermined epigenesis assumes that there is a uni-directional causal path from genes to structural brain changes to brain function and experience. In contrast, probabilistic epigenesis views the interactions between genes, structural brain changes, and function as bidirectional:

Predetermined epigenesis:
(Unidirectional structure–function development)
genes → brain structure → brain function → experience

Probablistic epigenesis:
(Bidirectional structure–function development)
genes ↔ brain structure ↔ brain function ↔ experience
(*Source*: Gottlieb, 1992)

Thus, by the predetermined epigenesis view the infant mind is viewed as being comparable to adults with focal brain injury. That is, specific cognitive mechanisms are either present or absent at a given age. For example, parallels have been drawn between infants and patients with frontal lobe deficits. This view shares common assumptions with the "marker task" method discussed earlier, and is commonly associated with a maturational viewpoint. Circuits that support components of the adult system are assumed to come "on-line" at various ages. However, while this approach is likely to provide a reasonable first approximation for normal developmental events, it is unlikely to provide a full account in the long run.

An alternative approach to investigating the relation between the developing brain and cognition is associated with a probabilistic epigenesis approach to biological development. This viewpoint assumes that development involves the progressive restriction of fate. Early in development a system, such as the brain/mind, has a range of possible developmental paths and end states. The developmental path and end state that result are dependent on the particular sets of constraints that operate. This type of analysis of ontogenetic development derives from work on the development of body structure by D'Arcy Thompson (1917) and C. H. Waddington (1975), among others.

Waddington (whose work greatly influenced Piaget) proposed that there are developmental pathways, or necessary epigenetic routes, which he termed "chreods." Chreods can be conceptualized as valleys in an epigenetic landscape such as that shown in figure 1.3. Self-regulatory processes (which Waddington called "homeorhesis") ensure that the organism (conceptualized as a ball rolling down the landscape) returns to its channel following small perturbations. Large perturbations, such as being reared in darkness, can result in a quite different valley route being taken, especially when these occur near a decision point. These decision points are regions of the epigenetic landscape where a small perturbation can lead to a different route being taken. Thus, while for the typically developing child the same end point will be reached despite the small perturbations that arise from slightly different rearing environments, a deviation from the normal path early in

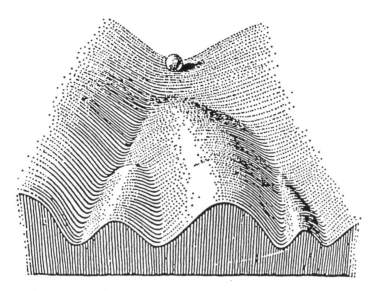

Figure 1.3   The epigenetic landscape of Waddington (1975).

development (high up the hill), at a decision point, or a major perturbation later in development, may cause the child to take a different developmental path and reach one of a discrete set of possible alternative end states (phenotypes).

Aside from Waddington's informal conceptualization, the constructivist (probablistic epigenesis) approach to development is currently more difficult to work with since we have few theoretical tools for understanding emergent phenomena in complex dynamic systems. By this view, developmental disorders are possible developmental trajectories that are responses to different sets of constraints. This implies that from the moment when the developmental trajectory deviates from the normal one, a variety of new factors and adaptations will come into play, making it likely that some re-organization of brain functioning will take place. In contrast to the maturational approach (causal epigenesis), therefore, applying the mapping between brain regions and functions found in normal adults to such cases may be only partially informative. It should be stressed that the constructivist view just outlined does not seek to downplay the role of genetic factors. Rather, it seeks to understand the emergence of new structures and functions through the complex interactions between genes and their different environments.

1.6 THREE VIEWPOINTS ON HUMAN FUNCTIONAL BRAIN DEVELOPMENT

Relating the neuroanatomical changes that occur during the development of the brain to the remarkable changes in motor, perceptual, and cognitive abilities during the first decade or so of human life presents a considerable challenge. Throughout this book, I will discuss evidence inspired by three distinct, but not necessarily incompatible, viewpoints on human functional brain development. These are: (1) a maturational perspective, (2) interactive specialization, and (3) a skill learning viewpoint.

As mentioned earlier, much of the research to date attempting to relate brain to behavioral development in humans has been from a maturational viewpoint in which the goal is to relate the "maturation" of particular regions of the brain, usually regions of the cerebral cortex, to newly emerging sensory, motor, and cognitive functions. Evidence concerning the differential neuroanatomical development of brain regions is used to determine an age when a particular region is likely to become functional. Success in a new behavioral task at this age may then be attributed to the maturation of this "new" brain region. By this view, functional brain development is the reverse of adult neuropsychology, with the difference that specific brain regions are added-in instead of being damaged.

Despite the intuitive appeal and attractive simplicity of the maturational approach, we will see during the course of this book that it does not successfully explain some major aspects of human functional brain development. Further, associations between neural and cognitive changes based on age of onset can be theoretically weak due to the great variety of neuroanatomical and neurochemical measures that change at different times in different regions of the brain.

In contrast to the above approach a specific constructivist viewpoint, "interactive specialization" (IS), assumes that postnatal functional brain development, at least within the cerebral cortex, involves a process of organizing patterns of inter-regional interactions (Johnson, 2001, 2002). According to this view, the response properties of a specific region are partly determined by its patterns of connectivity to other regions, and their patterns of activity. During postnatal development, changes in the response properties of cortical regions occur as they interact and compete with each other to acquire their role in new computational abilities. From this perspective, some cortical regions may begin with poorly defined functions, and consequently are partially activated in a wide range of different contexts and tasks. During development, activity-dependent interactions between regions hone the functions of regions such that their activity becomes restricted to a narrower set of circumstances (e.g. a region originally activated by a wide variety of visual objects may come to confine its response to upright human faces). The onset of new behavioral competencies during infancy will therefore be associated with changes in activity over several regions, and not just with the onset of activity in one or more additional region(s). I will expand further on this theory in chapter 10.

A third perspective on human functional brain development, skill learning, involves the proposal that the brain regions active in infants during the onset of new perceptual or motor abilities are similar, or identical, to those involved in complex skill acquisition in adults. For example, with regard to perceptual expertise, Gauthier and colleagues have shown that extensive training of adults with artificial objects (called "greebles") eventually results in activation of a cortical region previously associated with face processing, the "fusiform face area" (Gauthier, Tarr, Anderson, Skudlarksi, & Gore, 1999). This suggests that the region is normally activated by faces in adults, not because it is prespecified for faces, but due to our extensive expertise with that class of stimulus. Further, it encourages parallels with the development of face processing skills in infants (see Gauthier & Nelson, 2001). While it remains unclear how far parallels can be drawn between adult expertise and infant development, to the extent that the skill learning hypothesis is correct, it presents a clear view of a continuity of mechanisms throughout the life span. Finally, skill learning is not necessarily incompatible with interactive specialization, and sometimes they make similar predictions.

 ## 1.7 LOOKING FORWARD

The next chapter reviews the current state of knowledge regarding the pre- and postnatal development of the human brain. While the general sequence of developmental events is very similar for all mammals, the timing of human development, and especially human postnatal development, is protracted. This extended period of postnatal development is associated with a greater extent of area of the cerebral cortex, in particular the prefrontal regions. The more extended postnatal development observed in humans reveals differential rates of development in aspects of brain structure (e.g. different cortical areas and layers). The more differentiated picture of postnatal brain development in humans has also been used to make predictions about the emergence of function.

Focusing on the cerebral cortex, neurobiological and brain imaging studies indicate that the cortex probably does not possess innate representations (in the sense discussed earlier). Rather, early in life large-scale regions of cortex have approximate biases that make them best suited to supporting particular types of computations. The fairly consistent structure–function relations observed in the cortex of normal human adults appear to be the consequence of multiple constraints both intrinsic and extrinsic to the organism, rather than of detailed intrinsic genetic specification. In the following chapters a number of domains of perceptual, cognitive, and motor development that have been associated with neural development are reviewed. In each of these domains I attempt to reveal some of the sources of constraint on the representations that emerge within cortical circuits. Examples of combinations of constraints from the correlational structure of the external environment, the basic architecture of the cortex, and the influence of subcortical circuits are discussed.

Although atypical development is not the primary focus of this book, throughout the review of normal development evidence from atypical development is discussed where relevant (see appendix). Focusing in particular on three developmental disorders (dyslexia, autism, and Williams syndrome), we see that specific neurocognitive deficits can result from diffuse damage to multiple brain systems. Brain damage in prenatal development can divert the child from one develop-mental path to another. However, it is possible that different types of brain damage can result in the same adult end state (phenotype), somewhat like the discrete number of valleys in Waddington's epigenetic landscape. In contrast to this, brain damage in later life (perinatal and early postnatal) is commonly compensated for by other parts of the brain. Thus, at this later stage a focal brain lesion may have only mild diffuse cognitive consequences, resembling Waddington's self-organizing adaptation keeping the organism within a certain chreod and resulting in the same general phenotype.

In chapter 9, mechanisms and types of changes in representations during human postnatal development are discussed, and the IS viewpoint on human func-tional brain development is expanded further. The emergence of specific functions in cortical areas is seen as a product of interactions within the brain, and between the brain and its external environment. Just as the child develops within a social and physical environment, and the brain within a body ("embodiment"), each cortical area develops its functionality within the context of the whole brain ("embrainment"). In the final chapter a number of conclusions and recommenda-tions for future research are made.

2 BUILDING A BRAIN

This chapter describes several aspects of the pre- and postnatal development of the brain, with specific reference to humans where data permit. In the first section, some of the stages of prenatal brain development are outlined, including the proliferation, migration, and differentiation of cells such that they give rise to particular brain structures. Next, a basic overview of primate brain anatomy is provided with specific emphasis on the neocortex. A distinction is made between two dimensions of the cortex: its areal or regional structure, and its laminar (layered) structure. The following section on postnatal development reports that while human brain volume quadruples between birth and adulthood, this is mainly due to increases in nerve fiber bundles, and myelination, but not additional neurons. Further, some measures of structural and neurophysiological brain development, such as the density of synaptic contacts, show a characteristic "rise and fall" during postnatal development. The following section addresses the question of the extent to which the differentiation of the neocortex into areas or regions is prespecified. The "protomap" hypothesis states that the areal differentiation of the cortex is determined by intrinsic molecular markers or prespecification of the proliferative zone. In contrast, the "protocortex" hypothesis suggests that an initially undifferentiated protocortex is divided up largely as a result of input through projections from the thalamus and is activity-dependent. A review of currently available evidence supports a middle-ground view in which large-scale regions are prespecified, while small-scale functional areas require activity-dependent processes. This implies that cortical networks impose architectural constraints on the representations that emerge within them, but there are no innate representations. Further evidence in support of this conclusion comes from a variety of studies on cortical plasticity in newborn rodents. In some of these studies sensory inputs to cortical areas are diverted to other regions, or pieces of cortex are transplanted from one region to another. In both of these cases cortical tissue acquires representations according to the nature of the input, rather than its developmental origins. In some cases these representations can even be used to guide the behavior of the animal. With some caveats, I suggest that similar conclusions

*can be drawn about primate cortical development and plasticity. The next section
focuses on a clear area of difference between human cortical development and that
of other primates: the very extended period of postnatal development. This greatly
extended period reveals two differential aspects of cortical development not as
clearly evident in other primates: an inside-out pattern of development of layers,
and differences in the timing of development across regions. These differential aspects
of human cortical development will provide the basis for associations between brain
and cognitive development described in later chapters. The chapter concludes with
discussion of the postnatal development of some subcortical structures, and with a
brief review of our knowledge of the development of neurotransmitters and modula-
tors. The developmental levels of several neurotransmitters mirror aspects of the
differential structural development of cortex.*

2.1 PRENATAL BRAIN DEVELOPMENT

The sequence of events during the prenatal development of the human brain
closely resembles that of many other vertebrates. Shortly after conception a fertil-
ized cell undergoes a rapid process of cell division, resulting in a cluster of
proliferating cells (called the blastocyst) that somewhat resembles a bunch of
grapes. Within a few days, the blastocyst differentiates into a three-layered structure (the embryonic disk). Each of these layers will further differentiate into a
major organic system. The endoderm (inner layer) turns into the set of internal
organs (digestive, respiratory, etc.), the mesoderm (middle layer) turns into the
skeletal and muscular structures, and the ectoderm (outer layer) gives rise to the
skin surface and the nervous system (including the perceptual organs).

The nervous system itself begins with a process known as *neurulation.* A
portion of the ectoderm begins to fold in on itself to form a hollow cylinder called
the *neural tube.* The neural tube differentiates along three dimensions: length,
circumference, and radius. The length dimension gives rise to the major subdivisions of the central nervous system, with the forebrain and midbrain arising at
one end and the spinal cord at the other. The end which will become the spinal
cord differentiates into a series of repeated units or segments, while the front end
of the neural tube organizes differently with a series of bulges and convolutions
forming (see figure 2.1). By around 5 weeks after conception these bulges can be
identified as protoforms for major components of the mammalian brain. Proceed-
ing from front to back: the first bulge gives rise to the cortex (telencephalon),
the second gives rise to the thalamus and hypothalamus (diencephalon), the
third turns into the midbrain (mesencephalon), and others to the cerebellum
(metencephalon), and to the medulla (myelencephalon).

The circumferential dimension (tangential to the surface) in the neural tube is
critical, because the distinction between sensory and motor systems develops
along this dimension: dorsal (top-side) corresponds roughly to sensory cortex,

Figure 2.1 A sequence of drawings of the embryonic and fetal development of the human brain. The drawings of brains beneath 25–100 days are the same images but drawn to the same scale as those in the row below. The forebrain, midbrain, and hindbrain originate as swellings at the head end of the neural tube. In primates, the convoluted cortex grows to cover the midbrain, hindbrain, and parts of the cerebellum. Prior to birth, neurons are generated in the developing brain at a rate of more than 250,000 per minute.

ventral (bottom-side) corresponds to motor cortex, with the various association cortices and "higher" sensory and motor cortices aligned somewhere in between. Within the brain stem and the spinal cord, the corresponding alar (dorsal) and basal (ventral) plates play a major role in the organization of nerve pathways into the rest of the body.

Differentiation along the radial dimension gives rise to the complex layering patterns and cell types found in the adult brain. Across the radial dimension of the neural tube the bulges grow larger and become further differentiated. Within these bulges cells *proliferate* (are born), *migrate (travel)*, and *differentiate into particular types.* The vast majority of the cells that will compose the brain are born in the so-called *proliferative zones.* These zones are close to the hollow portion of the neural tube (which subsequently become the ventricles of the brain). The first of these proliferation sites, the *ventricular zone,* may be phylogenetically older (Nowakowski, 1987). The second, the *subventricular zone,* only contributes significantly to phylogenetically recent brain structures such as the neocortex (i.e. "new" cortex). These two zones yield separate glial (support and supply cells) and neuron cell lines and give rise to different forms of migration. But first we will consider how young neurons are formed within these zones.

FURTHER READING: TAKAHASHI. NOWAKOWSKI, & CAVINESS, 2001, NOWAKOWSKI & HAYES, 2002

Neurons and glial cells are produced by division of proliferating cells within the proliferative zones to produce clones (a clone is a group of cells which are produced by division of a single precursor cell – such a precursor cell is said to give rise to a lineage). *Neuroblasts* produce neurons, and *glioblasts* produce glial cells. Each of the neuroblasts gives rise to a definite and limited number of neurons, a point to which I will return later. In at least some cases particular neuroblasts also give rise to particular types of cell. For example, less than a dozen proliferating cells produce all the Purkinje cells of the cerebellar cortex, with each producing about 10,000 cells (Nowakowski, 1987).

After young neurons are born, they have to travel or *migrate* from the proliferative zones to the particular region where they will be employed in the mature brain. There are two forms of migration observed during brain development. The first, and more common, is *passive cell displacement.* This occurs when cells that have been generated are simply pushed further away from the proliferative zones by more recently born cells. This form of migration gives rise to an outside-in pattern. That is, the oldest cells are pushed toward the surface of the brain, while the most recently produced cells are pulled toward the inside. Passive migration gives rise to brain structures such as the thalamus, the dentate gyrus of the hippocampus, and many regions of the brain stem. The second form of migration is more active and involves the young cell moving past previously generated cells to create an "inside-out" pattern. This pattern is found in the cerebral cortex and in some subcortical areas that have a laminar structure (divided into parallel layers).

It is important to emphasize that prenatal brain development is not a passive process involving the unfolding of genetic instructions. Rather, from an early stage interactions between cells are critical, including the transmission of electrical signals between neurons. In one example, patterns of spontaneous firing of cells in the eyes (before they have opened in development) transmit signals that appear to specify the layered structure of the lateral geniculate nucleus (see O'Leary & Nakagawa, 2002; Shatz 2002). Thus, waves of firing intrinsic to the developing organism may play an important role in specifying aspects of brain structure before sensory inputs from the external world have any effect.

FURTHER READING: SHATZ, 2002

2.2 AN OVERVIEW OF PRIMATE BRAIN ANATOMY

The mammalian brain follows a basic vertebrate brain plan found in lower species such as salamanders, frogs, and birds. The major differences between these species and higher primates is in the dramatic expansion of the cerebral cortex together with associated structures such as the basal ganglia. Human brain development follows closely the sequence of events observed in other primates, albeit on a slower schedule. A model of the evolution of the brain that successfully predicts the timing of different neural development events in various mammalian species (Finlay & Darlington, 1995) has recently been extended to human prenatal development (Clancy, Darlington, & Finlay, 2000). The model predicts that the more delayed the general time course of brain development in a species, the larger the relative volume of the later developing structures (such as the cerebral cortex, and particularly the frontal cortex) will be. In accordance with this general prediction, the slowed rate of development in humans is associated with a relatively larger volume of cortex, and an especially large frontal cortex. But, as we will see later, the relatively delayed time course of human brain development has another important benefit. It allows a prolonged postnatal period during which interaction with the environment can contribute to the tuning and shaping of circuitry.

The rapid expansion of the area of cortex has resulted in it becoming increasingly convoluted. For example, the area of the cortex in the cat is about 100 cm^2, whereas that of the human is about 2,400 cm^2. This suggests that the extra cortex possessed by primates, and especially humans, is related to the higher cognitive functions they possess. However, the basic relations between principal structures of the brain remain similar from mouse to human. The neocortex of mammals is basically a thin (about 3–4 mm) flat sheet. Although complex, its general layered structure is relatively constant throughout its extent (see figure 2.2).

Most of the sensory inputs to the cortex pass through a structure known as the thalamus. Each type of sensory input has its own particular nuclei within this region. For example, the lateral geniculate nucleus (LGN) carries visual input to the cortex, while the medial geniculate nucleus (MGN) carries information from the auditory modality. Because of the crucial role of the thalamus in mediating inputs to the cortex, some have hypothesized that it also plays a crucial role in cortical development – an idea that will be discussed at greater length later. The flow of information between thalamus and cortex is not unidirectional, however,

Figure 2.2   A simplified schematic diagram which illustrates that, despite its convoluted surface appearance (top), the cerebral cortex is a thin sheet (middle) composed of six layers (bottom). The convolutions in the cortex arise from a combination of growth patterns and the restricted space inside the skull. In general, differences between mammals involve the total area of the cortical sheet, and not its layered structure. Each of the layers possesses certain neuron types and characteristic input and projection patterns (see text).

since most of the projections from lower regions into the cortex are matched by projections from the cortex back down. Some output projections from the cortex pass to regions that are believed to be involved in motor control, such as the basal ganglia and the cerebellum. However, most of the projections from the cortex to other brain regions terminate in roughly the same regions from which projections arrived (such as the thalamus). In other words, the flow of information to and from the cortex is largely bidirectional. For this reason, it is important not to confuse the terms "input" and "output" with "sensory" and "motor". All sensory and motor systems make extensive use of both input and output fibers, with information passing rapidly in both directions along collateral pathways.

The brain has two general types of cells, neurons and glial cells. Glial cells are more common than neurons, but are generally assumed to play no direct role in computation. However, as we shall see later they play a very important role in the development of the cortex. The computational unit of the brain has long been thought to be the neuron (Shepherd, 1972). Neurons come in many shapes, sizes, and types, each of which presumably reflects their particular computational function. There appear to be approximately 25 different neuronal types within the cortex, although several of these types are relatively rare, and some are restricted to particular layers. About 80 percent of neurons found in the cortex are *pyramidal cells*, so-called because of the distinctive pyramid shape of the soma (cell body) produced by the very large apical dendrite (input process), which is always tangential to the surface of the cortex (figure 2.3). These are the neurons whose long axons (output processes) are so often found in the fibers feeding into other cortical and subcortical regions. While pyramidal cells are found in many of the layers of the cortex (generally they are larger in the lower layers and smaller in

Dendrite

Cell Body

Axon

Figure 2.3   A typical cortical pyramidal cell. The apical dendrite is the long process that extends to the upper layers, and may allow the cell to be influenced by other neurons. An axon projects to subcortical regions.

the upper layers), their apical dendrites often reach into its most superficial layer, layer 1 (see below). This long apical dendrite allows the cell to be influenced by large numbers of cells from other (more superficial) layers and regions. This may be computationally important if the pyramidal cell is a very stable and inflexible class of cell whose output is modulated by groups of plastic and flexible inhibitory regulatory neurons. Figure 2.2 also shows a schematic section through an area of primate cortex cut at right angles to the surface of the cortex, revealing the layered structure. I will refer to this as the *laminar* structure of the cortex. As just noted, each of the laminae has particular cell types within it, and each layer has typical patterns of inputs and outputs.

Most areas of the neocortex (in all mammals) are made up of six layers. The basic characteristics that define each layer appear to hold in most regions of the cortical sheet. Layer 1 has few cell bodies. It is made up primarily of long white fibers running along the horizontal surface, linking one area of cortex to others some distance away. Layers 2 and 3 also contain horizontal connections, often projecting forward from small pyramidal cells to neighboring areas of cortex. Layer 4 is the layer where most of the input fibers terminate and it contains a high proportion of spiny stellate (star-shaped) cells on which these projections terminate. Layers 5 and 6 have the major outputs to subcortical regions of the brain. These layers contain a particularly high proportion of large pyramidal cells, with long descending axons. There are also many neurons involved in intrinsic cortical circuits.

Although this basic laminar structure holds throughout most of the neocortex, there are some regional variations. For example, the input layer (layer 4) is particularly thick and well developed in sensory cortex. Indeed, in the visual system, it is possible to distinguish at least four "sublayers" within layer 4. Conversely, layer 5 (one of the output layers) is particularly well developed in motor cortex, presumably due to its importance in sending output signals from the cortex. It is also clear that different parts of the cortex have different projection patterns to other parts of the cortex. While there may only be a small number of these characteristic projection patterns from one region of cortex to another, there is no single pattern that can be said to be characteristic of all cortical regions. Hence this is another dimension of variation that can contribute to regional specialization within the cortex. Further dimensions could include the presence of particular neurotransmitters, and the relative contribution of excitatory vs inhibitory neurotransmitters. Finally, as we will see later, regions may vary in the timing of key developmental events, such as the postnatal reduction in the number of synapses (Huttenlocher, 1990).

2.3 POSTNATAL BRAIN DEVELOPMENT

There are a number of ways to study the postnatal development of neuronal structure in the brain. Traditionally, investigators have used neuroanatomical analysis of postmortem tissue. Such analysis tends to be based on relatively small numbers of children due to the extensive work involved and the difficulties associated in gaining such tissue. Furthermore, those children who come to autopsy have often suffered from trauma or diseases that complicate generalizations to normal brain development. *In vivo* studies of adults using magnetic resonance imaging (MRI) (Courchesne, Hesselink, Jernigan, & Yeung-Courchesne, 1987; Jernigan, Press, & Hesselink, 1990) and PET scanning of infants and adults (Petersen, Fox, Posner, Mintun, & Raichle, 1988; Chugani, Phelps, & Mazziotta, 2002) can inform us about the structural development of the brain. But these techniques are expensive, and are usually restricted to children with clinical symptoms that justify neural imaging. Hence generalizations to normal brain development must be made with caution in these cases as well. Despite these difficulties, a number of progressive and regressive neuroanatomical and neurophysiological changes have been observed during postnatal development in children. Specifically, a number of measures of brain anatomy and function show a characteristic "rise and fall" developmental pattern during this period. While the progressive and regressive processes should not be viewed as distinct stages, for the purposes of exposition I will discuss them in sequence.

A number of lines of evidence indicate that substantive additive changes occur during postnatal development of the brain. At the most gross level of analysis, brain volume quadruples between birth and adulthood. This increase comes from a number of sources, but, in general, not from additional neurons. The formation of neurons and their migration to appropriate brain regions takes place almost entirely within the period of prenatal development in the human. Although there may be some addition of neurons in the hippocampus and elsewhere (see later), the vast majority are present by around the seventh month of gestation (Rakic, 1995). In contrast to the lack of new nerve cell bodies, there is dramatic postnatal growth of synapses, dendrites, and fiber bundles. Further, nerve fibers become covered in a fatty myelin sheath that adds further to the mass of the brain.

Perhaps the most obvious manifestation of postnatal neural development as viewed through the confocal microscope is the increase in size and complexity of the dendritic tree of most neurons. An example of the dramatic increase in dendritic tree extent during human postnatal development is shown in figure 2.4. While the extent and reach of a cell's dendritic arbor may increase dramatically, it also often becomes more specific and specialized. Less apparent through stand-ard microscopes, but more evident with electron microscopy, is a corresponding increase in measures of the density of synaptic contacts between cells.

Huttenlocher and colleagues have reported a steady increase in synaptic dens-ity in several regions of the human cerebral cortex (Huttenlocher, de Courten, Garey, & Van der Loos, 1982; Huttenlocher, 1990, 1994). While an increase in synaptogenesis begins around the time of birth for all cortical areas studied to date, the most rapid bursts of increase, and the final peak density, occur at different ages in different areas. In the visual cortex there is a rapid burst at 3 to 4 months, and the maximum density of around 150 per cent of adult level is

Figure 2.4 A drawing of the cellular structure of the human visual cortex based on Golgi stain preparations from Conel (1939–67).

reached between 4 and 12 months. A similar time course is observed in the primary auditory cortex (Heschl's gyrus). In contrast, while synaptogenesis starts at the same time in a region of the prefrontal cortex, density increases much more slowly and does not reach its peak until after the first year. (It should be noted at this point that there are a variety of possible measures of synaptic density – per cell, per unit dendrite, per unit brain tissue, etc. Careful selection of measures is required so that factors such as increases in dendritic length do not unduly influence the results. Huttenlocher, 1990, discusses some of these issues of appropriate measurement.)

FURTHER READING: BOURGEOIS, 2001, HUTTENLOCHER, 2002

Another additive process is myelination. Myelination refers to an increase in the fatty sheath that surrounds neuronal pathways, a process that increases the efficiency of information transmission. In the central nervous system, sensory areas tend to myelinate earlier than motor areas. Cortical association areas are known to myelinate last, and continue the process into the second decade of life (see later). Because myelination continues for many years after birth, there has been a great deal of speculation about its role in behavioral development (Yakovlev & Lecours, 1967; Parmelee & Sigman, 1983; Volpe, 1987). However, interest in the causal role of myelination has begun to wane in the last few years since it became clear that under-myelinated connections in the young human brain are still capable of transmitting signals.

FURTHER READING: SAMPAIO & TRUWIT, 2001

A positron emission tomography study of human infants (Chugani et al., 2002) reported a sharp rise in overall resting brain metabolism (glucose uptake) after the first year of life, with a peak approximately 150 per cent above adult levels achieved somewhere around 4–5 years of age for some cortical areas. While this peak occurred somewhat later than that in synaptic density, an adult-like *distribution* of resting activity within and across brain regions was observed by the end of the first year.

FURTHER READING: CHUGANI ET AL., 2002

I now turn to regressive events during human postnatal brain development. Such events are commonly observed by those studying the development of nerve cells and their connections in the vertebrate brain (for reviews see: Cowan, Fawcett, O'Leary, & Stanfield, 1984; Hopkins & Brown, 1984; Clarke, 1985; Purves & Lichtman, 1985; Janowsky & Findlay, 1986). That processes of selective loss have a significant influence on postnatal primate brain development is evident from a number of quantitative measures. For example, in the PET study just mentioned the authors found that the absolute rates of glucose metabolism rise postnatally until they exceed adult levels, before reducing to adult levels after about 9 years of age for most cortical regions.

Consistent with these PET findings, Huttenlocher (1990, 1994) reports quantitative neuroanatomical evidence from several regions of the human cortex that following the increase in density of synapses described above there is then a period of synaptic loss. Like the timing of bursts of synaptogenesis, and the subsequent peaks of density, the timing of the reduction in synaptic density varies between cortical regions. For example, synaptic density in the visual cortex returns to adult levels between 2 and 4 years, while the same point is not reached until between 10 and 20 years of age for regions of the prefrontal cortex. Huttenlocher (1990, 1994) suggests that this initial overproduction of synapses may have an important role in the apparent plasticity of the young brain, a matter that will be discussed in more detail later. There is no strong evidence for this pattern of rise and fall either for the density of dendrites or for the number of neurons themselves in humans or other primates. However, in rodents and other vertebrates cell loss may be more significant.

FURTHER READING: GREENOUGH ET AL., 2002

One explanation for the decrease in glucose uptake observed in the PET studies is that it reflects the decrease in synaptic contacts. This hypothesis was investigated in a developmental study conducted with cats (Chugani, Hovda, Villablanca, Phelps, & Xu, 1991). In this study, the peak of glucose uptake in cat visual cortex was found to coincide with the peak in overproduction of synapses in this region. However, when similar data from human visual cortex are plotted together (see figure 2.5), it is apparent that the peak of glucose uptake lags behind synaptic density. An alternative to the hypothesis that reduction of metabolic activity is the result of the elimination of neurons, axons, and synaptic branches is that the same activity may require less "mental effort" once a certain level of skill has been attained.

Most of the developments in the brain discussed so far concern aspects of the structure of the brain. However, there are also developmental changes in what has been known as the "soft soak" aspects of neural function, molecules involved in the transmission and modulation of neural signals. While these will be discussed in more detail in a later section, it is interesting to note at this point that a number of neurotransmitters in rodents and humans also show the rise and fall

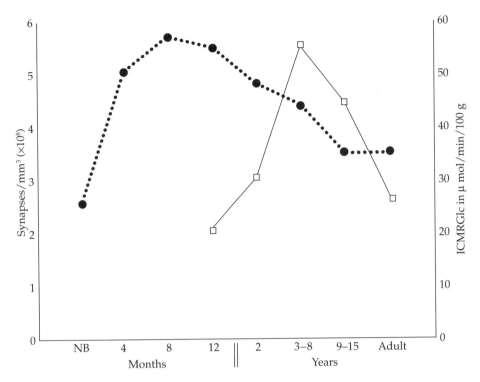

Figure 2.5 Graph showing the development of density of synapses in human primary visual cortex (dotted line: data taken from Huttenlocher, 1990), and resting glucose uptake in the occipital cortex as measured by PET (solid line: data taken from Chugani et al., 1987). ICMRGlc is a measure of the local cerebral metabolic rates for glucose.

developmental pattern (see Benes, 1994, for review). Specifically, the excitatory intrinsic transmitter glutamate, the intrinsic inhibitory transmitter GABA (Gamma-aminobutyric acid), and the extrinsic transmitter serotonin all show this same developmental trend.

FURTHER READING: BENES, 2001; CAMERON, 2001; BERENBAUM, MOFFAT, WISNIESKI, & RESNICK, 2003

Thus, the distinctive "rise and fall" developmental sequence is seen in a number of measures of structural and neurophysiological development in the human cortex. The number of measures and different laboratories in which this somewhat counter-intuitive developmental sequence has been observed leads to a degree of confidence in its validity. However, it should be stressed that (i) not all measures show this pattern (e.g. myelination); (ii) measures such as synaptic density are static snapshots of a dynamic process in which both additive and regressive processes are continually in progress: in other words, there are probably not distinct and separate progressive and regressive phases; and (iii) models which are exclusively dependent on regressive processes are unlikely to be adequate.

In addition to these caveats, all of the additive and subtractive events just described for normal human brain development must be weighed against a growing literature on individual differences within the normal range. As more sophisticated brain imaging techniques are developed, it becomes increasingly evident that there is considerable variation in structure and function in normal adult subjects. For example, Tramo and his colleagues (Tramo et al., 1994) reconstructed the cortical areas of two identical twins from MRI scans. Even in the case of genetically identical individuals, the variation in cortical areas was striking, with the occipital lobe occupying 13–17 percent of cortical area in one individual, and 20 percent in the other. These differences between individuals in brain structure may also extend to brain functioning. For example, using functional MRI, Schneider and colleagues studied the areas of activation following upper or lower visual field stimulation. While it had classically been assumed that the upper and lower visual field mapped on to the regions above and below the sulcus, there is in fact a lot of variation, with some normal subjects showing an upper/lower visual field cut that straddles this structure (Schneider, Noll, & Cohen, 1993). This new evidence for variability complements an older literature on individual differences in handedness and hemispheric organization for language (e.g. Kinsbourne & Hiscock, 1983; Hellige, 1993). In view of this variability in normal adults, efforts to construct a timetable for "normal" postnatal brain development in humans must be interpreted with caution.

2.4 THE DEVELOPMENT OF CORTICAL AREAS: PROTOMAP OR PROTOCORTEX?

An ongoing debate among those who study the developmental neurobiology of the cortex concerns the extent to which its structure and function are prespecified, in the sense that they are the result of genetic, molecular, and cellular level interactions and not determined by the pattern of firing of neurons. Orthogonal to the laminar dimension of cortical structure is its differentiation into regions or areas. Figure 2.6 illustrates one of the best-known schemes for dividing the cerebral cortex into areas. In the adult primate most of these cortical areas can be determined by very detailed differences in the laminar structure, such as the precise thickness of certain layers. Often, however, the borderlines between areas are indistinct and controversial. It is commonly assumed that these anatomically defined areas are also functionally distinct. While this has proved to be the case for early sensory and motor areas, there are many cases of functional regions or borders that do not neatly correspond to known neuroanatomical divisions. It

Figure 2.6 Cytoarchitectural map of the cerebral cortex. Some of the most important specific areas are as follows. Motor cortex: motor strip, area 4; pre-motor area, area 6; frontal eye fields, area 8. Somatosensory cortex: areas 3, 1, 2. Visual cortex: areas 17, 18, 19. Auditory cortex: areas 41 and 42. Wernicke's speech area: approximately area 22. Broca's speech area: approximately area 44 (in the left hemisphere) (from Brodmann, in Brodal, 1981).

should be stressed that the division of the cortex into areas with differing functional specializations is not an exact science in that the detailed features of neuroanatomy relevant for supporting different functions are unknown.

Despite these caveats, a century of neuropsychology has taught us that the majority of normal adults tend to have similar functions within approximately the same areas of cortex. This observation has lead to a common assumption that the division of the cerebral cortex into structural and functional areas is genetically prespecified. However, as we will see, this assumption is, at best, only partially correct.

The framework outlined in chapter 1 can be used to ask whether aspects of cortical structure are specified prior to postnatal experience. This question can be asked of both the laminar and the areal structure of cortex. Of course the two dimensions of cortical structure are not entirely independent, since structural areal divisions are partly specified by detailed differences in laminar structure. However, the framework in chapter 1 allowed for the possibility that while the basic architecture of a network is innate (basic circuitry, learning rules, type and number of cells, etc.), the detailed patterns of (dendritic and synaptic) connectivity are dependent upon experience. In such a case we may say that while the *network imposes architectural constraints on the representations that emerge within it, there are no innate representations.*

In the review that follows I will suggest that several aspects of the structure of the cerebral cortex, including the general laminar structure and large-scale regions, do not require neural activity to be established. Crucially, however, much of the fine-scale division into functional areas involves activity-dependent processes. I begin by returning to the prenatal development of cortex, and arguably the most complete theory of the development of cortical structure: the radial unit model proposed by Pasko Rakic (1988).

As mentioned earlier, most cortical neurons in humans are generated outside the cortex itself in a region just underneath what becomes the cortex, the "proliferative zones." This means that these cells must migrate to take up their locations within the cortex. How is this migration accomplished? Rakic has proposed a "radial unit model" of neocortical differentiation that gives an account of how *both* the areal and the layered structure of the mammalian cerebral cortex arise (Rakic, 1988). According to the model, the laminar organization of the cerebral cortex is determined by the fact that each proliferative unit (in the subventricular zone) gives rise to about one hundred neurons. The progeny from each proliferative unit all migrate up the same radial glial fibre, with the latest to be born travelling past their older relatives. A radial glial fibre is a long process that stretches from top to bottom of the cortex and originates from a glial cell. Thus, radial glial fibres act like a climbing rope to ensure that cells produced by one proliferative unit all contribute to one radial column within the cortex. Rakic's proposed method of migration is illustrated in figure 2.7.

FURTHER READING: RAKIC, 2002

There are some consequences of the radial unit model for the role of genetic regulation in species differences. For example, Rakic (1988) has pointed out that a single round of additional symmetric cell division at the proliferative unit formation stage would double the number of ontogenetic columns, and hence the area of cortex. In contrast, an additional single round of division at a later stage, from the proliferative zones, would only increase the size of a column by one cell (about 1 per cent). There is very little variation between mammalian species in the layered structure of the cortex, while the total surface area of the cortex can vary by a factor of 100 or more between different species of mammal. It seems likely, therefore, that species differences originate (at least in part) in the timing of cell development (i.e. the number of "rounds" of cell division that are allowed to take place within and across regions of the proliferative zones).

A related view on the evolution of mammalian brain has been put forward by Finlay and Darlington (1995). These authors compared data on the size of brain

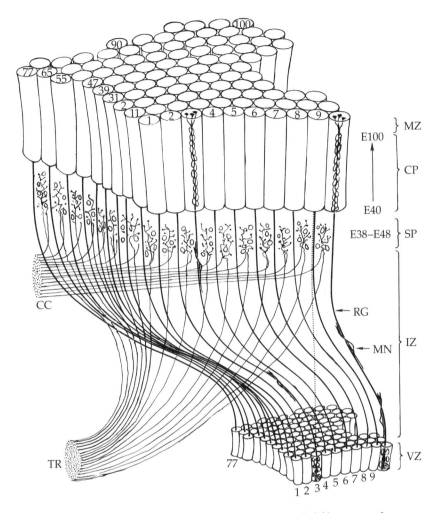

Figure 2.7 The radial unit model of Rakic (1987). Radial glial fibers span from the ventricular zone (VZ) to the cortical plate (CP) via a number of regions: the intermediate zone (IZ) and the subplate zone (SP). RG indicates a radial glial fiber, and MN a migrating neuron. Each MN traverses the IZ and SP zones that contain waiting terminals from the thalamic radiation (TR) and corticocortico afferents (CC). As described in the text, after entering the cortical plate, the neurons migrate past their predecessors to the marginal zone (MZ).

structures from 131 mammalian species, and concluded that the order of neurogenesis is conserved across a wide range of species and correlates with the relative enlargement of structures as overall brain size increases. Specifically, disproportionately large growth occurs in the late-generated structures such as the neocortex. By this analysis, the structure most likely to differ in size in the relatively slowed neurogenesis of primates is the neocortex.

Rakic's model explains how cortical cells arrange themselves into the thickness of the cortex, but how does the differentiation into specific layers emerge? While we are far from being able to answer this question definitively at this point, one view is that differentiation into particular cell types occurs *before* a neuron reaches its final location. That is, a cell "knows" what type of neuron it will become (pyramidal, spiny stellate, etc.) before it reaches its adult location within the cortex. Some evidence suggests that cells do indeed begin to differentiate before they reach their final vertical location. For example, in genetic mutant "reeler" mice, cells that acquire inappropriate laminar positions within the cortex still differentiate into neuronal types according to their time of origin, rather than the types normally found at their new location. This implies that the information required for differentiation is present at the cell's birth in the proliferative zones; it is not dependent upon their distance from the proliferative zones, or on the characteristics of the neighborhood in which that cell ends up. That is, in the proliferative zones for the neocortex, some cell types may be determined at the stage of division.

Although in many cases a cell's identity may be determined before it leaves the proliferative zones, some of the properties that distinguish among cell types may form later. For example, Marin-Padilla (1990) has proposed that the distinctive apical dendrite of pyramidal cells, which often reaches into layer 1, is a result of the increasing distance between this layer and other layers resulting from the inside-out pattern of growth. Specifically, the increasing separation between layer 1 and the subplate zone which results from young neurons moving into what will become layers 2 to 6 means that cells which have their processes attached to layer 1 will become increasingly "stretched" – that is, their leading dendrite will become stretched tangential to the surface of the cortex, resulting in the elongated apical dendrite so typical of cortical pyramidal cells. As mentioned earlier, this long apical dendrite allows the cell to be influenced by large numbers of cells from other (more superficial) layers.

Another aspect of the laminar structure of cortex that appears to be regulated by intrinsic cellular and molecular interactions concerns the major connections between cells, in particular the inputs from the thalamus. As mentioned earlier, the main input layer in the cortex is layer 4. A series of experiments by Blakemore and colleagues established that the termination of projections from the thalamus in layer 4 is governed by molecular markers. Slices of brain tissue are able to survive and grow in a Petri dish for several days under the appropriate conditions. Indeed, pieces of thalamus of the appropriate age will actually innervate other pieces of brain placed nearby. Molnar and Blakemore (1991) investigated if and how a piece of visual thalamus (LGN) would innervate various types of cortical and non-cortical brain tissue.

In initial experiments they established that when a piece of thalamus (LGN) and a piece of visual cortex were placed close together in the dish, afferents from the LGN not only invaded a piece of visual cortex of the appropriate age, but also terminated in the appropriate layer 4. Thus, layer 4 appears to contain some molecular stop signal that tells the afferents to stop growing and form connections at that location. Next, they conducted a series of choice experiments in which the visual thalamus had a piece of visual cortex and some other piece of brain placed nearby. The thalamic afferents turned out to dislike cerebellum, rarely penetrating it, but the afferents did grow into hippocampus. However, the growth into hippo-campus (a piece of brain that is closely related to neocortex – see section 2.8) was not spatially confined in the way it had been for visual cortex, suggesting that it was just a "growth-permitting substrate."

The evidence discussed so far indicates that the laminar structure of cortex probably arises from local cellular and molecular interactions, rather than it being shaped as a result of thalamic and sensory input. That is, the identity and location of neurons are determined before birth. Similarly, incoming fibers "know" in which layer to stop and make synaptic contacts. I now turn to the question of whether the areal structure of the cortex is determined in a similar way.

There are two possibilities that have been put forward to account for the division of cortex into areas:

1　The areal differentiation of cortex is due to a *protomap* (Rakic, 1988). By this view, differentiation into cortical regions occurs early in the formation of the cortex, and is due to intrinsic (to the cortex or its proliferative zones) factors. The activity of neurons is not required. The cortex is viewed as a mosaic from the start such that each cortical area has individually specified features par-ticularly suitable for the input it will receive or the functions it will perform.

2　The different areas of cortex arise out of an undifferentiated *protocortex*. By this view, differentiation occurs later in the development of cortex, and it depends on extrinsic factors like input from other parts of the brain or sensory systems. The activity of neurons is required (O'Leary, 2002; Killackey, 1990). The division of cortex into areas in the adult brain is influenced by informa-tion relayed from the thalamus, and from interactions with other areas of cortex via inter-regional connectivity.

FURTHER READING: O'LEARY, 2002; RAKIC, 2002

There is a large, complicated, and sometimes apparently conflicting literature on the areal differentiation of neocortex (for recent reviews see: Kingsbury & Finlay, 2001; Pallas, 2001; Ragsdale & Grove, 2001). Some recent experiments appear, at first sight, to be compelling evidence for the protomap view. For example, the newborns of a strain of "knockout" rodent (see chapter 1) that genetically lack connections between the thalamus and the cortex still have normal, well-defined regional gene-expression boundaries within their cortex (Miyashita-Lin, Hevner, Wassarman, Martinez, & Rubinstein, 1999) and some other characteristics of wild-type mice. In another example, *in vitro* studies in which cortical tissue is maintained in culture, and thus isolated from potential extrinsic patterning cues, still show patterns of gene expression consistent with the development of the hippocampus (Tole, Goodreau, Assimacopoulos, & Grove, 2000). Despite these and other studies supporting the idea of genetically specified regionalization of cortex, there are some important caveats, and also a surprising amount of evidence in support of the opposing protocortex view.

1   Most of the patterns of gene expression thought to contribute to the differentiation of cortex do not show clearly defined boundaries, but rather show graded expression across large extents of cortex. This suggests that regionalization of cortex could emerge from a combination of different gradients of gene expression. Kingsbury and Finlay (2001) refer to this as a "hyperdimensional plaid" and contrast this with a "mosaic quilt" (protomap) view.

2   At present, there are few examples of clear regionalization that map on to functional areas, and there are good reasons to believe that these cases are exceptions to the general rule. For example, comparisons across a large number of species have led several experts to argue that primary sensory areas that receive direct input from the primary sensory thalamic nuclei are less susceptible to change between species than most of the rest of the cortex (e.g. Krubitzer, 1998). In particular, the primary visual cortex in primates has unique characteristics that have led some to propose that it is the most recently evolved part of cortex. In the primary visual cortex, inputs from the visual thalamus may regulate the extent of cell proliferation in the ventricular zone (see Kennedy & Dehay, 1993), ensuring that this area of cortex has a rate of neuron production nearly twice that in neighboring areas. The entorhinal cortex, the region of cortex most closely associated with the hippocampus, shows some differentiation from surrounding cortex as early as 13 weeks after gestation (Kostovic, Petanjek, & Judas, 1993). However, for the majority of cortex in the mouse, and the vast majority in humans, there is currently no evidence for cortical divisions arising through the expression of a single gene.

3   Despite primary sensory regions being the best candidates for genetic prespecification, we will see in the next section of this chapter that even these regions can have their properties significantly changed through experience. Thus, input may be vital for the maintenance of cortical divisions.

4   Evidence for cortical differentiation prior to birth does not allow us to conclude that neuronal activity is not important since spontaneous neural activity within the brain is known to be important for differentiation (Shatz 2002).

FURTHER READING: SHATZ, 2002

To summarize so far, the basic laminar structure of the cerebral cortex in mammals appears to be very general. Cellular and molecular level interactions determine many aspects of the layered structure of cortex and its patterns of connectivity. Cortical neurons are often differentiated into specific computational types before they reach their destination (although some of the characteristic features of cell types are shaped by their journey to that site, e.g. the long apical dendrite that typifies pyramidal cells reflects a literal "stretching" of processes during the migration process). However, this does not mean that cells in a particular area are prespecified for processing certain kinds of information. The division of cortex into distinct regions and areas takes place along the areal dimension. Recent reviews of the evidence converge on a view mid-way between the protomap and protocortex hypotheses (Kingsbury & Finlay, 2001; Pallas, 2001; Ragsdale & Grove, 2001). This view is that graded patterns of gene expression potentially create large-scale regions with combinations of properties that may better suit certain computations (protomap). It is within these large-scale regions that smaller scale functional areas arise through mechanisms associated with the protocortex view. A hypothetical example is that one region may receive particular thalamic input, overlaid with a certain pattern of neurotransmitter expression, and the presence of certain neuromodulators. This combination of circumstances, combined with neural activity, may then induce further unique features such as particular patterns of short-range or long-range connectivity. Differentiation into smaller areas within the larger regions may occur through the selective pruning of connections (see chapter 10).

A good example of how a region of cortex can become differentiated comes from work on the so-called "barrel fields" that develop in the somatosensory cortex of rodents. Each barrel field is an anatomically definable functional grouping of cells that responds to a particular whisker on the animal's snout (see figure 2.8). Barrel-fields are an aspect of the areal structure of cortex that emerges postnatally, and are sensitive to whisker-related experience over the first days of life. For example, if a whisker is removed, then the barrel field that normally corresponds to that whisker does not emerge, and neighboring ones may occupy some of the cortical space normally occupied by it (for review see Schlaggar & O'Leary, 1993). Figure 2.8 illustrates how the areal divisions of the cortex arise as

Face   Ganglion V   Brain stem   Thalamus   Cortex

Figure 2.8 Patterning of areal units in somatosensory cortex. The pattern of "barrels" in the somatosensory cortex of rodents is an isomorphic representation of the geometric arrangement of vibrissae found on the animal's face. Similar patterns are present in the brain stem and thalamic nuclei that relay inputs from the face to the barrel cortex.

a result of similar divisions in structures closer to the sensory surface. In this case, it is almost as if the sensory surface *imposes* itself on to the brain stem, thence to the thalamus, and finally on to the cortex itself. The barrel field compartments emerge in sequence in these areas of the brain, with those closest to the sensory surface forming first, and the cortex patterns emerging last. While there is little evidence that barrel fields are prespecified in the cortex (but see Cooper & Steindler, 1986), a map of sensory space comes to occupy the somatosensory cortex in a reliable and replicable way.

In this section I have reviewed some of the literature on laminar and areal specification of cortex during normal development, concluding that there is evidence for both the protomap and protocortex views. This apparently conflicting evidence can be reconciled by the notion that large-scale regions of cortex have particular combinations of graded gene expression that are then refined into smaller areas through activity-dependent processes.

2.5 CORTICAL PLASTICITY

While some differentiation of cortex may occur early in development through intrinsic molecular and genetic factors, the nature of the information entering a region of cortex may be important in ensuring the maintenance and further progression of this differentiation. Further, neural activity driven by inputs may be able to change the function and detailed neuroanatomy of a region. Indeed, a number of experiments have shown that regions of the mammalian cerebral cortex can support a variety of different representations early in development. The evidence for this includes the following:

1   Reducing of the extent of thalamic input to a region of cortex early in life influences the subsequent size of that region (Rakic, 1988; Dehay, Horsburgh, Berland, Killackey, & Kennedy, 1989; O'Leary, 2002). Conversely, changing the quantity of cortex available for thalamic innervation changes the overall pattern of cortical differentiation and not just the affected region.
2   When thalamic inputs are "re-wired" such that they project to a different region of cortex from normal, the new recipient region develops some of the properties of the normal target tissue (e.g. auditory cortex takes on visual representations – Sur, Garraghty, & Roe, 1988; Sur, Pallas, & Roe, 1990).
3   When a piece of cortex is transplanted to a new location, it develops projections characteristic of its new location rather than its developmental origin (e.g. transplanted visual cortex takes on the representations that are appropriate for somatosensory input – O'Leary & Stanfield, 1989).

I will now consider each of these in more detail.

(1)   The effect on the cortex of manipulating the extent of sensory input (via the thalamus) to an area has been investigated in experiments where the thalamic input to an area of cortex is surgically reduced (Dehay, Kennedy, & Bullier, 1988). Surgical intervention in newborn macaque monkeys can reduce the thalamic projections to the primary visual cortex (area 17) by 50 percent. This reduction results in a corresponding reduction in the extent of area 17 in relation to area 18. That is, the border between areas 17 and 18 shifts such that area 17 becomes much smaller. Despite this drastic reduction in the radial size of area 17, it is important to note that its laminar structure remains normal. Further, the area which is still area 17 looks identical to its normal structure, and the region which becomes area 18 has characteristics normally associated with that area, and none of those unique to area 17 (Rakic, 1988). Thus, there is (surprisingly) little effect of reducing the extent of sensory projections to area 17 on the subsequent laminar structure of areas 17 and 18. The specific effect of this manipulation is to reduce the *area* of 17 relative to 18, despite the evidence of some prespecification of neuron numbers in this particular region discussed earlier. This indicates that even those cortical areas for which there is some evidence for prespecification can be subsequently modified.

Even the outputs characteristic of areas 17 and 18 follow the shift in border between them. For example, while area 18 normally has many callosal projections to the other hemisphere, area 17 does not. The region which is normally area 17, but becomes area 18 in the surgically operated animals, has the callosal projection pattern characteristic of normal area 18. A reasonable conclusion reached on the basis of these observations is that the region of cortex that would normally mature into area 17 develops properties that are characteristics of the adjacent area 18 as a result of reducing its thalamic input. Thus, at least some of the area-specific characteristics of cortex appear to be regulated by extrinsic factors, even for regions that show the greatest degree of prespecification.

In the converse experiment to those just discussed, when the cortical sheet is surgically reduced (in the opossum embryo), it produces a complete, although smaller and distorted, area map (Huffman et al., 1999). Relatedly, in genetically altered strains of mice that lack certain regulatory genes (Emx2 or Pax6), the resulting area map is distorted (Bishop et al., 2000; Mallamaci, Muzio, Chan, Parnavelas, & Boncinelli, 2000). Specifically, regions where these genes are normally expressed at high levels become "compressed" while other regions expand. These experiments illustrate that gradients of gene expression set up scaffolding which then interacts with thalamic input to result in functional areas. However, in atypical situations resulting from surgical or genetic manipulation, thalamic inputs can also shape regions that are not their normal targets.

(2)   Cross-modal plasticity of cortical areas has now been demonstrated at the neurophysiological level in several mammalian species (for review see Pallas, 2001). For example, in the ferret, projections from the retina can be induced to project to auditory thalamic areas, and thence to auditory cortex. Following a

technique initially developed by Frost (1990), this is done by placing lesions in the normal visual cortex and in the lateral geniculate (the thalamic target of retinal projections). Lesions are also placed such that auditory inputs do not innervate their normal thalamic target, the medial geniculate. Under these pathological conditions, retinal projections will re-route to innervate the medial geniculate nucleus (MGN). Projections from the MGN then project to the auditory cortex as normal. The experimental question concerns whether the normally auditory cortex becomes visually responsive (i.e. in accord with its input), or whether it retains features characteristic of auditory cortex. The answer turns out to be that auditory cortex does become visually responsive. Furthermore, cells in what would have been auditory cortex also become orientation- and direction-selective, and some become binocular.

While these observations are provocative, they do not provide evidence that the auditory cortex as a whole becomes functionally similar to the visual cortex. It is possible, for example, that the visually driven cells in the auditory cortex would fire in isolation from the activity of their colleagues. That is, there may be no organization above the level of the individual neuron. In order to address this issue, evidence that there is a spatial map of the visual world formed across this area of cortex is needed. In order to study this issue, Sur and colleagues recorded from single neurons in a systematic way across the re-wired cortex (Sur et al., 1988; Roe, Pallas, Hahm, & Sur, 1990). These experiments revealed that the previously auditory cortex had developed a two-dimensional retinal map. In normal ferrets, the primary auditory cortex contains a one-dimensional representation of the cochlea. Along one axis of the cortical tissue electrode penetrations revealed a gradual shift from responses to low frequencies to responses to high frequencies (see figure 2.9). Along the orthogonal dimension of cortex, frequency remained constant (the isofrequency axis). In contrast, the visual representation developed in the re-wired animals occupied both dimensions (elevation and azimuth). The authors conclude: "Our results demonstrate that the form of the map is not an intrinsic property of the cortex and that a cortical area can come to support different types of maps" (Roe et al., 1990)

Although these neuroanatomical and neurophysiological data support the idea that the auditory cortex can support visual representations, it remains to be established whether these representations can be used to guide the behavior of the animal in the normal way. To investigate this question, Sur and colleagues trained adult ferrets, re-wired in one hemisphere at birth, to discriminate between visual and auditory stimuli presented to the normal hemisphere. After this they probed the functioning of the re-wired hemisphere by presenting visual stimuli that activated only the re-wired pathway. The ferrets reliably interpreted the visual stimulus as visual rather than auditory (von Melchner, Pallas, & Sur, 2000). These results indicate that visual inputs can direct the construction of the appropriate processing circuitry.

(3) Additional evidence for cortical plasticity comes from studies on rodents in which pieces of cortex are transplanted from one region to another early in

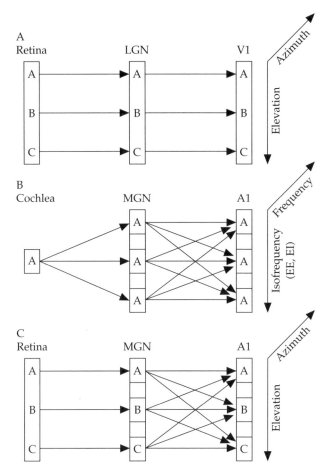

Figure 2.9 Schematic representation and summary of projections from the sensory receptor surface through the thalamus to the cortex in (A) the normal visual system, (B) the normal auditory system, and (C) lesioned ferrets with retinal projections induced into the auditory pathway.

development. These experiments allow neurobiologists to address the question of whether transplanted areas take on representations appropriate for their *developmental origins*, or the function of the *new location* in which they find themselves.

Pieces of fetal cortex have been successfully transplanted into other regions of newborn rodent cortex. For example, visual cortex neurons can be transplanted into the sensorimotor region and vice versa. Experiments such as these, conducted by O'Leary and Stanfield (1985, 1989), among others, have revealed that the projections and structure of such transplants develop according to their new spatial location rather than their developmental origins. For example, visual cortical neurons transplanted to the sensorimotor region develop projections to the spinal cord, a projection pattern characteristic of the sensorimotor cortex, but not the visual cortex. Similarly, sensorimotor cortical neurons transplanted to the visual cortical region develop projections to the superior colliculus, a subcortical target of the visual cortex, but not characteristic of the sensorimotor region. Thus, the inputs and outputs of a transplanted region take on the characteristics of their new location.

A further question concerns the internal structure of the transplanted region. As discussed earlier, the somatosensory cortex of the rat (and other rodents) possesses characteristic internal structures known as "barrel fields." Barrel fields are an aspect of the areal structure of the cortex, and are clearly visible under the microscope. Each of the barrels corresponds to one whisker on the rat's face. Barrels develop during postnatal growth, and can be prevented from appearing in the normal cortex by cutting the sensory inputs to the region from the face. Furthermore, barrel structure is sensitive to the effects of early experience such as repeated whisker stimulation, or whisker removal (see Schlaggar & O'Leary, 1993, for review). The question then arises whether transplanted slabs of visual cortex take on the barrel field structures that are typical of somatosensory cortex in the rat.

Schlaggar and O'Leary (1991) conducted a study in which pieces of visual cortex were transplanted into the part of the somatosensory cortex that normally forms barrel fields in the rodent. They found that when innervated by thalamic afferents, the transplanted cortex developed barrel fields very similar to those normally observed. Thus, not only can a transplanted piece of cortex develop inputs and outputs appropriate for its new location, but the inputs to that location can organize the internal structure of the cortical region.

At this stage, mention should be made of two caveats to the conclusion that the majority of cortical tissue is largely equipotent early in life. First, most of the transplant and re-wiring studies have involved primary sensory cortices. Some authors have argued that primary sensory cortices may share certain common developmental origins that other types of cortex do not (Galaburda & Pandya, 1983; Pandya & Yeterian, 1990; Krubitzer, 1998). It is possible that certain lineages of cortex which differ in detailed ways from other areas of cortex may be more suited for dealing with certain types of information processing. With regard to the transplant experiments discussed earlier, it may be that cortex is only equipotential within a lineage (e.g. primary-to-primary or secondary-to-secondary).

The second caveat to the conclusion that cortex is equipotential is that while transplanted or re-wired cortex may look very similar to the original tissue in terms of function and structure, it is rarely absolutely indistinguishable from the original. For example, in the re-wired ferret cortex studied by Sur and colleagues the mapping of the azimuth (angle right or left) is at a higher resolution (more detailed) than the mapping of the elevation (angle up or down) (Roe et al., 1990). In contrast, in the normal ferret cortex azimuth and elevation are mapped in equal detail.

2.6 DIFFERENTIAL DEVELOPMENT OF HUMAN CORTEX

The main phylogenetic changes in cortical development in primates appear to be in the extent of cortical tissue and the more prolonged period of development in primates and humans. Even between *Homo sapiens* and other primates there is a wide difference in timing, with human postnatal cortical development being extended (roughly by a factor of four) longer than other primates. As discussed earlier, this prolonged postnatal development in humans stretches out differential laminar and regional cortical developments that are more compressed in time in other species. In the case of laminar development, although most cortical neurons are in their appropriate locations by the time of birth in the primate, the "inside-out" pattern of growth observed in prenatal cortical development extends into postnatal life. Extensive descriptive neuroanatomical studies of cortical development in the human infant by Conel over a thirty-year period lead him to the conclusion that the postnatal growth of cortex proceeds in an "inside-out" pattern with regard to the extent of dendrites, dendritic trees, and myelination (Conel, 1939–67). Conel's general conclusions have been validated with more modern neuroanatomical methods (e.g. Purpura, 1975; Rabinowicz, 1979; Becker, Armstrong, Chan, & Wood, 1984), and a modern re-analysis of Conel's original data has deemed it to be highly consistent and reliable (Shankle, Kimball, Landing, & Hara, 1998). In particular, the maturation of layer 5 (deeper) in advance of layers 2 and 3 (superficial) seems to be a very reliably observed sequence for many cortical regions in the human infant (Rabinowicz, 1979; Becker et al., 1984). For example, the dendritic trees of cells in layer 5 of primary visual cortex are already at about 60 per cent of their maximum extent at birth. In contrast, the mean total length for dendrites in layer 3 is only at about 30 per cent of their maximum at birth. Furthermore, higher orders of branching in dendritic trees are observed in layer 5 than in layer 3 at birth (Becker et al., 1984; Huttenlocher 1990). Interestingly, this inside-out pattern of growth is not evident in the later occurring rise and fall in synaptic density. For this measure, there are no clear differences between cerebral cortical layers.

Differential development in human postnatal cortical growth is also evident in the areal dimension. Huttenlocher (1990, 1994; Huttenlocher & Dabholkar, 1997) reports clear evidence of a difference in the timing of postnatal neuroanatomical events between the primary visual cortex, the primary auditory cortex, and the frontal cortex in human infants, with the latter reaching the same developmental landmarks considerably later in postnatal life than the first two. It is worth noting that this differential development within the cerebral cortex has not been reported in other primate species (Rakic, Bourgeois, Eckenhoff, Zecevic, & Goldman-Rakic, 1986; Bourgeois, 2001). Rakic et al. report that all areas of cortex appear to reach their peak in synaptic density about the same time – around 2–4 months in the rhesus monkey, roughly corresponding to from 7 to 12 months in the human child. Contrary to Huttenlocher's findings, this suggests that there may be a common genetic signal to increase connectivity across all brain regions, simultaneously, regardless of their current maturational state. A sudden event of this kind stands in marked contrast to known region-by-region differences in the time course of cell formation, migration, myelination, and metabolism in the human cortex (Conel, 1939–1967; Yakovlev & Lecours, 1967). The most likely difference between the human results and those from the macaques is that the protracted postnatal development of humans means that regional differences are more evident. In the macaque, however, possible regional differences are compressed into a much shorter time, making them harder to detect (Huttenlocher, 1994). However, Goldman-Rakic (1994) suggests that the differences between the macaque and human results may be due to the neuroanatomical techniques used. Further, the decline in synaptic density in the human brain may not differ between regions, but occur simultaneously at puberty (Bourgeois, 2001).

FURTHER READING: BOURGEOIS, 2001; HUTTENLOCHER, 2002

Consistent with the reports from human postmortem tissue, a study in which the functional development of the human brain was investigated by PET has also found differential development between regions of cortex (Chugani & Phelps, 1986; Chugani et al., 2002). In infants under 5 weeks of age glucose uptake was highest in sensorimotor cortex, thalamus, brain stem, and the cerebellar vermis. By 3 months of age there were considerable rises in the parietal, temporal, and occipital cortices, basal ganglia, and cerebellar cortex. Maturational rises were not found in the frontal and dorsolateral occipital cortex until approximately 6 to 8 months. These developments are shown in figure 2.10.

In addition to the formation of dendritic trees and their associated synapses, most fibers become myelinated during postnatal development. As described earlier, myelin is a membrane wrapping around axons that improves conduction. Owing to the increased lipid content of the brain caused by myelination of fibers, structural MRI images can reveal a clear gray–white matter contrast, and this allows quantitative volume measurements to be made during development (see Sampaio & Truwit, 2001). While some controversy remains about the interpretation of images from infants under 6 months (due to a higher than adult water content in both gray and white matter at this age), there is consensus that the appearance of brain structures is similar to that of adults by 2 years of age, and that all major fiber tracts can be observed by 3 years of age (Huttenlocher & Dabholkar, 1997; Bourgeois, 2001). Some reports suggest that after a rapid increase in gray matter volume up to about 4 years of age, there is then a prolonged period of slight decline that extends into adult years (Chugani et al., 2002; but see Huttenlocher & Dabholkar, 1997). Whether this decline in gray matter is due to dendritic and synaptic pruning remains unknown, although in some studies the time course of the rise and fall coincides (Huttenlocher & Dabholkar, 1997).

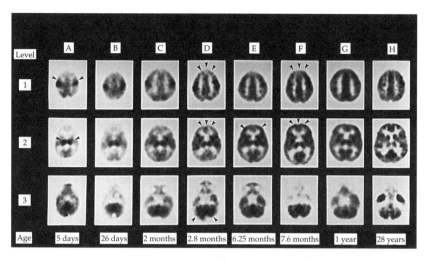

Figure 2.10 PET images illustrating developmental changes in local cerebral metabolic rates for glucose (ICMRGlc) in the normal human infant with increasing age. Level 1 is a superior section, at the level of the cingulate gyrus. Level 2 is more inferior, at the level of caudate, putamen, and thalamus. Level 3 is an inferior section of the brain, at the level of cerebellum and inferior position of the temporal lobes. Gray scale is proportional to ICMRGlc with black being highest. Images from all subjects are not shown on the same absolute gray scale of ICMRGlc; instead, images of each subject are shown with the full gray scale to maximize gray scale display of ICMRGlc at each age. (A) In the 5-day-old, ICMRGlc is highest in sensorimotor cortex, thalamus, cerebellar vermis (arrows), and brain stem (not shown). (B, C, D) ICMRGlc gradually increases in parietal, temporal, and calcarine cortices; basal ganglia; and cerebellar cortex (arrows), particularly during the second and third months. (E) In the frontal cortex, ICMRGlc increases first in the lateral prefrontal regions by approximately 6 months. (F) By approximately 8 months, ICMRGlc also increases in the medial aspects of the frontal cortex (arrows), as well as the dorsolateral occipital cortex. (G) By 1 year, the ICMRGlc pattern resembles that of adults (H).

Changes in the extent of white matter are of interest since they presumably reflect inter-regional communication in the developing brain. While increases in white matter extend through adolescence into adulthood, particularly in frontal brain regions (Huttenlocher et al., 1982), the most rapid changes occur during the first 2 years. Myelination appears to begin at birth in the pons and cerebellar peduncles, and by 3 months has extended to the optic radiation and splenium of the corpus callosum. Around 8–12 months the white matter associated with the frontal, parietal, and occipital lobes becomes apparent.

FURTHER READING: SAMPAIO & TRUWIT 2001

The differential laminar and regional development observed in the human, as described in this section, provides the basis for many of the associations between brain growth and cognitive change to be described in the following chapters. But first we need to review some other aspects of postnatal brain development.

2.7 POSTNATAL BRAIN DEVELOPMENT: THE HIPPOCAMPUS AND SUBCORTICAL STRUCTURES

This chapter has focused primarily on the cerebral neocortex since this is the part of the brain that shows most protracted postnatal development. However, other brain structures such as the hippocampus and cerebellum also show some post-natal development and, as we will see, have been associated with cognitive changes in infancy and childhood. The postnatal development of some subcortical struc-tures (such as the hippocampus, cerebellum, and thalamus) poses something of a paradox: on the one hand, there is much behavioral and neural evidence to indicate that these structures are functioning at birth, while, on the other, they all show some evidence of postnatal development and/or functional re-organization. One explanation for this is that as the neocortex develops postnatally, its interac-tions with subcortical regions undergo certain changes. Thus, while some subcortical structures are capable of functioning relatively independently of the cortex early in life, the increasing development of the cortex requires some structural and functional adjustment.

The limbic system is normally taken to include the amygdala, the hippocampus, and the limbic regions of cortex (cingulate gyrus and parahippocampal gyrus [entorhinal cortex]). While these latter cortical regions follow the same develop-mental timetable as other regions of the cortex, they are differentiated from the rest of cortex at an early stage, and are therefore unlikely to show the same degree of plasticity. As discussed earlier, gyral development (folding) does not necessarily indicate architectural specificity. Nevertheless, the gyral folding asso-ciated with the cingulate region is discernible as early as 16–19 weeks of gesta-tional age in humans and the parahippocampal gyrus within the temporal lobe at 20–3 weeks gestational age (Gilles, Shankle, & Dooling, 1983). In contrast, other prominent gyri in the cortex do not emerge until 24–31 weeks. The major nuclear components of the limbic system, such as the hippocampus, start to differentiate from the developing temporal lobe around the third and fourth months of fetal development. After this, further differentiation of the hippocampus takes place, resulting in it becoming a rolled structure tucked inside the temporal lobe and surrounded by tissue known as the dentate gyrus (see Seress, 2001, for review). It has been known for some time that in rodents neurogenesis continues into postnatal life in the dentate gyrus region (Wallace, Kaplan, & Werboff, 1977). Recently, it has been confirmed in humans that granule neurones continue to be produced throughout adulthood (for review see Tanapat, Hastings, & Gould, 2001).

This new production of neurons is influenced by hormones (see next section), and, at least in rats, some types of learning enhance the number of new neurons produced. The computational importance of adult neurogenesis in this region remains to be determined.

FURTHER READING: SERESS, 2001; TANAPAT ET AL., 2001

The cerebellum is a brain structure thought to be involved in motor control, but which probably also plays a role in some aspects of "higher" cognitive functioning. Within 2 months after conception the cerebellum has formed its three primary layers, the ventricular (V), intermediate (I), and marginal (M) layers. However, its development is prolonged and neurogenesis in this region continues postnatally with only about 17 percent of the final number of granule cells present at birth, and neurogenesis possibly continuing until 18 months (Spreen et al., 1995). Despite being one of the few regions of the human brain to show postnatal neurogenesis, cerebellar functional development as measured by resting PET shows high glucose metabolic activity as early as 5 days old (postnatal), the same schedule as other sensorimotor regions such as the thalamus, brain stem, and sensorimotor cortex (Chugani, 1994).

2.8 NEUROTRANSMITTERS AND NEUROMODULATORS

The aspects of brain development discussed so far have mainly concerned its neurons and "wiring." However, there are also developmental changes in what has been referred to as "soft soak" aspects of neural function. Soft soak refers specifically to the chemicals involved in the transmission and modulation of neural signals. Neurons and their dendrites can be thought of as lying in a bath composed of various chemicals that modulate their functioning. In addition, other chemicals play a vital role in the transmission of signals from one cell to another. Neurotransmitters in the cerebral cortex may be classified into those that arise within the cortex (intrinsic), and those that arise from outside the cortex (extrinsic) (see Benes, 1994). The intrinsic transmitters can be further divided according to whether they have an excitatory effect or inhibitory effect on postsynaptic sites.

The intrinsic excitatory transmitter glutamate is thought to play an important role in the axons of pyramidal cells that project to intrinsic cortical microcircuits, other cortical regions, and subcortical regions (Streit, 1984). In rats, the developmental time course of different glutamatergic pathways varies considerably. In general, however, it is the receptors for the transmitter, rather than the quantity of the transmitter, that increase with postnatal age. This development seems to follow the rise and fall pattern seen in other aspects of neural development. Specifically, in the rat between postnatal days 10 and 15 the amount of glutamate binding in cortical regions increases rapidly and reaches a peak around ten times the levels observed in adults (Schliebs, Kullman, & Bigl, 1986). By day 25 these levels have reduced drastically.

GABA (Gamma-aminobutyric acid) is probably the most important intrinsic inhibitory transmitter in the mammalian brain. While there are a variety of ways to measure GABA activity which sometimes give differing results (see Benes, 1994), in the human the same overall pattern of rise and fall seen for glutamate is also observed for GABA. Specifically, the density of GABA receptors increases rapidly in the perinatal period and doubles over the first few weeks before later declining (Brooksbank, Atkinson, & Balasz, 1981). The extent to which the rise and fall in these intrinsic neurotransmitters mirrors that observed in the structural measures discussed earlier such as glucose uptake and synaptic density is currently unclear and requires further research. It is clear, however, that the levels of GABA can be influenced by the extent of sensory experience (Fosse, Heggelund, & Fonnum, 1989).

Extrinsic neurotransmitters arise from a number of different subcortical locations. One of these transmitters, acetylcholine, originates mainly from the basal forebrain (Johnston, McKinney, & Coyle, 1979). Interestingly, the innervation of cortex by cholinergic fibers follows the "inside-out" pattern of growth described earlier, with the deeper cortical layers being innervated before the more superficial ones. In humans, this cholinergic innervation begins prenatally, though adult levels are not reached until about 10 years old (Diebler, Farkas-Bergeton, & Wehrle, 1979). However, the binding sites within the cortex for this transmitter decrease from birth onwards, possibly due to synaptic pruning (Ravikumar & Sasatry, 1985).

Another neurotransmitter with origins outside the cortex is norepinephrine (or noradrenaline), which originates in a cluster of nuclei called the locus coeruleus. As well as its role as a neurotransmitter, norepinephrine has been associated with cortical plasticity (Kasamatsu & Pettigrew, 1976). In several mammals there is an extensive network of noradrenergic fibers in the cortex at birth which may be more dense than that seen in adults (Coyle & Molliver, 1977). Currently, little developmental information is available on this transmitter in primates (Benes, 1994).

Serotonin originates in the brainstem raphe nuclei, and in both rats and primates the level increases rapidly over the first few weeks of life (Johnston, 1988). In rhesus monkeys the adult pattern of projection of serotonin fibers is reached by the sixth week postnatal, though levels of serotonin continue to rise after this (Goldman-Rakic & Brown, 1982). There is some evidence (from specific binding sites) of a later decrease in serotonin in human cortex and hippocampus (Marcusson, Morgan, Winblad, & Finch, 1984). Like acetylcholine, serotonin is found mainly in the deeper cortical layers at birth, consistent with the structural inside-out gradient of development discussed earlier.

The fourth main extrinsic cortical transmitter, dopamine (which originates in the substantia nigra), likewise shows an inside-out pattern around the time of birth, at least in rats (Kalsbeek, Voorn, Buijs, Pool, & Uylings, 1988). Dopaminergic fibers show the adult pattern of projection into the frontal and cingulate cortex through extended postnatal development in rats (Bruinink, Lichtensteiger, & Schlumpf, 1983).

In summary, it appears that:

- Most intrinsic and extrinsic transmitters are present in the cortex at birth, at least in rats and probably also in humans, but show changes in distribution and overall levels for some time after birth.
- Several transmitters of both intrinsic and extrinsic origins show the characteristic rise and fall evident in some measures of structural neuroanatomical development. Owing to a paucity of human data, it is currently not possible to say to what extent these developmental patterns overlap.
- Several transmitters of extrinsic origin show the same inside-out gradient of cortical development observed in structural measures.
- Neurotransmitters may play multiple roles during development. For example, noradrenaline may also regulate cortical plasticity.
- Some transmitters show a differential distribution throughout the cortex. This differential distribution may play some role in the subsequent specialisation of regions of cortex for certain functions.

FURTHER READING: BENES, 2001; CAMERON, 2001; BERENBAUM ET AL., 2003; RICHARDS, 2003

2.9 GENERAL SUMMARY AND CONCLUSIONS

This chapter has reviewed the pre- and postnatal development of the human brain. While many of the landmarks of development are similar between humans and other mammals, the timing of human brain development is characterized by being slower and more protracted. According to some theories, this slowed development allows the building of relatively more cortex, and particularly frontal cortex. One major feature of human postnatal development is that brain volume quadruples between birth and adulthood, mainly due to increases in nerve fiber bundles, dendrites, and myelination. Another major feature is that several measures of structure and neurophysiology, such as the density of synaptic contacts, show a characteristic "rise and fall" during postnatal development.

The issue was raised as to whether the differentiation of the neocortex into anatomical and functional areas is prespecified. The "protomap" hypothesis states that the differentiation of the cortex into areas is determined by intrinsic molecular markers or prespecification of the proliferative zones. The "protocortex" hypothesis states that an initially undifferentiated protocortex is divided up largely as a result of input through projections from the thalamus and is activity-dependent. A review of currently available evidence supports a middle-ground view in which large-scale regions are prespecified, while the establishment of small-scale functional areas require activity-dependent processes.

The very extended period of postnatal development seen in the human brain reveals two differential aspects of cortical development not as clearly evident in other primates: an inside-out pattern of development of layers, and differences in the timing of development across regions. These differential aspects of human cortical development will provide the basis for associations between brain and cognitive development described in later chapters.

3 VISION, ORIENTING, AND ATTENTION

This chapter reviews selected topics in vision, visual orienting, and visual attention for which attempts have been made to relate brain development to behavioral change. The contribution of peripheral systems (retinal) development in the emergence of basic visual functions is briefly alluded to before discussion of the neural basis of the development of binocular vision. Neuroanatomical and computational modeling evidence highlights the importance of the segregation of inputs to layer 4 cells in the primary visual cortex. This increased segregation of inputs from the two eyes can be viewed as the result of a self-organizing neural network constrained by certain intrinsic and extrinsic factors. A compelling behavioral test of the increased segregation hypothesis is discussed. Moving on from sensory processing to sensorimotor integration, the following section describes an attempt to use the developmental neuroanatomy of the cortex to make predictions about transitions in orienting behavior in infants. A number of behavioral marker tasks for cortical regions involved in oculomotor control are reviewed and discussed in relation to the maturational model. Recent neuroimaging and behavioral studies require modifications to the original model. Finally, experiments concerned with the development of covert (internal) attention shifts in infants and children are described. A number of changes in the flexibility and speed of shifting attention are shown to originate in infancy but continue into childhood.

3.1 THE DEVELOPMENT OF VISION

Visual pathways, and especially the visual cortex, are among the most studied regions of the brain. More than twenty-five visual areas of the primate cortex have been identified, and, by means of single-cell recording, neuroimaging, and neuropsychological studies, attempts have been made to understand the functions of these regions. On the behavioral side, much is known about visual psychophysics, and our knowledge about visual cognitive abilities is rapidly expanding. Vision would therefore seem to be a good starting place for studying the functional consequences of the developing brain.

Immediately we begin to consider this issue it becomes obvious that it is hard to determine whether changes in visual abilities during development are due to limitations in the periphery, such as the structure of the eye, lens, or eye muscles, or whether they are due to changes within the brain. It is clear that immaturities in peripheral sensory systems place limits on the perceptual capacities of young infants. For example, it is well known that immaturity of the retina limits spatial acuity. Some have even argued that such limitations are necessary to prevent overwhelming developing visual circuits with too much data too soon (Turkewitz & Kenny, 1982). The issue remains, however, whether peripheral limitations provide the major constraints on the development of perception, or whether development of visual pathways within the brain is the primary limiting factor. While this issue continues to be debated, Banks and colleagues (e.g. Banks & Shannon, 1993) conducted an "ideal observer" analysis in which the morphology of neonatal photoreceptors and optics was compared to that of adults. This analysis generated estimates of the contribution of optical and receptor immaturity, as opposed to central immaturities, to deficits in infant spatial and chromatic vision. Observed differences in these aspects of vision between adults and infants turn out to be significantly greater than would be predicted on the basis of peripheral limitations only, indicating that central nervous system pathway development is an important contributing factor in the development of vision. Given that central nervous system factors play an important role even in the development of spatial acuity, we can inquire further into the nature and source of these constraints. Figure 3.1 summarizes some of the steps in visually guided behavior that will be discussed in the next few chapters. Processing related to perceiving and acting on objects is discussed in the next chapter. The processing of social visual stimuli, such as faces, is discussed in chapter 5. In the present chapter we focus on some aspects of visual processing, orienting, and attention.

> *FURTHER READING: DANNEMILLER, 2001; MAURER & LEWIS, 2001; ATKINSON & BRADDICK, 2003*

Alongside evidence from behavioral and psychophysiological measures of visual abilities, in recent years investigators have begun to use functional imaging to see which visual pathways and structures can be activated at different ages. Owing to the difficulties of keeping young infants still for long enough, functional MRI studies with this population typically involve sedated infants being scanned for clinical reasons. Nevertheless, the studies have demonstrated that sedated and

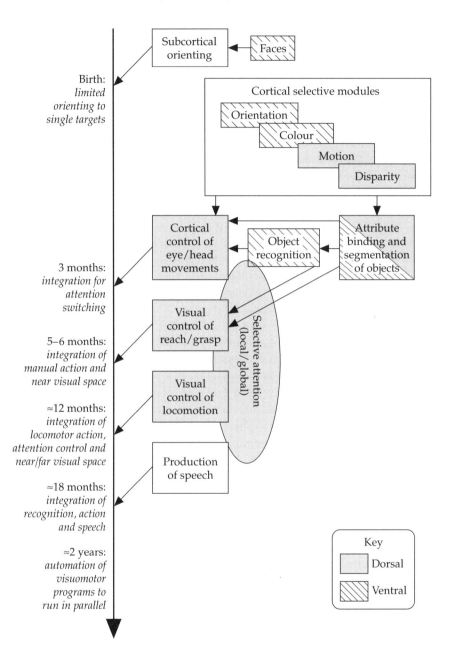

Figure 3.1 Diagram of the developmental sequence of visual behavior (left of vertical line) and ventral- and dorsal-stream neural systems contributing to this (right of vertical line).

sleeping infants respond to visual stimulation in some of the same visual cortical regions as adults (Born, Rostrup, Leth, Peitersen, & Lou, 1996; Born, Rostrup, Miranda, Larsson, & Lou, 2002; Yamada et al., 1997, 2000). These findings have been confirmed in healthy awake infants using the new technique of optical imaging (NIRS). Following on from an earlier study with a single site (Meek et al., 1998), Taga and colleagues used a multi-channel optical system to study blood oxygenation in occipital and frontal sites while 2 to 4-month-olds viewed dynamic schematic face-like patterns (Taga, Asakawa, Maki, Konishi, & Koizumi, 2003). The results demonstrated that a localized area of the occipital cortex responded to brief changes in luminance contrasts in the form of event-related changes in blood oxygenation similar to those seen in adults. More importantly, this study has helped establish that this technique can be used in the near future to explore visual function during early infancy.

The central visual field of most primates is binocular, requiring integration of information between the two eyes. This integration is achieved in the primary visual cortex. Functional and anatomical structures observed in layer 4 of the primary visual cortex, so-called "ocular dominance columns," are thought to be important for binocular vision (see figure 3.2). These columns arise from the segregation of inputs from the two eyes. In other words, neurons in a single ocular dominance column are dominated by input from one eye in adult mammals. Ocular dominance columns are thought to be the stage of processing necessary to achieve binocular vision and, subsequently, detection of disparities between the two retinal images. Owing to the fact that ocular dominance columns are known to have a sensitive period for their formation, and to be sensitive to the differential extent of input from the two eyes, they have become a popular model system for developmental neurobiology (e.g. Kasamatsu & Pettigrew, 1976; Bear & Singer, 1986; Rauschecker & Singer, 1981).

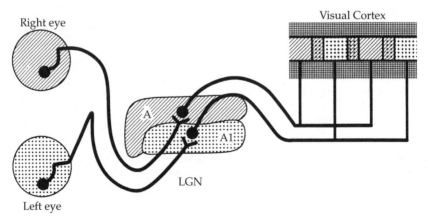

Figure 3.2 Simplified schematic diagram illustrating how projections from the two eyes form ocular dominance columns in the visual cortex.

Held (1985) reviewed converging evidence that binocular vision develops at approximately the end of the fourth month of life in human infants. Visually evoked potential measures (short latency ERPs elicited by a conspicuous visual stimulus) with dynamic correlograms find evidence for binocularity around 3 months (see Atkinson & Braddick, 2003, for review). One of the abilities associated with binocular vision, stereoacuity, increases very rapidly from the onset of stereopsis, such that it reaches adult levels within a few weeks. This is in contrast to other measures of acuity, such as grating acuity, which increase much more gradually. Held suggested that this very rapid spurt in stereoacuity requires some equally rapid change in the neural substrate supporting it. On the basis of evidence from animal studies, he proposed that this substrate is the development of ocular dominance columns found in layer 4 of the primary visual cortex. While Held's proposal was initially based on a simple causal association between the formation of ocular dominance columns and the onset of binocularity, other research in his laboratory has been concerned to describe a link between the process of change at the two levels.

As mentioned in the previous chapter, processes of selective loss commonly contribute to the sculpting of specific pathways in the cortex. Neurophysiological evidence indicates that the inputs from the two eyes to the cortex are initially mixed so that they synapse on common cortical neurons in layer 4 (see figure 3.3). These layer 4 cells project to disparity-selective cells (possibly in cortical layers 2 and 3). During ontogeny, geniculate axons originating from one eye withdraw from the region, leaving behind axons from the other eye. Held suggested that it is these events at the neural level that give rise to the sudden increase in stereoacuity observed by behavioral measures in the human infant.

This process of selective loss has the information-processing consequence that information from the two eyes which was previously combined in layer 4 of the primary visual cortex becomes segregated (Held, 1993). Specifically, there will be a certain degree of integration between the eyes that will decline once each neuron receives innervation from only one eye. Held and colleagues elegantly demonstrated this increasing segregation of information from the two eyes by showing that infants under 4 months can perform certain types of integration between the two eyes that older infants cannot. In this experiment, Held and his colleagues presented a grating to one eye of an infant, and an orthogonal grating to the other eye (Shimojo, Birch, & Held, 1983). Infants under 4 months perceived a single grid-like representation instead of two sets of gratings that were orthogonal to each other. This is because, presumably, synaptic inputs from the individual eyes have not segregated into ocular dominance columns. As a result, a given cortical layer 4 neuron may have synaptic inputs from each eye and will effectively "see" the image from each eye simultaneously. That is, information from the two eyes would be summed in layer 4, resulting in an averaging of the two signals. Since the inputs from each eye summate, in the case of the orthogonal gratings a grid was perceived. Older infants (older than 4 months of age) do not perceive this grating because neurons in cortical layer 4 of striate cortex only

Figure 3.3 (A) Afferents from both eyes synapse on the same cells in layer 4, thereby losing information about the eye of origin. (B) Afferents are segregated on the basis of eye origin (R and L), and consequently recipient cells in layer 4 may send their axons to cells outside of that layer so as to synapse on cells that may be disparity-selective.

receive inputs from one eye. The inputs to layer 4 have been segregated from one another, and a given layer 4 neuron will receive input from one eye or the other.

The loss of these connections is probably due to the refinement of synapses by selective loss. This refinement most likely occurs through activity-dependent neural mechanisms since it has been shown that the formation of ocular dominance columns can be experimentally blocked by reducing neuronal activity (Stryker & Harris, 1986). Monocular deprivation (Wiesel & Hubel, 1965) also results in atypical ocular dominance columns; in this case, the eye that is preserved takes over more than its normal share of cortical area. The increasing segregation of inputs through selective pruning of connections is a developmental process that recurs in several of the domains of cognition that we will discuss in later chapters.

While at first sight the rapid onset of binocular function and its hypothesized neural basis makes it seem an attractive candidate for the maturational approach, computational modeling efforts suggest that in this case an activity-dependent (interactive specialization) approach may be more appropriate. For example, Miller and his colleagues (Miller, Keller, & Stryker, 1989; Miller, 1990) developed a neural network model of ocular dominance column development. They found that "ocular dominance columns" emerged robustly under a variety of starting conditions and learning rules (see figure 3.4). The purpose of such modeling is to understand the core requirements or constraints for the formation of a structure. In this case, Miller and colleagues identified several critical factors for the formation of this pattern. The first of these was that the projection pattern from each LGN cell to cortical cells needs to be such that cortical cells at the center of the projection fan receive stronger input than do those at the edge of the projection. The second critical factor identified by Miller and colleagues was that the projections within the cortex need to be locally excitatory and inhibitory for longer distances. Intuitively, it is obvious that this arrangement will ensure that cells that respond to similar inputs will cluster together and "push apart" from those that have different response properties. The third critical factor is that correlations of firing from LGN cells within each eye must be greater than between the two eyes. In other words, inputs from within one eye tend to correlate more highly in their activity than those between the two eyes. Miller and colleagues suggest that this is the case because spontaneous activity (firing) in the retina and LGN is likely to be more correlated within each eye than between the two eyes.

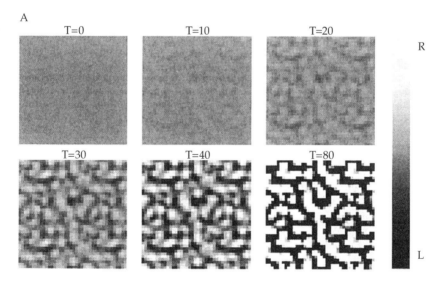

Figure 3.4 Typical development of ocular dominance patches of cortex at time-steps T = 0, 10, 20, 30, 40, 80. Each pixel represents a single cortical cell. The shades represent ocular dominance of each cell, that is, the difference between the total (summed) strength of right eye and of left eye geniculate inputs to the cell. White indicates complete dominance by the right eye; black indicates complete dominance by the left eye; and gray represents equality of the two eyes.

To generalize the conclusions from the work of Miller and colleagues, for the ocular dominance columns to develop, critical factors from three sources must all be present: first, the correlational structure of the input is important (in this case to ensure that the correlations within an eye projection are greater than those between the two eyes); second, the intrinsic microcircuitry of cortex (in this case the relative distribution of excitatory and inhibitory projections); and, third, constraints imposed by subcortical circuitry (in this case the projection patterns from the LGN). We will see that these three sources of constraint play a role in shaping the representations and areal structures that emerge in other examples of cortical development. While ocular dominance columns and binocular vision may seem at first sight like a prime example of the maturation of the brain causing a behavioral change, on closer inspection we have seen that viewing the process in terms of interactive specialization may be more fruitful.

3.2 THE DEVELOPMENT OF VISUAL ORIENTING

In the previous section attempts to relate brain development of an aspect of sensory processing were discussed. In this section we move to a domain, visual orienting, which allows the study of the effects of brain development on the integration between sensory input and motor output. Visual orienting involves moving the eyes and head in response to, or in anticipation of, a new sensory stimulus. Most of the tasks to be described involve stimuli that are well within the visual capacities for infants, and involve a form of action (movements of the eyes) which infants can readily accomplish. Thus, while there is continuing development of both sensory and motor processing throughout infancy, through carefully designed experiments we are able to focus more on the integration between sensory input and motor output.

There are also other reasons for studying the development of visual orienting. One of these is that over the first year of life it is the human infant's primary method of gathering information from its environment. These shifts of gaze allow the infant to select particular aspects of the external world for further study and learning. For example, as we will see in chapter 5, simply by shifting the head and eyes infants can ensure that they are exposed to faces more than to other stimuli. In addition, most of what we have learned about mental processes in infants has come from tasks in which some measure of looking behavior, such as preferential looking or habituation to a repeatedly presented stimulus, is used (see chapter 1).

Despite the importance of shifts of eye gaze in early infancy, however, until the past decade very little was known about how the development of the brain relates to changes in visual orienting abilities. This was despite a substantial literature on the neural basis of saccades (eye movements) which comes from neuropsychological and neuroimaging studies of human adults, as well as single-cell recording and lesion studies in non-human primates (see Andersen, Batista, Snyder, Buneo, & Cohen, 2000 for review).

In one of the first attempts to relate brain development to behavioral change in the human infant, Gordon Bronson (1974, 1982) argued that the early development of vision and visual orienting could be attributed to a shift from subcortical visual processing to processing in cortical visual pathways over the first 6 months of life. Specifically, Bronson cited evidence from electrophysiological, neuroanatomical, and behavioral studies that the primary (cortical) visual pathway is not fully functioning until around 3 months postnatal. As discussed earlier, it has more recently become evident that there is some, albeit limited, cortical activity in newborns, and that the onset of cortical functioning probably proceeds by a series of graded steps, rather than in an all-or-none manner. Meanwhile, neurophysiological research on monkeys and neuropsychological research with human adults has revealed that there are multiple pathways involved in oculomotor (eye movement) control and attention shifts in the primate brain. A number of the structures and pathways involved in oculomotor control in primates are illustrated in figure 3.5.

FURTHER READING: DANNEMILLER, 2001; JOHNSON, 2002; ATKINSON & BRADDICK, 2003; RICHARDS, 2001, 2003

Most of the pathways and structures illustrated in figure 3.5 are known to be involved in particular types of information processing related to the execution and

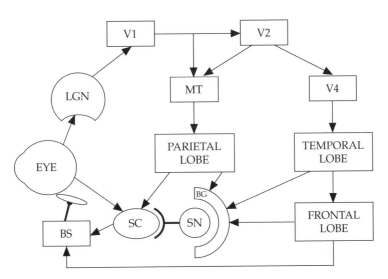

Figure 3.5 Diagram representing some of the main neural pathways and structures involved in visual orienting and attention. BS, brain stem; LGN, lateral geniculate nucleus; V1, V2, and V4, visual cortical areas; MT, middle temporal area; SC, superior colliculus; SN, substantia negra; BG, basal ganglia; FEF, frontal eye fields.

planning of eye movements. When considering the integration between sensory inputs and motor outputs it is important that the pathways discussed can be traced from the source of the input (the eye) to the muscles that shift the eyes. A diagram of such pathways may look different from one that just shows pathways for sensory processing. In chapter 4 we will discuss the dissociation between visual pathways for action and perception.

Four brain pathways will be discussed here. The first is the pathway from the eye to the superior colliculus. This subcortical pathway has input mainly from the temporal visual field (the peripheral or outer half of the field of each eye), and is involved in the generation of rapid reflexive eye movements to easily discriminable stimuli. The other three pathways to be discussed here share a projection from the eye to cortical structures via the midbrain (thalamic) visual relay, the lateral geniculate nucleus (LGN), and the primary visual cortex (V1). The first of these goes both directly to the superior colliculus from the primary visual cortex and also via the middle temporal area (MT). Some of the structures on this pathway are thought to play an important role in the detection of motion and the smooth tracking of moving objects. The next pathway proceeds from V1 to other parts of the visual cortex and thence to the frontal eye fields (FEF). As we will see later, this FEF pathway is thought to be involved in more complex aspects of eye movement planning such as anticipatory saccades and learning sequences of scanning patterns. Finally, there is a more complex and less well understood pathway that involves tonic (continual) inhibition of the superior colliculus (via subcortical structures called the substantia nigra and basal ganglia). Schiller (1985) proposed that this pathway ensures that the activity of the colliculus can be regulated. Others suggest that this oculomotor pathway forms an integrated system with the frontal eye fields and parietal lobes (e.g. Alexander, DeLong, & Strick, 1986) and that it plays some role in the regulation of the subcortical oculomotor pathway by the other cortical pathways.

The challenge has been to relate the development of these various pathways to the visuomotor competence of the infant at different ages. The three perspectives on the development of human brain function offer different views on this. According to the maturational view, we need to relate the sequential development of the different pathways to the onset of new functions as assessed by marker tasks. According to the skill learning view, the infant's brain needs to acquire the sensorimotor skill of generating accurate and informative saccades, and so areas involved in skill acquisition will be important. Finally, according to the interactive specialization view, some of the pathways will initially have poorly defined borders and functions (a lack of specialization) and only with experience will they become dissociable.

Of these three approaches, the maturational view has held sway with regard to visual orienting. To date, this has involved two complementary approaches: predictions about the sequence of development of the pathways from developmental neuroanatomy (Atkinson, 1984; Johnson, 1990), and the administration of marker tasks (see chapter 1) to ascertain the functional development of particular structures or pathways. An example of the first approach was originally presented over a decade ago (Johnson, 1990). In this analysis I proposed that, first, the characteristics of visually guided behavior of the infant at particular ages are determined by which of the pathways (shown in figure 3.5) are functional, and, second, which of the cortical pathways are functional is influenced by the developmental state of the primary visual cortex. The basis of this claim at the neuroanatomical level lies in three sets of observations. First, the primary visual cortex is the major (though not exclusive) "gateway" for input to most of the cortical pathways involved in oculomotor control (Schiller, 1985). Second, the primary visual cortex shows a postnatal continuation of the prenatal "inside-out" pattern of cortical growth described in chapter 2, with the deeper layers (5 and 6) showing greater dendritic branching, length, and extent of myelination than more superficial layers (2 and 3) around the time of birth. Third, there is a restricted pattern of inputs and outputs from the primary visual cortex (e.g. the projections to V2 depart from the upper layers – see chapter 2). By combining these observations with information about the developmental neuroanatomy of the human primary visual cortex, I hypothesized the following sequence of development of cortical pathways underlying oculomotor control: the subcortical pathway from the eye directly to the superior colliculus (probably including cortical projections from the deeper layers of V1 to superior colliculus), followed by the cortical projection which inhibits the superior colliculus pathway, followed by the pathway through cortical structure MT, and finally the pathway involving the frontal eye fields and related structures.

Following these predictions derived from developmental neuroanatomy, we can return to behavioral experiments to see if the transitions here support the predicted sequence of pathway development. Beginning with the newborn infant, evidence from measures of the extent of dendritic arborization and myelination indicate that only the deeper layers of the primary visual cortex are likely to be capable of supporting organized information-processing activity in the human newborn. Since the majority of feed-forward intracortical projections depart from outside the deeper layers (5 and 6), most of the cortical pathways involved in oculomotor control will only be receiving weak or disorganized input at this stage. However, evidence from various sources, such as visually evoked potentials, indicate that information from the eye is entering the primary visual cortex in the newborn. Thus, while some of the newborn's visual behavior can be accounted for in terms of processing in the subcortical pathway, I argued in my 1990 paper that there is also information processing occurring in the deeper cortical layers at birth. At least two characteristics of visually guided behavior in the newborn are consistent with predominantly subcortical control such as saccadic pursuit tracking and preferential orienting to the temporal field. To go through these in more detail:

- The ability of infants to track a moving stimulus in the first few months of life has two characteristics (Aslin, 1981). The first is that the eye movements follow the stimulus in a "saccadic" or step-like manner, as opposed to the smooth pursuit found in adults and older infants. The second characteristic is that the eye movements tend to lag behind the movement of the stimulus, rather than predicting its trajectory. Therefore, when a newborn infant visually tracks a moving stimulus, it could be described as performing a series of saccadic eye movements. Such behavior is consistent with subcortical control of orienting.

- Newborns much more readily orient toward stimuli in the temporal, as opposed to the nasal (the half of the visual field of each eye closer to the nose), visual field (e.g. Lewis, Maurer, & Milewski, 1979). Posner and Rothbart (1981) suggest that midbrain structures such as the colliculus can be driven most readily by temporal field input. This proposal has been confirmed in studies of adult "blindsight" patients by Rafal, Smith, Krantz, Cohen, and Brennan (1990), who established that distracter stimuli placed in the temporal "blindfield" had an effect on orienting into the good field, whereas distracter stimuli in the nasal blindfield did not. Evidence from studies of infants in which a complete cerebral hemisphere has been removed (to alleviate epilepsy) indicate that the subcortical (collicular) pathway alone is capable of generating saccades toward a peripheral target in the cortically "blind" field (Braddick et al., 1992).

Around 1 month of age infants show "obligatory attention" (Stechler & Latz, 1966; Johnson, Posner, & Rothbart, 1991; Hood, 1995). That is to say, they have great difficulty in disengaging their gaze from a stimulus in order to make a saccade to another location. Sometimes an infant around 1 month of age can spend as long as several minutes fixedly gazing at a seemingly uninteresting aspect of the environment, such as a section of carpet, before bursting into tears! Although this phenomenon is still poorly understood, I suggested that it was due to the development of tonic inhibition of the colliculus via the substantia nigra (see figure 3.5). Since this pathway projects from the deeper layers of the primary visual cortex to the colliculus, it is hypothesized to be the first strong cortical influence on oculomotor control. This (as yet) unregulated tonic inhibition of the colliculus has the consequence that stimuli impinging on the peripheral visual field no longer elicit an automatic exogenous saccade as readily as in newborns.

By around 2 months of age infants begin to show periods of smooth visual tracking, although their eye movements still lag behind the movement of the stimulus. At this age they also become more sensitive to stimuli placed in the nasal visual field (Aslin, 1981) and also more sensitive to coherent motion (Wattam-Bell, 1990). I proposed that the onset of these behaviors coincides with the functioning of the pathway involving structure MT. The enabling of this route of eye movement control may provide this cortical stream with the ability to regulate activity in the superior colliculus.

Associated with further dendritic growth and myelination within the upper layers of the primary visual cortex strengthening the projections from V1 to other cortical areas, around 3 months of age the pathways involving the frontal eye fields may become functional. This development may greatly increase the infant's ability to make "anticipatory" eye movements and to learn sequences of looking patterns, both functions associated with the frontal eye fields. With regard to the visual tracking of a moving object, now not only do infants show periods of smooth tracking, but their eye movements often predict the movement of the stimulus in an anticipatory manner. A number of experiments by Haith and colleagues have demonstrated that anticipatory eye movements can be readily elicited from infants by this age. For example, Haith, Hazan, and Goodman (1988) exposed 3.5-month-old infants to a series of picture slides which appeared either on the right- or on the left-hand side of the infant. These stimuli were either presented in an alternating sequence with fixed inter-stimulus interval (ISI), or with an irregular alternation pattern and ISI. It was observed that the regular alternation pattern produced more stimulus anticipations and faster reaction times to make an eye movement than in the irregular series. Haith and colleagues concluded from these results that infants of this age are able to develop expectancies for non-controllable spatiotemporal events. Canfield and Haith (1991) tested 2- and 3-month-old infants in an experiment which included more complex sequences (such as left–left–right, left–left–right, etc.). Consistent with the predictions from developmental neuroanatomy, while they failed to find significant effects with 2-month-olds, 3-month-olds were able to acquire at least some of the more complex sequences.

Given that this survey of the behavioral evidence pertaining to the development of visual orienting was broadly consistent with the predictions from developmental neurobiology (see table 3.1 for a summary), the next step was to develop and consider marker tasks for some of these and other parts of the cortex with a role in oculomotor control. Table 3.2 shows a number of marker tasks that have recently been developed for the functioning of structures involved in oculomotor control and visual attention (next section) shifts.

Table 3.1 Summary of the relation between developing oculomotor pathways and behavior

Age	Functional anatomy	Behavior
Newborn	SC pathway + layer 5 and 6 pyramidal output to LGN and SC	Saccadic pursuit tracking Preferential orienting to temporal visual field "Externality effect"
1 months	As above + inhibitory pathway to SC via BG	As above + "obligatory" attention
2 months	As above + MT (magnocellular) pathway to SC	Onset of smooth pursuit tracking and increased sensitivity to nasal visual field
3 months and over	As above + FEF (parvocellular) pathway to SC and BS	Increase in "anticipatory" tracking and sequential scanning patterns

SC, superior colliculus: LGN, lateral geniculate nucleus; BG, basal ganglia; MT, middle temporal area; FEF, frontal eye fields; BS, brain stem.

Table 3.2   Marker tasks for the development of visual orienting and attention

Brain region	Marker task	Studies
Superior colliculus	Inhibition of return	Clohessy, Posner, Rothbart, & Vecera (1991); Simion, Valenza, Umilta, & Dalla Barba (1995)
	Vector summation saccades	Johnson, Gilmore, Tucker, & Minister (1995)
Middle temporal area	Coherent motion detection; structure from motion	Wattam-Bell (1991)
	Smooth tracking	Aslin (1981)
Parietal cortex	Spatial cueing task	Hood & Atkinson (1991); Hood (1993); Johnson (1994); Johnson & Tucker (1996)
	Eye-centered saccade planning	Gilmore & Johnson (1997)
Frontal eye fields	Inhibition of automatic saccades	Johnson (1995)
	Anticipatory saccades	Haith et al. (1988)
Dorsolateral prefrontal cortex	Oculomotor delayed response task	Gilmore & Johnson (1995)

Marker tasks for several cortical regions thought to play a role in oculomotor control, the parietal cortex, frontal eye fields (FEF), and dorsolateral prefrontal cortex (DLPC), have been developed, and show rapid development between 2 and 6 months of age in human infants. Starting with marker tasks for the FEF, frontal cortex damage in humans results in an inability to suppress involuntary auto-matic saccades toward targets, and an apparent inability to control volitional saccades (Guitton, Buchtel, & Douglas, 1985; Fischer & Breitmeyer, 1987). For example, Guitton et al. (1985) studied normal participants and patients with frontal lobe lesions or temporal lobe lesions in a so-called "anti-saccade" task. In this task participants are instructed to *not* look at a briefly flashed cue, but rather to make a saccade in the opposite direction (Hallett, 1978). Guitton et al. (1985) reported that while normal participants and patients with temporal lobe damage could do this task with relative ease, patients with frontal damage, in particular those with damage around the FEF, were severely impaired. Patients with frontal damage had particular difficulty in suppressing unwanted saccades toward the cue stimulus.

I have developed a version of the anti-saccade task for use with infants (Johnson, 1995). Clearly, one cannot give verbal instruction to a young infant to look to the opposite side from where the cue stimulus appears. Instead, infants are motivated by making the second stimulus reliably more dynamic and colorful than the first. Thus, after a number of such trials infants may learn to inhibit their tendency to make a saccade to the first stimulus (the cue) when it appears, in order to respond as rapidly as possible to the more attractive second stimulus (the target). A group of 4-month-old infants showed a significant decrease in their frequency of looking to the first (cue) stimulus over a number of such trials (Johnson, 1995). A second experiment demonstrated that this decrement was not due to differential habituation to the simpler stimulus. Since 4-month-olds are able to inhibit saccades to a peripheral stimulus, it is reasonable to infer that their frontal eye field circuit is functioning by this age. Similar experiments are currently being run with younger infants.

Other tasks recently conducted with infants are consistent with an increasing prefrontal cortex endogenous control over shifts of attention and saccades around 6 months of age. For example, Funahashi, Bruce, and Goldman-Rakic (1989, 1990) devised an oculomotor delayed response paradigm to study the properties of neurons in the DLPC of macaque monkeys. In this task the monkey plans a saccade toward a particular spatial location, but has to wait for a period (usually between 2 and 5 seconds) before actually executing the saccade. Single-unit recording in the macaque indicates that some cells in the DLPC code for the direction of the saccade during the delay. Further, reversible microlesions to the area result in selective amnesia for saccades to a localized part of the visual field. A subsequent PET study on human participants has confirmed the involvement of DLPC (and parietal cortex) in this task (Jonides et al., 1993).

Gilmore and Johnson (1995) devised an infant version of the oculomotor delayed response task: a marker task for DLPC (see figure 3.6). The results obtained to date indicate that 6-month-old human infants can perform delayed saccades successfully with delays of up to 5 seconds, suggesting some influence of the prefrontal cortex on eye movement control by this age.

In terms of the three viewpoints on human functional brain development outlined earlier, the Johnson (1990) model of the development of visual orienting could be described as a maturational hypothesis. The emphasis of this model was on how maturational changes in neuroanatomy cause or allow new brain pathways to become active.

FURTHER READING: RICHARDS, 2001, 2003; JOHNSON, 2002

Data collected more recently suggest that the original model requires some modification, and that it may be beneficial also to consider skill learning perspectives. A more direct assessment of the hypotheses advanced in the Johnson model

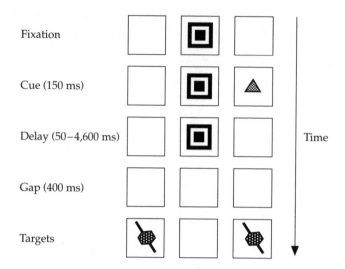

Figure 3.6 The oculomotor delayed response task as designed for use with infants. Infant subjects face three computer screens on which brightly colored moving stimuli appear. At the start of each trial a fixation stimulus appears on the central screen. Once the infant is looking at this stimulus, a cue is briefly flashed up on one of the two side screens. Following the briefly flashed cue, the central stimulus stays on for between 1 and 5 seconds, before presentation of two targets on the side screens. By measuring delayed looks to the cued location prior to the target onset, Gilmore and Johnson (1995b) established that infants can retain information about the cued location for several seconds.

can be provided by event-related potential measures (time-locked to the initiation of the eye movements: Balaban & Weinstein, 1985; Csibra, Johnson, & Tucker, 1997). By time-locking to the onset of eye movements we can examine the brain events that precede the production of this simple action. In adults such experiments reveal characteristic pre-saccadic components recorded over the parietal cortex prior to the execution of saccades. The clearest of these components is the pre-saccadic "spike potential" (SP), a sharp positive-going deflection which precedes the saccade by 8–20 ms (Csibra et al., 1997). The spike potential is observed in most saccade tasks in adults, and is therefore thought to represent an important stage of cortical processing required to generate a saccade.

Csibra, Tucker, and Johnson (1998) investigated whether there are pre-saccadic potentials recordable over parietal leads in 6-month-old infants. Given the prediction that by this age infants have essentially the same pathways active for saccade planning as do adults, we were surprised to find no evidence of this component (see figure 3.7) in our infant participants (see also Vaughan & Kurtzberg, 1989). This finding suggests that the target-driven saccades performed by 6-month-olds in our study were controlled largely by subcortical routes for visually guided responses mediated by the superior colliculus.

6-month-olds   12-month-olds   Adults

Figure 3.7 Grand-average saccade-locked potentials at Pz in (a) 6-month-old infants, (b) 12-month-old infants, and (c) adults. The vertical bar marks the saccade onset, a spike potential is evident in adults and 12-month-olds, but not at 6 months.

Because this result was surprising, we decided to conduct two follow-up studies. In one of these we tested 12-month-olds with the same procedure. These older infants did show a spike potential like that observed in adults though somewhat smaller in amplitude (see fig 3.7). The other study explored whether the dorsal pathway could be activated in very young infants through a more demanding saccade task. Specifically, we compared ERPs before reactive (target-elicited) and anticipatory (endogenous) saccades in 4-month-old infants (Csibra, Tucker, & Johnson, 2001). We were not able to record any reliable posterior activity prior to either reactive or anticipatory eye movements. Thus, even when the saccade is generated by cortical computation of the likely location of the next stimulus, as in the case of anticipatory eye movements, posterior cortical structures do not seem to be involved in the planning of this action.

In all these infant ERP studies, while there was a lack of evidence for posterior structure control over eye movements in our experiments with 6-month-olds, we observed effects recorded over frontal leads. These saccade-related effects were consistent with the frontal eye field disinhibition of subcortical (collicular) circuits when a central foveated stimulus is removed (Csibra et al., 1998, 2001). In brief, we interpreted these findings in terms of the frontal eye fields helping to maintain fixation on to foveated stimuli by inhibiting collicular circuits. This is consistent with the predictions of the Johnson (1990) model. However, when saccades to peripheral stimuli are made, the ERP evidence indicated that these are largely initiated by collicular circuits, sometimes as a consequence of inhibition being released by the frontal eye fields. In a converging line of thinking, Canfield and colleagues argued on the basis of behavioural and further neuroanatomical evidence that the FEF pathway would precede the more posterior pathways developmentally (Canfield, Smith, Brezsnyak, & Snow, 1997). This early involvement of the FEF pathway could be consistent with a skill learning hypothesis in which more anterior structures get activated earlier than posterior circuits. By this interpretation, there is greater involvement of frontal cortex circuitry in infants because they are still acquiring the skill of planning and executing eye movements.

The third perspective on functional brain development, interactive specialization, could also be brought to bear on this data. From this perspective, the pathways involved in visual orienting are initially less distinct from both surrounding tissue and each other (see Dannemiller, 2001). Further, rather than the onset of a new ability being associated with the onset of functioning in a "new" area, the interactive specialization approach encourages the view that there will be widespread changes across one or more pathways associated with new abilities. In a study where functional activity in children and adults was assessed by fMRI during the onset of demanding saccade tasks, multiple cortical and subcortical areas appeared to change their response pattern (Luna et al., 2001), rather than one or two previously silent regions becoming active (mature).

One cortical area involved in oculomotor control for which a more experience-dependent approach has been taken is the parietal cortex. This is a region of the primate cortex which has been implicated in aspects of saccade planning in monkey cellular recording studies, human functional neuroimaging studies, and neuropsychological studies of brain-damaged patients. It is also a region of cortex that undergoes marked developmental changes between 3 and 6 months of age, as demonstrated in both neuroanatomical studies of postmortem brains (Conel, 1939–67) and PET (Chugani et al., 1987). Andersen and colleagues have recorded from single cells in parts of the macaque monkey parietal cortex, and many of these cells code for saccades within an eye- or head-centered frame of reference. In other words, their receptive fields respond to combinations of eye or head position, on the one hand, and retinal distance from the fovea to the target, on the other. This is in contrast to parts of the superior colliculus in which cells commonly respond according to the retinal distance and direction of the target from the fovea.

Zipser and Andersen (1988; Andersen & Zipser, 1988) constructed a connectionist model in which the hidden layer units developed response properties which closely resembled those observed within regions of the primate parietal cortex. While the details of this neuroconnectionist model need not concern us here, the fundamental point to note is that the representations for generating saccades within an eye- or head-centered frame of reference emerged as a result of training, and did not require to be "hard-wired" into the network. An important question that remains is whether infants only develop the ability to use extra-retinal coordinates to plan saccades during postnatal life. If they do, this would be consistent with the assumption underlying the model that representations controlling eye- or head-centered action need to be constructed postnatally, and result from constraints imposed by the network structure and its interaction with the external environment.

With Rick Gilmore, I conducted several experiments designed to ascertain whether the ability of infants to use extra-retinal frames of reference to plan saccades emerges over the first few months of life. In one of these experiments we exposed 4- and 6-month-old infants to two simultaneously flashed targets on a large monitor screen. The targets were flashed so briefly that they were gone before the infant started to make a saccade to them. We then studied the saccades which infants made in response to these targets (see figure 3.8). In many trials they made two saccades, the first of these being to the location of one of the two targets. Having made a saccade to one of the two targets, we examined whether the second

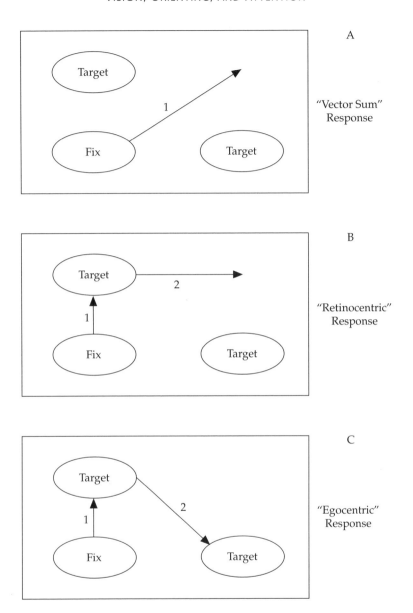

Figure 3.8 Three types of saccades made by young infants in response to two targets briefly flashed as shown. (A) A "vector summation" saccade in which eye movement is directed between the two targets. (B) A "retinocentric" saccade in which the second saccade is directed to the location corresponding to the retinal error when the flash occurred. (C) An "egocentric" saccade which corresponds to the use of extra-retinal information to plan the second saccade. Between birth and 6 months, infants shift from the first two types of response to the third.

saccade that they made was to the actual location of the second target, or whether it was to the retinal location (the location on the retina at which that target had originally appeared). To make the second saccade to the correct spatial location requires infants to be able to take into account the fact that their eyes had shifted position, and then compute the saccade necessary given the new eye position. The results indicated that for 4-month-olds the majority of second saccades were directed to the retinal location in which the target had appeared. In contrast, for the 6-month-olds, the majority of second saccades were made to the correct spatial location for the other target. These results suggest that the ability to use extra-retinal cues to plan saccades emerges through the first six months of life. However, saccades based on retinal location (and thought to be subcortical in origin) are probably present from birth (Gilmore & Johnson, 1997).

FURTHER READING: JOHNSON ET AL., 2001

In sum, while even newborns are capable of simple target-driven saccades, oculomotor skills continue to develop throughout the first year. Influential maturational models have been only partially supported by recent ERP and neuroimaging evidence. In particular, the finding that frontal regions may be more important than more posterior areas presents a challenge to the maturational approach.

3.3 VISUAL ATTENTION

Our discussion so far has concerned *overt* shifts of attention due to eye and head movements. However, adults are also capable of shifting their attention *covertly* (i.e. without moving the eyes or other sensory receptors). This allows us to enhance our processing of some spatial locations or objects within our visual field, to the exclusion of others.

One way in which evidence for covert attention has been provided in adults is by studying the effect on detection of cueing saccades to a particular spatial location. A briefly presented cue serves to draw covert attention to the location, resulting in the subsequent facilitation of detection of targets at that location (Posner & Cohen, 1980; Maylor, 1985). While detection of and responses to a covertly attended location are *facilitated* if the target stimulus appears very shortly after the cue offset, with longer latencies between cue and target, saccades toward that location are *inhibited*. This latter phenomenon, referred to as "inhibition of return" (Posner, Rafal, Choate, & Vaughan, 1985), may reflect an evolutionarily important mechanism which prevents attention returning to a recently processed spatial location. In adults facilitation is reliably observed when targets appeared at the cued location within about 150 ms of the cue, whereas targets appearing between 300 and 1300 ms after a peripheral (exogenous) cue result in longer detection latencies (e.g. Posner & Cohen, 1980, 1984; Maylor, 1985).

Following lesions to the posterior parietal lobe, adults show severe neglect of the contralateral visual field. According to Posner and colleagues, this neglect is due to damage to the "posterior attention network." This refers to a brain circuit which includes not only the posterior parietal lobe, but also the pulvinar and superior colliculus (Posner, 1988; Posner & Petersen, 1990; see figure 3.5 for all but the pulvinar). Damage to this circuit is postulated to impair participants' ability to shift covert attention to a cued spatial location. The involvement of these regions in shifts of visual attention has been confirmed by PET studies. As mentioned above, both neuroanatomical (Conel, 1939–67) and PET (Chugani et al., 1987) evidence from the human infant indicate that the parietal lobe is undergoing substantive and rapid development between 3 and 6 months after birth. The question arises, therefore, as to whether infants become capable of covert shifts of attention during this time.

Since infants do not accept verbal instruction and are poor at motor responses used to study spatial attention in adults, such as a key press, the only response available to demonstrate facilitation and inhibition of a cued location is eye movements. That is, overt shifts are used to study *covert* shifts of attention by examining the influence of a cue stimulus (which is presented so briefly that it does not normally elicit an eye movement) on infants' subsequent saccades toward conspicuous target stimuli. Using these methods, Hood and Atkinson (1991; see Hood, 1995) reported that 6-month-old infants have faster reaction times to make a saccade to a target when it appears immediately after a brief (100 ms) cue stimulus than when it appears in an uncued location. A group of 3-month-old infants did not show this effect. Johnson (1994; Johnson & Tucker, 1996) employed a similar procedure in which a brief (100 ms) cue was presented on one of two side screens, before bilateral targets were presented either 100 ms or 600 ms later. It was hypothesized on the basis of the adult findings that the 200 ms stimulus onset asynchrony (SOA) would be short enough to produce facilitation, while the long SOA trials should result in preferential orienting toward the opposite side (inhibition of return). This result was obtained with a group of 4-month-old infants, suggesting the possibility that infants are capable of covert shifts of attention at this age. Consistent with the previous findings, these effects were not observed in a group of 2-month-old infants.

Another manifestation of covert attention concerns so-called "sustained" attention. Sustained attention refers to the ability of participants to maintain the direction of their attention toward a stimulus even in the presence of distracters. Richards (2001, 2003) has developed a heart rate marker for sustained attention in infants. The heart-rate-defined period of sustained attention usually lasts for between 5 and 15 seconds after the onset of a complex stimulus (see figure 3.9).

In order to investigate the effect of sustained attention on the response to exogenous cues, Richards (2001, 2003) used an "interrupted stimulus method" in which a peripheral stimulus (a flashing light) is presented while the infant is

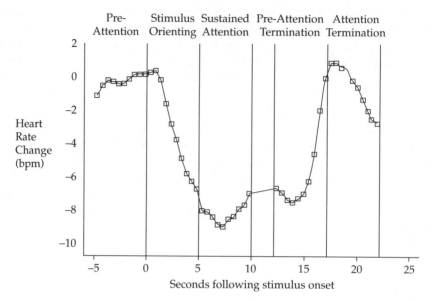

Figure 3.9 Heart-rate-defined phases of sustained attention.

gazing at a central stimulus (a TV screen with a complex visual pattern). By varying the length of time between the onset of the TV image and the onset of the peripheral stimulus, he was able to present the peripheral stimulus either within the period of sustained covert attention, or outside it. Richards found that during the periods when heart rate was decreased (sustained endogenous attention) it took twice as long for the infant to shift their gaze toward the peripheral stimulus as when heart rate had returned to pre-stimulus levels (attention termination). Further, those saccades that are made to a peripheral stimulus during sustained attention are less accurate than normal, and involve multiple hypometric saccades, a characteristic of collicular-generated saccades (Richards, 1991). Thus, the lack of distractibility during periods of sustained attention is likely to be due to cortically mediated pathways inhibiting collicular mechanisms.

FURTHER READING: RICHARDS, 2001, 2003

A number of studies have traced developments in visual attention during childhood using purely cognitive methods, but have described the continuation of similar transitions to those observed in early infancy. Three transitions that have been described are the greater ability to expand or constrict a field of attention (e.g. Chapman, 1981; Enns & Girgus, 1985), the greater ability to disengage attention from distracting information or invalid cueing (Akhtar & Enns, 1989; Enns & Brodeur, 1989), and a faster speed of shifting attention (Pearson & Lane, 1990).

Enns and Girgus (1985) tested school-age children and adults in speeded classification tasks involving a stimulus composed of two elements that varied in distance (visual angle). Participants had to classify stimuli on the basis of one of the two elements. Younger children (6–8 years) experienced more interference when the elements were closely spaced than did older children (9–11 years) and adults. The same stimuli were used for a second task in which both of the elements had to be taken into account. In this task the younger children had difficulty when the elements were separated by large visual angles. The authors conclude that younger children have problems in contracting and expanding the size of attentional focus. An ERP study of auditory attention also concluded that there is a development in the ability to narrow attentional focus during childhood (Berman & Friedman, 1995).

An observation that may be related is that older children and adults are often reported as being able to shift their attention more rapidly than younger ones. For example, Pearson and Lane (1990) using a spatial cueing paradigm observed that younger infants took longer to covertly shift their attention to more peripheral targets, whereas they were almost as fast as adults to shift to targets very close to fixation. This indicates that it is the speed of shifting, rather than the latency to elicit a covert shift, which improves with age. The increasing speed of shifting attention with age has also been reported during infancy (Johnson & Tucker, 1996), indicating that this developmental transition may be a gradual one that begins early in life.

In several studies, younger children and infants have been argued to have greater difficulty in disengaging from distracting stimuli or invalid spatial cues. For example, Enns and Brodeur (1989) used a spatial cueing paradigm to cue either neutrally (all locations cued), unpredictably (random cueing), or predictably (cue predicts target presentation). The results from participants aged 6, 8, and 20 years indicated that while all age groups automatically oriented attention to the cued location, the children processed targets in non-cued locations more slowly than did adults, and did not take advantage of the predictability of the cues. Thus the costs and benefits of cueing were greater in the younger participants due to an increased cost imposed by invalid cueing. Tipper, Bourque, Anderson, and Brehaut (1989) suggest that these deficits are due to the relative inability to inhibit irrelevant stimuli, a conclusion that is consistent with more recent findings (Brodeur & Boden, 2000; Wainwright & Bryson, 2002). Once again, similar developmental trends have been observed in infancy experiments where younger infants are more likely to fail to disengage from competing stimuli, such as obligatory attention described earlier.

Research on the neural basis of the development of covert attention in childhood has only just begun, and has been based on three topics: (a) ERP studies, (b) effects of early cortical damage, and (c) developmental disorders of genetic origin. Richards (2003) describes several experiments in which he has used the spatial cueing procedure while recording ERPs from infants in order to detect neural signatures of covert attention. In one study he examined the "P1 validity effect" in young infants. The P1 is a large positive ERP component that occurs around 100 ms after stimulus presentation. Studies with adult participants have shown that the P1 is enhanced in scale in valid trials (where the cue correctly predicts the target) (Hillyard, Mangun, Woldorff, & Luck, 1995). This is of interest since this short-latency component reflects early stages of visual processing, demonstrating that shifts of covert attention modulate early sensory processing of the target. Richards (2003) reports that while there was little ERP evidence for covert attention shifts in 3-month-old infants, by 5 months the pattern of ERP data resembled that in adults, indicating that infants at this age were shifting attention to the cued location covertly.

Another way to examine the neural basis of covert orienting in development has been to assess the consequences of perinatal damage to the cerebral cortex. In collaboration with Joan Stiles and colleagues, we examined spatial cueing in infants who had unfortunately suffered perinatal damage to one of four quadrants of the cortex (Johnson, Tucker, Stiles, & Trauner, 1998). The results were some-what surprising in that the posterior lesions that would normally cause deficits in adults had no effect on the infants. In contrast, frontal damage did have a measurable effect on spatial cueing. While surprising, these results fit well with work from other laboratories. For example, Craft, Schatz, and colleagues have studied the consequences of perinatal brain injury (sometime associated with sickle cell anemia) on performance in spatial cueing tasks during childhood. In several studies deficits were observed following anterior (frontal) damage, and not (or less) with posterior damage (Craft, White, Park, & Figiel, 1994; Schatz, Craft, Koby, & DeBaun, 2000; Schatz, Craft, White, Park, & Figiel, 2001).

A third way to address the neurodevelopment of covert attention is to study disorders of this process in groups of atypically developing children. ADHD (atten-tion deficit/hyperactivity disorder) is characterized by inattention, hyperactivity, and impulsivity beginning before 7 years of age (Karatekin, 2001). Estimates for its prevalence run as high as 3–5 percent of school children in the USA, although this figure varies enormously across cultures. Despite the title of the disorder, there is no general agreement about specific deficits in components of attention in these children. Rather, they appear to have mild difficulties in some tests of sustained and selective attention that may reflect difficulties in processing attended stimuli and/or in maintaining attention in tasks that make demands on cognitive resources (see Karetekin, 2001, for review). Another disorder that has been linked to deficits in attention is autism (see appendix and chapter 5 for an introduction to autism). As one example of this approach, Courchesne and colleagues (Akshoomoff & Courchesne, 1994; Townsend & Courchesne 1994) have tested individuals with autism on a variety of spatial cueing and attention switch-ing tasks. They report, on the basis of autopsy and structural MRI data, that most participants with autism have developmental damage to their cerebellum. In a number of tasks they have associated this damage with reduced ability to switch attention, and a slower shifting of covert spatial attention. Another neural deficit observed in at least some participants with autism is bilateral parietal damage. Townsend and Courchesne (1994) have proposed that this damage gives rise to a

narrowed focus of spatial attention, such that targets presented within the narrowed "spotlight" are detected more rapidly than normal. In contrast, targets
presented at small eccentricities from fixation that would be responded to rapidly
by typical participants are responded to much more slowly by autistic participants
since they are outside the narrow attentional focus.

3.4 GENERAL SUMMARY AND CONCLUSIONS

This chapter began with a discussion of the contribution of peripheral systems
(retinal) development in the emergence of basic visual functions. Retinal development
can only partially explain improvements in basic visual functions, indicating that
brain changes are important also. With regard to binocular vision, neuroanatomical
and computational modeling evidence highlights the importance of the segregation
of inputs to layer 4 cells in the primary visual cortex. This increased segregation
of inputs from the two eyes can be viewed as the result of a self-organizing neural
network constrained by certain intrinsic and extrinsic factors. Thus, while the onset
of binocular vision may initially appear to be a good example of a maturational
process, activity-dependent factors appear to be important.

Moving from sensory processing to sensorimotor integration, we proceeded to
describe an attempt to use the developmental neuroanatomy of the cortex to make
predictions about developmental changes in visual orienting in infants. A number
of behavioral marker tasks for cortical regions involved in oculomotor control were
reviewed and discussed in relation to the maturational model. Recent neuroimaging
and behavioral studies require modifications to the original model, and suggest
that an interactive specialization view may eventually prove more fruitful.

Finally, experiments concerned with the development of covert (internal) attention
shifts in infants and children were described. A number of changes in the flexibility
and speed of shifting attention were shown to originate in infancy but continue
into childhood. Some developmental disorders, such as autism, may involve deficits
in shifting covert attention.

4 PERCEIVING AND ACTING ON THE PHYSICAL WORLD
OBJECTS AND NUMBER

Objects are special in our sensory world since they are both recognized and manipulated. Neuroscience evidence suggests that these two functions are computed by two different pathways: a ventral recognition pathway and a dorsal sensorimotor action pathway. Preliminary attempts to relate these two pathways to human development are discussed, and simple computational models are presented. Bursts of high-frequency neural oscillations have been related to the binding of features to compose objects and to the retention of objects following occlusion. Two number-relevant systems in the primate brain are discussed. One of these is an analog-magnitude system similar to that active in time or length judgments, while the other is a system engaged by tracking small numbers of objects (object-files). Both systems appear to be active in young infants, and may underlie their ability to perform simple numerical computations with small numbers of objects. Some suggest that more sophisticated computations with large numbers require language-mediated integration between these two systems.

Physical objects are special in our sensory world since – unlike landscapes, faces, and sounds – they are not only recognized and categorized, but are also often manipulated using our hands and feet. As adults, perceiving and acting on everyday objects seems easy. However, further consideration reveals that complex computations and rich representations need to underlie these processes. For example, objects have to be recognized from multiple different viewpoints, and under conditions where they are partially obscured (partial occlusion) or in front of complex backgrounds (object parsing). Our fingers and hands have to be adjusted according to the anticipated size and weight of the object, and our wrists oriented appropriately to let us grasp the object in the appropriate place and correct orientation. While there have been many behavioral studies conducted on object processing in infants and young children, only recently has evidence from cognitive neuroscience been used to inform and constrain theories of this domain of cognitive development.

4.1 THE DORSAL AND VENTRAL VISUAL PATHWAYS

In chapter 3 we discussed several pathways that underlie visual orienting and attention. There is now a substantive body of evidence that visual information processing about objects is divided into two relatively separate streams in the brain. The detailed connectivity of these cortical routes is very complex (see van Essen, Anderson, & Felleman, 1992), but, in simplified terms, one pathway (the ventral route) extends from the primary visual cortex through to parts of the temporal lobe, while the other pathway (the dorsal route) goes from the primary visual cortex to the parietal cortex (see figure 4.1). The exact point at which the routes separate is still debated. For reasons we will discuss below, the ventral route is sometimes called the *What* or *Perception* pathway, while the dorsal route is often called the *Where* or *Action* pathway. We will start our discussion with the dorsal route.

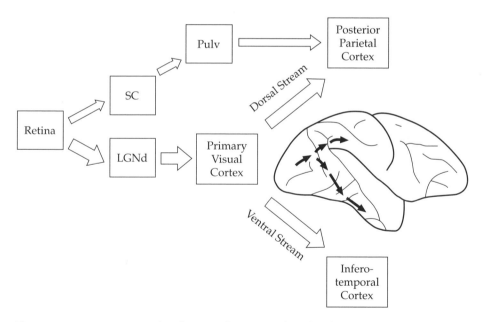

Figure 4.1 Major routes whereby retinal input reaches the dorsal and ventral streams. The diagram of the brain on the right of the figure shows the approximate routes of the projections from primary visual cortex to posterior parietal and the inferotemporal cortex, respectively. LGNd: lateral geniculate nucleus, pars dorsalis; Pulv: pulvinar; SC: superior colliculus.

All visually guided actions take place in space, but the spatial processing required will differ according to the action to be performed. Evidence for multiple spatial systems can be seen in the spatial coding shown by neurons in the dorsal stream. For example, as we heard in chapter 3, some cells in the parietal cortex anticipate the retinal consequences of saccadic eye movements and update the cortical (body-centered) representation of visual space to provide continuously accurate coding of the location of objects in space. Other cells have gaze-dependent responses. That is, they mark where the animal is looking with respect to eye-centered coordinates systems. Both of these provide egocentric spatial codings that are only useful over very short periods of time since every time the animal moves the coordinates have to be re-computed.

In the real world target objects are often moving. Hence, it is not only necessary for us to track that motion in order to localize the object in space, but it is also necessary to anticipate the object's movement. Some cells in the parietal cortex appear to be involved in the tracking of moving objects. Moreover, many of these cells continue to respond after the stimulus has disappeared (Newsombe, Wurtz, & Komatsu, 1988). In addition, there is selectivity in other parts of the dorsal stream for relative motion and size changes when an object moves toward or away from the viewer. Many neurons on the dorsal pathway are also driven by large-scale optical flow fields, suggesting that self-motion is being computed. Cells in the dorsal pathway also code size, shape, and orientation, which are necessary for the proper reaching for and grasping of an object.

There is also evidence suggesting that the different spatial-temporal systems described above are partially segregated into different regions and routes within the dorsal pathway. Thus the dorsal stream could be viewed as a pathway with many parallel computations of different spatial-temporal properties occurring at once. Different streams compute different-spatial temporal analyses in different coordinate systems, possibly with different effector systems in mind. Milner and Goodale (1995) argue that the cells of the parietal cortex are neither sensory nor motor, but rather sensorimotor. They are involved in transforming retinal information (sensory) into motor coordinates (motor), and in transducing perceptual input into motor actions.

The properties of neurons in the adult ventral stream seem complementary to those in the dorsal stream. As one proceeds along the ventral stream, cells respond to more and more complex clusters of features. At the higher levels, the complex cells show remarkable selectivity in their firing. These neurons are all selective to the figural and surface properties of objects (i.e. the internal object features). More importantly, many of the cells have very large receptive fields on the retina. That means that, although they can process feature information, they lose much of their spatial resolution on the retina. In effect, these cells develop spatially invariant representations of objects by responding to the presence of a consistent feature cluster independently of its position. Some cells seem to respond maximally to a preferred object orientation (independently of position) thereby computing a "view-centered representation." Other cells respond equally to an object in any orientation. That is, they have developed a transformation-invariant representation. Thus, the properties of neurons along the ventral pathway are entirely consistent with what would be expected of a system concerned with recognizing objects, scenes, and individuals with enduring characteristics rather than the moment-to-moment changes in the visual array that occur in a natural setting. Transformation-invariant representations could provide the basic raw material for recognition memory and other long-term representations of the visual world.

Why should such different streams of processing be present in adult primates? If the representations in the dorsal stream are closely linked to the functions of the motor system, then it is not surprising that spatial-temporal information is at a premium down this pathway. Motor actions involve localizing targets within a three-dimensional spatial-temporal world. In contrast, recognition or identification of objects requires that spatial-temporal variability be minimized. Early work in machine vision found that view-invariant recognition (i.e. the ability to recognize an object as the same independently of orientation and location) was a very difficult computational problem. One of the most efficient ways of doing this is to factor out spatial variability. However, removing spatial information from the object representation is completely at odds with the requirements of the motor system. Hence the need for two distinct object classes of object representations.

FURTHER READING: DANNEMILLER, 2001; JOHNSON ET AL., 2001; ATKINSON & BRADDICK, 2003

The three approaches discussed in chapter 1 cast a different light on developmental hypotheses about the dorsal and ventral pathways. According to a maturational viewpoint, we need to consider which of the pathways develops first, and whether this can explain aspects of behavioral development of object processing. For example, Atkinson (1998) argued, on the basis that infants and children can perceive coherent forms prior to judging motion coherence, that the dorsal pathway develops later than the ventral. However, evidence from developmental neuroanatomy in human infants is not compelling in this regard. For example, in resting (with no task) PET studies of glucose uptake, virtually identical overall patterns of developmental change are seen in the temporal and parietal cortex (Chugani et al., 2002). Resting blood flow measurements and structural neuroanatomy studies cannot inform us directly about function. In chapter 3 we reviewed several functional imaging studies with young infants showing activity in primary visual and some ventral pathway structures. However, these tasks involved passive viewing of 2D visual patterns or faces and were thus unlikely to evoke dorsal pathway activity even in adults. In non-human primates, there is evidence of ventral pathway functioning from as young as 6 weeks of age. Rodman and colleagues (Rodman, Skelly, & Bross, 1991) established that neurons within the superior temporal sulcus were activated by complex visual stimuli, including faces, from the earliest age at which they could record – 6 weeks. Unfortunately, equivalent data are not available for dorsal pathway functions, and so no comparison is possible. Thus, there is currently very little direct evidence relevant to the question available.

From a skill learning perspective, we need to inquire into the acquisition of perceptual recognition skills in the ventral pathway, and the emergence of sensorimotor integration skill in the dorsal pathway. Further, we might investigate whether interactions between processing in the two pathways is acquired during development. The third perspective outlined in chapter 1, interactive specialization, suggests yet another theoretical possibility for the dorsal and ventral visual pathways: that as the two pathways become more specialized, and acquire representations appropriate for either recognition or action, they become less interactive and tend to be co-activated less often. This view would also predict that the two pathways initially begin inter-mixed and hard to dissociate, but with development the dissociation becomes more complete. Further, from this perspective, the complementary specialization of the two pathways emerges during the development of the individual.

4.2 HIDDEN OBJECTS

It was Jean Piaget who originally noticed some unusual "errors" in the way that young children thought about, and acted on, objects that were out of view. Specifically, Piaget (1954) reported that infants fail to retrieve objects partly occluded by a surface until 7–8 months, fail to search manually for fully occluded objects until several months later, and fail to trace the spatial-temporal trajectory of a hidden object to its final destination until $1^1/_2$ years of age. Piaget proposed that these developmental changes reflect a conceptual revolution in the first years of life that results in the construction of the first true object representation: an "object concept."

More recently, studies of the early development of object perception have qualified Piaget's original account. Experiments that rely on measures of looking, rather than manual reaching, have shown that even 4-month-olds perceive that a partly occluded object continues behind its occluder. For example, after familiarization with an object moving behind a central occluder, infants generalized to (i.e. looked less at) a fully visible complete object relative to a fully visible display with a gap where the occluder had been (Kellman & Spelke, 1983; Slater, Mattock, & Brown, 1990; Johnson & Nanez, 1995; Johnson & Aslin, 1996). Two-month-old human infants were not found to perceive complete objects over occlusion when tested with the displays used with 4-month-olds, but they performed like the older infants when tested with enhanced displays in which the occlusion and motion relationships were easier to detect (Johnson & Aslin, 1995). In recent studies using even more enhanced displays, abilities to perceive the complete shapes of partly occluded displays have been extended to 3-week-old human infants (Kawabata, Gyoba, Inoue, & Ohtsubo, 1999).

These findings provide evidence that human perceptual systems rapidly come to detect one kind of invariance in natural scenes: the invariant shape of an object over changing patterns of occlusion and background. Experiments in psychophysics and in cognitive neuroscience provide evidence that adults detect many other invariant properties of objects as well, including the invariant view-dependent shape of an object over changes in object size and position (e.g. Grill-Spector et al., 1998). These abilities also appear to have their roots in infancy, where some evidence for size and shape constancy has been obtained even with newborn infants (Slater, 1982). All these findings cast doubt on Piaget's claim that the ability to perceive objects depends on a process akin to scientific reasoning. They raise the question whether infants might also be able to represent objects that they cannot see, when they are tested with looking methods. Evidence from several laboratories indicate that in looking tasks infants represent fully occluded objects long before they pass Piaget's object permanence tasks (e.g. Spelke, Breinlinger, Macomber, & Jacobsen, 1992; Baillargeon, 1993), although scattered negative findings also have been reported using this method (see Haith & Benson, 1998, for review). Given that different results are obtained with looking methods compared to other infant behavioral testing paradigms, several groups have turned to cognitive neuroscience theories and methods to resolve this paradox. Studies in cognitive neuroscience suggest several potential answers to this issue that are currently under active investigation: (1) the extent of integration of the dorsal and ventral visual pathways, (2) the changing strength of representations of objects in the brain, and (3) the possible inability of infants to plan the necessary actions to retrieve hidden objects. Since the second of these possibilities is discussed in chapter 10, and the third in chapter 8, we will focus here on explanations associated with the dorsal and ventral visual pathways.

Mareschal and colleagues chose to explore the hypothesis that the discrepancy between looking and reaching tasks is due to a relative lack of integration between the dorsal and ventral visual pathways in early infancy (Mareschal, Plunkett, & Harris, 1999). The logic behind this hypothesis is that object-directed action toward hidden objects requires a degree of interaction between the two pathways. This idea was initially explored through a connectionist model designed to simulate some of the computational properties and development of the dorsal and ventral pathways. Figure 4.2 shows a schematic outline of this "dual route" processing model. Consistent with the neurophysiology reviewed above, the model has an object recognition route (equivalent to the ventral pathway) and a trajectory prediction route (dorsal pathway). The former route develops a spatially invariant representation of an object to which it is exposed (using the unsupervised learning algorithm developed by Foldiak [1996]), while the latter learns to predict the next "retinal" position of the object. Through recurrent connections, both pathways have some degree of memory. A third component of the model is a response integration network that corresponds to the infant's ability to coordinate and use

Figure 4.2 A diagram showing the object processing model of Mareschal et al. (1999).

the information it has about object position and object identity. This network integrates the internal representations generated by the two pathways as required by a retrieval response task.

The model embodies the basic architectural constraints on visual cortical pathways revealed by contemporary neuroscience: an object recognition network that develops spatially invariant feature representations of objects; a trajectory prediction network that is blind to surface features and computes appropriate spatial-temporal properties even if no actions are undertaken towards the object; and a response module that integrates information from these two networks for use in voluntary actions.

A prediction of the above model has recently been tested (Mareschal & Johnson, 2003). In this behavioral experiment infants viewed an array presented on a video monitor in which two different objects moved behind, and then re-appeared from behind, an occluding surface. In some conditions these objects were potentially graspable toys, while other conditions involved stimuli more likely to engage ventral pathway function such as faces (see chapter 5). When the objects re-appeared following removal of an occluder, the objects concerned could have either their features switched (e.g. color, or the identity of a face), or their spatial location, or both. If infants were surprised (looked longer) when just features were changed, this was taken to indicate ventral (recognition) pathway processing, whereas if surprise was shown when only the location of the objects changed, this was taken to indicate dorsal pathway retention. The results indicated that infants were able to encode either the surface features, or the spatial location, but not both. This suggests that infants are only capable of activating either the dorsal or the ventral pathway, but, unlike adults, not both at the same time. As yet, behavioral evidence such as this does not conclusively decide between the view that there is increasing integration between the two visual pathways, or the contrary idea that there may be increasing dissociation between the two pathways (Jacobs, Jordan, & Barto, 1991; O'Reilly, 1998).

The ideas behind the Mareschal model have also been extended by Kaufman, Mareschal, and Johnson (2003), who reviewed some of the apparently inconsistent findings from behavioral experiments on object perception in infants in terms of the potential graspability or other properties of the objects involved. The logic behind this analysis was that behavioral tasks that involve objects that are the appropriate size, shape, and distance to be grasped are more likely to activate the dorsal pathway. Thus, the information that infants encode about these objects relates to their spatial location and shape, and not their color or other surface features. In contrast, tasks that involve objects that are too large, or too far away, to be grasped by the infant may lead to object processing centered on the surface features important for visual recognition. Future work to explore these ideas will require ERP, event-related oscillations (see below), or other forms of functional imaging.

4.3 NEURAL OSCILLATIONS AND OBJECT PROCESSING

A third general direction for understanding object processing and permanence in the infant brain comes from animal and human research on neural oscillations. A number of electrophysiological studies in animals and scalp-recorded EEG studies in humans have identified sharply timed bursts of high-frequency oscillatory activity that relate to aspects of visual processing and cognition (see Singer & Gray, 1995, for review). For example, Tallon-Baudry and colleagues found a burst of "Gamma" frequency EEG oscillations (around 40 Hz) when adults had to bind together spatially separate features to compose a single object (Tallon-Baudry, Bertrand, Peronnet, & Pernier, 1998). This team proposed that such bursts of Gamma EEG reflect the computational process of "perceptual binding."

The question of at what age infants are able to bind together separate features to compose a unitary object has been controversial based on behavioral experiments (e.g. Kavsek, 2002). Therefore, with my colleagues, we set out to determine when infants will show a Gamma burst when viewing a Kanisza figure (a well-known illusory figure; Csibra et al., 2000). We found that a group of 8-month-old infants showed a clear burst of Gamma activity over left frontal channels at around the same time after the beginning of stimulus presentation as we would expect to see it in adults. This burst was not evident to the control, "pacmen," stimulus, which could not be bound into a single object. We also tested a group of younger infants who showed a general tendency for higher Gamma EEG in response to the Kanisza stimulus, but this was not structured as a single burst and seemed to be smeared over a long time period of brain computation.

Given the possible role of Gamma EEG in object processing, a further question that can be asked is whether these high-frequency oscillations are sustained when

Figure 4.3 Gamma-band EEG activity recorded from infants in the Kaufman, Csibra, and Johnson (2003) experiment. (a) Time-frequency analysis of the average EEG at three electrodes over the right temporal cortex (around T4) during the phase in which the tunnel was lifted showed higher activations when the object should have been below the tunnel. Black asterisks below the maps indicate a significant difference from baseline; red asterisks indicate a significant difference between conditions in the average gamma activity in 200 ms-long bins. (b) A topographical map of the between-condition difference of Gamma-band (20–60 Hz) activity during the occlusion-related peak Gamma activity (from –400 to –200 ms) revealed a right-temporal focus. Circles signify right-temporal electrode sites. (See also colour plate.)

an object is being "kept in mind." This may entail the brain keeping active a representation of an object through oscillatory neural activity (for computationally minded readers, a recurrent network). This issue was addressed by recording EEG while presenting infants with visual arrays in which objects appeared or disappeared behind occluders (Kaufman, Csibra, & Johnson, 2003). A sustained Gamma response over temporal lobe channels was observed when infants saw an object pass behind an occluder without re-appearing (see figure 4.3). Interestingly, results suggest that this response was enhanced when an occluder was removed and the object had unexpectedly disappeared. The finding suggests the possibility that active object representations are enhanced (at least temporarily) when the visual pathways of the brain are faced with conflicting visual input. By this view sustained Gamma is a neural signature of an "active" object representation that needs to be strengthened or weakened depending on the extent to which it conflicts with the current visual input. If Gamma EEG lives up to its early promise as a marker for stages of object processing in the infant brain, it will be worthwhile to explore the two visual pathways with this method.

    ## 4.4 NUMBER

Alongside language, number processing and mathematical thinking offer the most likely candidates for uniquely human abilities. They are also topics within developmental cognitive neuroscience that potentially offer application to education and remediation of developmental disorders. Research by comparative psychologists and animal behavior experts reveals two systems for representing number in several animal species. First, a diverse collection of animals, including birds, rodents, and primates, have been found, in laboratory training studies, to represent the approximate numerosity of large sets of objects and to respond to changes in numerosity when other continuous variables are controlled (see Gallistel, 1990; Dehaene, 1997, for reviews). This ability has been termed "analog-magnitude" representation, and is thought to represent quantity by a representation that reflects physical magnitude proportional to the items being enumerated. In such a system, "numerical" comparisons are made in a similar way to length or time comparisons. Three signatures of these analog-magnitude representations are: (1) that discriminability is proportional to magnitude, in accord with Weber's Law (e.g. 1 and 2 are more discriminable than 7 and 8); (2) that successful representations are formed only when all members of a set are perceptually available at once (for visual/spatial arrays) or in immediate succession (for sequences of lights or sounds); and (3) that these representations can be transfered both across modalities (auditory and visual) and across formats (spatial and temporal).

  Second, both trained and untrained birds and primates have been found to represent the exact numerosity of very small sets of objects (e.g. Hauser, MacNeilage, & Ware, 1996). Some have suggested that this system is an "object-file" system that originally evolved to allow us to track up to about four moving objects at a time (Carey, 2001). Three signatures of these exact number representations are (1) that they are limited to set sizes of 3 or 4, (2) that successful representations can be formed and maintained even when different members appear successively and then are occluded, and (3) that these representations are as abstract as large number representations, for they are impaired by simultaneous variation in continuous quantitative variables such as area or contour length (Carey & Spelke, in press).

FURTHER READING: CAREY, 2001

While both of the above systems are number-domain-relevant, they are not domain-specific in that they can be engaged by non-numerical tasks. Behavioral studies of human infants provide evidence that both these systems exist in humans and emerge early in development (see Carey, 2001, for review). By 6 months of age, infants discriminate between large numerosities when all other continuous variables are controlled, both in visual spatial arrays and in auditory temporal arrays. Like other animals, infants discriminate between large numerosities only when the ratio difference is large: they discriminate arrays of 8 vs 16 dots or sequences of 8 vs 16 sounds but fail, in each case, to discriminate 8 from 12 elements (Xu & Spelke, 2000; Lipton & Spelke, 2003).

Experiments from several laboratories indicate that young infants discriminate between small numbers of objects exactly, both in visible arrays and in arrays in which each object is successively revealed and occluded (see Wynn, 1998, for review). For example, young infants and even newborns can discriminate between 2 and 3 dots, sounds, or objects, and 5-month-olds can track simple transformations of object arrays, such as addition and subtraction (Wynn, 1992). However, like monkeys, human infants fail to discriminate between large approximate numerosities when elements are successively revealed and occluded, fail to discriminate numerosities exactly for arrays of more than 3–4 objects (Chiang & Wynn, 2000), and they form representations that are robust over variations in continuous quantities for large but not small numerosities (Feigenson, Carey, & Spelke, 2002). These findings suggest that both infants and other animals have separate systems for representing large approximate numerosity and small exact numerosity. It is important to note that some of the human infant experiments remain open to alternative (non-numerical) explanations (e.g. see Cohen & Marks, 2002), and that the capacity for successful behavior in small exact numerosity tasks may depend on a system that, while domain-relevant, is not necessarily domain-specific (see Carey, 2001).

There is evidence that both the analog-magnitude and the object-file systems exist in human adults and are associated with bilateral activity in the inferior parietal lobes. This finding is consistent with the sensitivity of the dorsal pathway to the spatial-temporal aspects of object processing. Evidence for the analog-magnitude system comes from experiments in which adults must rapidly (i.e. without counting) discriminate between numerosities in visual spatial arrays, visual sequences (light flashes), or auditory sequences. In these types of tasks, discriminability follows Weber's Law and is independent of stimulus modality, as found in animals (Barth, Kanwisher, & Spelke, 2003; Whalen, Gallistel, & Gelman, 1999). Evidence for the object-file system comes from experiments in which adults must enumerate or attentively track several objects (Pylyshyn & Storm, 1988; Trick & Pylyshyn, 1994). In these studies of object-files there is usually a limit of four objects, and performance is unimpaired by occlusion, as in studies of infants and animals (see Carey, 2001). As yet there are no functional imaging experiments on infants' number perception, but given that the "object-file" system may be activated in both object and number tasks, progress within the next few years seems likely.

When children attend school and learn elementary arithmetic, however, they must work with a different system of number representation: a system that does not have an upper limit, that is not constrained by the Weber fraction, that is not constrained by perception, and that can be related to language including number words. This system has been termed an "integer-list" representation (Carey, 2001). Studies of highly trained birds and primates so far provide no evidence that any non-human animal can acquire such a system (although some animals impressively expand their ability to use the two building-block systems described above: see, e.g., Matsuzawa, 1985, 1991; Pepperberg, 1987; Brannon & Terrace, 2000). How do human children construct this system?

One idea, advanced by Elizabeth Spelke and Susan Carey, is that children construct a new concept of number and gain arithmetic skills by bringing together their two initial systems of number representation, and that language – the number words and the verbal counting routine – plays a central role in orchestrating these systems. There are several lines of evidence in support of this view. First, when children learn the number words and the counting routine, they first map "one" to the object-file system and all other number words to the analog-magnitude system indiscriminately: for example, they respond correctly when they are presented with arrays of one and of four objects and are asked to point to the array with "one" vs "four", but they respond at chance when presented with arrays of two vs four or eight objects and asked to point to the array with "two" vs "four" or "eight" (Wynn, 1992). Next, children coordinate the systems together to learn the meanings of "two" and "three," while continuing to use all other number words indiscriminately to mean, roughly, "some" (Wynn, 1992; Condry, Smith, & Spelke, 2000). Finally, children surmise that each word in the count sequence refers to an array that includes one more entity, and a larger overall set size, than the array picked out by the previous word in the count sequence (Wynn, 1992).

Further evidence that the natural number concepts result from the coordination, through the language of counting, of the analog-magnitude and object-file systems comes from studies of human adults. When adults make judgments about number words or symbols (e.g. whether a given number word is larger or smaller than five), they activate analog-magnitude representation as well as exact numerosity, and therefore judge more quickly numbers that are more distant from the comparison number (Dehaene, 1997). This finding, and many other findings from behavioral studies of normal adults, behavioral studies of neuropsychological patients, and neuroimaging studies of normal adults, provides evidence that approximate number representations are activated in tasks requiring representations of the number concepts picked out by the counting words (see Dehaene, 1997, for review). Moreover, when bilingual adults learn new information about exact numerosity, their learning is language-specific: there is a cost in response time when the information is queried in the language not used in training. In contrast, when the same adults learn new information about exact numerosity, their learning shows full transfer across languages. This finding, and parallel findings from neuroimaging studies, provides evidence that representations of large, exact numerosities depend on language for adults, whereas representations of large approximate numerosities do not (Dehaene, Spelke, Pinel, Stanescu, & Tsivkin, 1999).

Problems with number come in several forms. Sometimes children with otherwise normal intelligence show particular problems with arithmetic. This is usually called "dyscalculia," and contrasts with cases where deficits in mathematical abilities co-occur with low IQ and other cognitive problems that result from genetic disorders. Dyscalculia may not be as specific as originally supposed since it often co-occurs with dyslexia and attention deficit disorders (see Ansari & Karmiloff-Smith, 2002, for review). In genetic disorders such as Williams syndrome, numeracy deficits are quite commonly observed (Ansari & Karmiloff-Smith, 2002). Further, performance in number tasks is often worse than reading scores, suggesting that number may be a particularly vulnerable cognitive domain in the atypically developing child.

FURTHER READING: TAGER-FLUSBERG, 2003

 4.5 GENERAL SUMMARY AND CONCLUSIONS

In adults, there is evidence that the dorsal and ventral visual pathways perform different computations on objects, with the ventral pathway involved in identification and recognition, and the dorsal pathway in actions on objects. Preliminary attempts to relate these two pathways to changes in infant behavior were discussed, and a simple computational model of the changing degree of integration between the pathways was presented. While models such as this can account for some behavioral data, further progress will depend on functional imaging studies. Bursts of high-frequency neural oscillations have been related to the binding of features to compose objects and to the retention of objects following occlusion. Recent studies have used these neural oscillations to study object processing in infants, and may provide a direct marker for active representations of occluded objects in infants.

Two number-relevant systems in the primate brain were discussed. One of these is an analog-magnitude system similar to that active in time or length judgements, while the other is a system engaged by tracking small numbers of objects (object-files). Both systems appear to be active in young infants, and may underlie their ability to perform simple numerical computations with small numbers of objects. Some suggest that more sophisticated computations with large numbers requires language-mediated integration between these two systems. Overall, the research to date on number suggests that mathematical thinking, and perhaps other forms of uniquely human thinking, results from the coordination of functionally and neurologically distinct subsystems that emerge early in human development and have homologs in other animals. This in turn suggests that developmental disabilities in the domain of mathematics may result either from impairments to one of the subsystems or from impairments to the system, related to language, that coordinates their functioning. Continued investigations, using the newly emerging tools of developmental cognitive neuroscience, may yield major insights into both normal and impaired cognitive functioning through continued investigation of the building-block systems in humans and other animals and through investigation, in developing children, of the processes by which these building blocks are assembled into mature cognitive skills.

5 PERCEIVING AND ACTING ON THE SOCIAL WORLD

Cognitive neuroscience studies in adults have revealed a network of structures involved in the perception and processing of social stimuli, including interpreting the thoughts and intentions of other humans. However, considerable debate remains about the developmental origins of this brain network. Perhaps the most basic aspect of the visual social brain is the perception of faces. One extreme view is that there is an innate cortical module for face processing (maturational view). At the opposite extreme is the view that expertise for faces is acquired in the same way as visual expertise for non-social stimuli (skill learning view). By considering evidence from an animal model (chicks), behavior, and neuroimaging, I argue that a primitive bias ensures that infants orient frequently to faces. This early exposure to faces allows this stimulus to capture dedicated regions of neural tissue. This process of specialization for faces appears to take months or years. The remainder of the chapter addresses other aspects of social cognition such as perceiving and acting on information from the eyes, and attributing intentions or goals to other humans. Evidence from two developmental disorders, autism and Williams syndrome, initially appears to provide support for a social module that can be selectively impaired (autism) or spared in the face of other deficits (Williams syndrome). On closer inspection, however, it becomes apparent that such a clean dissociation is not borne out by the evidence, and that social information processing emerges as a result of constraints from interactions with other conspecifics, initial biases toward social stimuli, and the basic architecture of the brain.

5.1 THE SOCIAL BRAIN

One of the major characteristics of the human brain is its social nature. As adults, we have areas of the brain specialized for processing and integrating sensory information about the appearance, behavior, and intentions of other humans.

Sometimes this processing is also extended to other species, such as the family cat, or even to inanimate objects such as our desktop computer. A variety of cortical areas have been implicated in the "social brain," including the superior temporal sulcus (STS), the "fusiform face area" (FFA – see further below), and orbitofrontal cortex (for recent review see Adolphs 2003) (see figure 5.1). One of the major debates in cognitive neuroscience concerns the origins of the "social brain" in humans, and theoretical arguments abound about the extent to which this is acquired through experience. Mentalistic understanding of others' behavior ("theory of mind") has been associated with various neural structures, including the amygdala and the temporal pole, the superior temporal gyrus and the temporo-parietal junction, and parts of the prefrontal cortex (mainly orbitofrontal and medial areas). According to Frith and Frith (2003), the neural activity in these regions may reflect different aspects of mental state understanding: the amygdala is involved in understanding emotions through empathy; parts of the temporal lobe represent biological motion and actions; and regions of the frontal cortex play a role in understanding "intentional" referential mental states, including mental states of the self. The question I will address in this chapter is how these regions develop their functionality and become parts of the human social brain.

The three perspectives on human functional brain development discussed in chapter 1 lead to different expectations about the origins of the social brain.

Superior Temporal Sulcus/Gyrus (1)   Left Frontal Operculum (2)

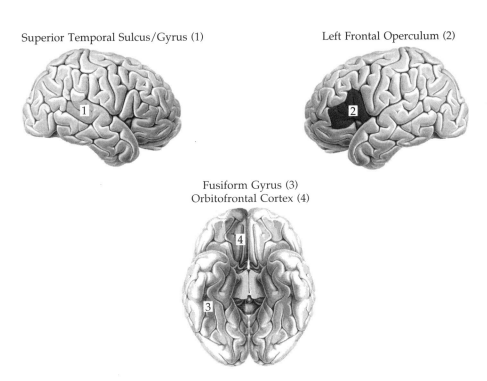

Fusiform Gyrus (3)
Orbitofrontal Cortex (4)

Figure 5.1   Some of the regions involved in the human social brain network.

According to the maturational view, through evolution, specific parts of the brain and areas of cortex have become dedicated to processing social information. Plausibly, some of the circuits are present and functioning at birth, while other components of the network become available through maturation later in development. For example, prefrontal areas associated with "theory of mind" computations may be the last component of the social brain to mature. While the maturational timetable may be accelerated or decelerated by experience, the sequence of maturation and the domain-specific wiring patterns are not. According to the skill learning view, at least some parts of the social brain are engaged by social stimuli because these tend to be the visual inputs with which we are most experienced. In other words, we tend to develop a higher level of perceptual expertise for socially relevant visual inputs. By this view we would not expect newborns to have any specific responses to social stimuli, and we should observe parallels between the development of face processing in infancy and the acquisition of perceptual expertise for other stimuli in adults. The third view, interactive specialization, predicts that the social brain will emerge as a network that becomes increasingly finely tuned to relevant stimuli and events in an activity-dependent manner. We should anticipate interactions between more primitive brain systems, cortical areas, and the environment, to produce the end result of a social brain.

In this chapter we initially examine these issues with perhaps the most fundamental visual function of the social brain – the perception and processing of faces. In later sections we go beyond this to examine some of the evidence available on more dynamic aspects of social cognition, such as interpreting eye gaze and the actions of other humans.

5.2 FACE RECOGNITION

The ability to detect and recognize faces is commonly considered to be a good example of human perceptual abilities, as well as being the basis of our adaptation as social animals. There is a long history of research on the development of face recognition in young infants extending back to the studies of Fantz more than forty years ago (e.g. Fantz, 1964). Over the past decade numerous papers have addressed the cortical basis of face processing in adults, including identifying areas that may be specifically dedicated to this purpose (Kanwisher, McDermott, & Chun, 1997; but see Haxby et al., 2001). Despite these bodies of data, surprisingly little remains known about the developmental cognitive neuroscience of face processing.

Face recognition skills may be divided into a number of components, including the ability to recognize a face as such, the ability to recognize the face of a particular individual, the ability to identify facial expressions, and the ability to use the face to interpret and predict the behavior of others. In a review of the available literature in the late 1980s, Johnson and Morton (1991) revealed two apparently contradictory bodies of evidence: while the prevailing view, and most of the evidence, supported the idea that infants gradually learn about the arrangement of features that compose a face over the first few months of life (for reviews see also Maurer, 1985; Nelson & Ludemann, 1989), the results from at least one study indicated that newborn infants, as young as 10 minutes old, will track a face-like pattern further than various "scrambled" face patterns (Goren, Sarty, & Wu, 1975). Evidence that newborns showed a preferential response to faces was used by some to bolster nativist views of infant cognition (maturational view). In contrast, the evidence for the graded development of face processing abilities over several months tended to be cited by theorists who believed that such skills need to be learned, and result from experience of the world (skill learning view). To translate these views into the framework introduced in chapter 1, while some believed that the brain possesses innate representations of faces, others took the view that face representations resulted from the information structure of the environment.

Since the study with newborn infants remained controversial for methodological reasons, my colleagues and I attempted to replicate it (Johnson, Dziurawiec, Ellis, & Morton, 1991). As in the original study, newborn infants (this time around 30 minutes old) were required to turn their head and eyes to keep a moving stimulus in view. This measure contrasts with more standard procedures in which the infant views one or more stimuli in static locations and the length of time spent looking at the stimuli is measured. In the first experiment we conducted, three of the four stimuli used in the original Goren et al. (1975) study were used: a schematic face pattern, a symmetric "scrambled" face, and a blank face outline stimulus. While we were unable to replicate preferential head turning to follow the face pattern, we did successfully replicate the preferential response to the face using a measure of eye movements (see figure 5.2).

This experiment confirmed that the brain of the newborn human infant contains some information about faces. Several more studies on face preferences in newborns have been published since 1991. While there are some differences reached in the conclusions of these authors, all of the studies found some evidence for sensitivity to face-like patterns. These have led to three hypotheses about the basis of this newborn preference behavior. Further, these three hypotheses may be associated with the three perspectives on functional brain development mentioned earlier.

FURTHER READING: DE HAAN, 2001

The sensory hypothesis: This is the hypothesis that the visual preferences of newborns, including face preferences, are determined by low-level psychophysical properties of the stimuli. This hypothesis is consistent with the skill learning

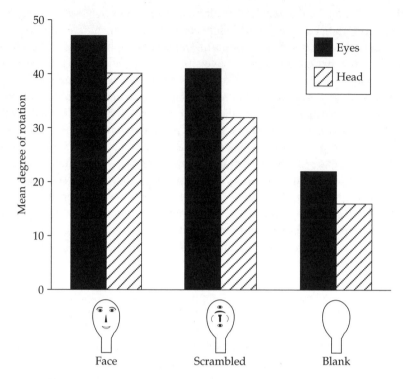

Figure 5.2   Data showing the extent of newborns' head and eye turns in following a schematic face, a scrambled face, and a blank (unpatterned) stimulus. The infants tracked the face significantly further than the other stimuli (Johnson & Morton, 1991).

perspective since it does not assume any domain-specific bias early in life. The hypothesis that face patterns are preferred due to their amplitude spectrum better suiting the infants' visual system (Kleiner, 1993) was initially rejected since face patterns always fare better than would be predicted on the basis of amplitude alone (Johnson & Morton 1991). However, Acerra, Burnod, and de Schonen (2002) recently suggested that minor differences in the exact schematic face stimuli used in critical experiments could regenerate the sensory hypothesis. Most recently, Bednar and Miikkulainen (2003) have criticized this analysis, and suggested that the overall pattern of data better fits a face-biasing system (see below for details).

Newborns have complex face representations: Empirical results have led some to the hypothesis that newborns already have complex representations of faces. This hypothesis is most consistent with the maturational view of functional brain development, since it presumably requires domain-specific circuits to be established prior to experience. These findings include the preference for attractive faces, and data indicating that newborns are sensitive to the presence of eyes in a face (Batki, Baron-Cohen, Wheelwright, Connellan, & Ahluwalia, 2001), and prefer to orient toward faces with direct (mutual) eye gaze (Farroni, Csibra, Simion, & Johnson, 2002). However, inspection of images of such stimuli through the appropriate spatial frequency filters for the newborn visual system reveals that a mechanism sensitive to low-spatial frequency components corresponding to the spatial arrangement of a face (below) could account for these seemingly more complex preferences.

Face-biasing system ("Conspec"): These hypotheses argue that the newborns' brain contains a system that biases it to orient to faces. Johnson and Morton (1991) referred to such a system as "Conspec." This hypothesis is most consistent with the interactive specialization view. In contrast to the last hypothesis, the functioning of a cortical face module is not assumed. Rather, the bias is presumed to be close to the minimum necessary for picking out faces from a natural environment. In contrast to the sensory hypothesis, the spatial relations between face features are thought to be important, even though the representation underlying this prefer-ence may not exactly map on to a face (Simion, Macchi Cassia, Turati, & Valenza, 2003). In one variant of this hypothesis, Johnson and Morton (1991) argued that their "Config" stimulus (see figure 5.3) was the minimal sufficient representation to ensure this preference. In recent neural network simulations, Bednar and Miikkulainen (2003) found that such a representation could account for the vast majority of documented newborn preferences between schematic and realistic face stimuli (see figure 5.3).

In conclusion, it appears that a primitive face-biasing system (Conspec) can, at present, account for the vast majority of data currently available on face pre-ferences with newborns. While this does not rule out some influence of sensory factors, it does mean that a simple version of the skill learning view is an unlikely explanation for the development of face processing.

Surprisingly, many other studies which used more conventional infant testing methods have not found a preference for face patterns over others until 2 or 3 months after birth (for review see also Maurer, 1985; Nelson & Ludemann, 1989). For example, Maurer and Barrera (1981) used a sensitive "infant control" testing procedure, in which participants view a series of singly presented static stimuli, and established that while 2-month-olds looked significantly longer at a face-like pattern than at various scrambled face patterns, 1-month-olds had no such pref-erence. Using the same method, Johnson, Dziurawiec, Bartrip, and Morton (1992) replicated this result and extended the original findings by including in the stimulus set the "de-focused" face arrangement stimulus used in the newborn studies earlier. The results replicated entirely the previous findings: the face was looked at longer than any of the other stimuli by 10-week-olds, but a group of 5-week-old infants showed no preference. This evidence was consistent with the

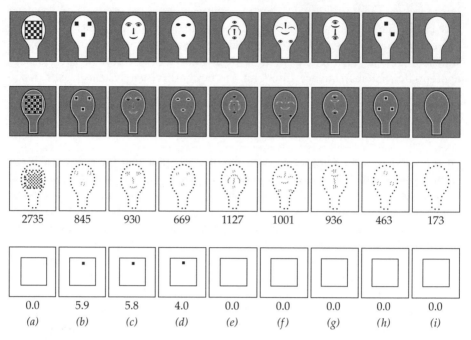

| 2735 | 845 | 930 | 669 | 1127 | 1001 | 936 | 463 | 173 |

| 0.0 | 5.9 | 5.8 | 4.0 | 0.0 | 0.0 | 0.0 | 0.0 | 0.0 |
| (a) | (b) | (c) | (d) | (e) | (f) | (g) | (h) | (i) |

Figure 5.3 A summary of human newborn and model responses to schematic images. The top row represents some of the schematic patterns presented to both newborns and the "retina" of the neural network model. The next two rows illustrate the LGN and visual cortex stages of the models processing. The bottom row indicates the output of the model, with the prefered stimuli being *b, c,* and *d.* The preferences of the model correspond well to the results obtained with newborn infants.

alternative claim that infants gradually construct representations of faces as a result of repeated exposure to them over the first few months of life (Gibson, 1979). Clearly, these apparently contradictory findings raised a problem for theories of the development of face recognition that involved only one process (either learning or innate face representations). In an attempt to interpret this apparently conflicting behavioral data, Johnson and Morton (1991) turned to evidence from two areas of biology: ethology and brain development.

The primary source of evidence from other species (ethology) that Johnson and Morton used to interpret the human infancy results concerned filial imprinting in the domestic chick. Imprinting in chicks was selected because it is well studied both in terms of behavior and in terms of its neural basis. Filial imprinting is the process by which young precocial birds such as chicks recognize and develop an attachment for the first conspicuous object that they see after hatching (for reviews see Bolhuis, 1991; Johnson & Bolhuis, 1991). While imprinting has been reported in the young of a variety of species, including spiny mice, guinea pigs, chicks, and ducklings, only in precocial species (those that are mobile from birth) can we measure it using the conventional measure of preferential approach.

 ## 5.3 FILIAL IMPRINTING IN CHICKS

In the laboratory, 1-day-old domestic chicks will imprint onto a variety of objects such as moving colored balls and cylinders. After even a few hours of exposure to such a stimulus, chicks develop strong and robust preferences for the training object over novel stimuli. In the absence of a mother hen this learning is relatively unconstrained: virtually any conspicuous moving object larger than a matchbox will serve as an imprinting stimulus, and will come to be preferred over any other.

A particular region of the chick forebrain (thought to correspond to mammalian cortex) has been shown to be critical for imprinting, a region known as the intermediate and medial part of the hyperstriatum ventrale (IMHV) (for reviews see Horn, 1985; Horn & Johnson, 1989). Lesions to IMHV placed before or after training on an object severely impair preference for that object in subsequent choice tests, but do not affect several other types of visual and learning tasks (McCabe, Cipolla-Neto, Horn, & Bateson, 1982; Johnson & Horn, 1986, 1987). Similar size lesions placed elsewhere in the chick forebrain do not result in significant impairments of imprinting preference (McCabe et al., 1982; Johnson & Horn, 1987).

The next step in analyzing the neural basis of imprinting was to study the microcircuitry of the region involved. Although the bird forebrain lacks the laminar organization of mammalian cortex, the relation of the forebrain to subcortical structures is similar following the basic higher vertebrate brain design (chapter 2). Evidence from a variety of vertebrate species supports the suggestion that the avian forebrain is a site of plasticity, and not the location of inbuilt, automatic, types of behavior which are located in other structures (MacPhail, 1982; Ewert, 1987).

Figure 5.4 illustrates the location of IMHV within the chick brain. It is worth noting that this region corresponds to, or overlaps with, regions critical for auditory imprinting and song learning (e.g. Maier & Schiech, 1983). The area occupies about 5 percent of total forebrain volume. Its main inputs come from visual projection areas (hyperstriatum accessorium and the optic tectum), and some of its projections go to regions of the bird brain thought to be involved in motor control (such as the archistriatum). Thus, the area is well placed to integrate visual inputs and motor outputs.

After identifying features of the basic microcircuitry of IMHV, the next step was to take a synthetic approach and build a computational model of the circuit concerned (Bateson & Horn, 1994; O'Reilly & Johnson 1994). In one of these models, Randall O'Reilly and I constructed a connectionist model based on two

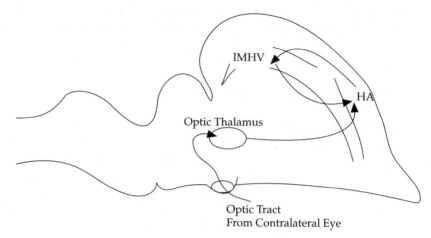

Figure 5.4 Outline sagittal view of the chick brain showing the main visual pathway to IMHV (HA, hyperstriatum accessorium). There are other routes of visual input to IMHV which are not shown in this figure (see Horn, 1985). The brain of a 2-day-old chick is approximately 2 cm long.

characteristics of the cytoarchitectonics of IMHV: the existence of positive feed-back loops between the excitatory principle neurons, and the extensive inhibitory circuitry mediated by the local circuit neurons. The detailed architecture of the model is shown in figure 5.5. (For further details of the model and neuroanatomy, see O'Reilly & Johnson, 2002.)

FURTHER READING: O'REILLY & JOHNSON, 2002

In the laboratory a wide range of objects, such as moving red boxes and blue balls, are as effective for imprinting as are more naturalistic stimuli, such as a moving stuffed hen. However, in the wild, precocial birds such as chicks invariably imprint on their mother, and not on other moving objects. These observations raise the question as to what constraints ensure that this plasticity in the chick brain is normally guided to encode information about conspecifics (the mother hen), rather than other objects in its environment.

An answer to this question became evident from the results of a series of experiments in which stimulus-dependent effects of IMHV lesions were observed (Horn & McCabe, 1984). Groups of chicks trained on an artificial stimulus such as a rotating red box were severely impaired by IMHV lesions placed either before or after training on an object. However, groups of chicks exposed to a stuffed hen were only mildly impaired in their preference. Other neurophysiological manipulations also show differences between the hen-trained and box-trained birds (see

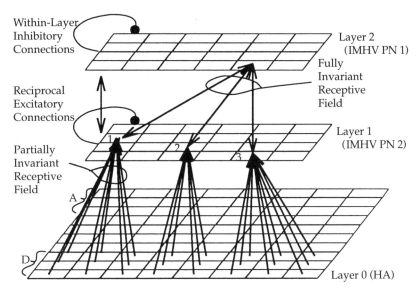

Figure 5.5 The detailed architecture of the model is designed around the anatomical connectivity of IMHV and its primary input area, the hyperstriatum accessorium (HA). The model is based on a set of layers, each of which has lateral inhibition within it. The "input" layer of the network, layer 0, represent HA. HA then projects to one subpopulation of IMHV projection neuron (PN) cells, which we assume to be type 1 PNs (see O'Reilly & Johnson, 2002). This is layer 1 of the IMHV component of the model. Note that the laminar distinction in the model between these two component cells of IMHV is not intended to suggest that the cells are arranged as such in the IMHV itself, but rather serves to reflect the functional distinction between the two types of PN. The axons from the type 1 neurons project to the type 2 projection neurons, as well as onto the local inhibitory neurons. This comprises the second layer of the model's "IMHV" component. The type 2 PNs then send a bifurcating axon both back to the type 1 PNs and the inhibitory cells (layer 2), and to other areas, which are not modeled. Within each layer of the model, strong lateral inhibition exists in the form of relatively large negative weights between all units in the layer. This reflects the presence of a large number of GABAergic inhibitory interneurons in IMHV (Tombol et al., 1988), and its relatively low levels of spontaneous activity. The strong inhibition in this layer of the model resulted in only one unit in each layer becoming active at any time.

table 5.1). For example, administration of the neurotoxin DSP4, which depletes forebrain levels of the neurotransmitter norepinephrine (see chapter 2), resulted in a severe impairment of preference in birds trained on the red box, but only a mild impairment in birds trained on the stuffed hen (Davies, Horn, & McCabe, 1985). In contrast, plasma levels of the hormone testosterone correlate with preference for the stuffed hen, but not preference for the red box (Bolhuis, McCabe, & Horn, 1986).

These results led Johnson and Horn (1988) to seek experimental evidence for an earlier suggestion (Hinde, 1961) that naturalistic objects such as hens may be more effective at eliciting attention in young chicks than are other objects. A

Table 5.1   Stimulus-dependent effects of neurophysiological manipulations

Treatment	Hen-trained chicks	Box-trained chicks
Bilateral IMHV lesions	Mild impairment	Severe impairment
DSP4 treatment	Mild impairment	Severe impairment
Plasma testosterone levels	Correlated with preference	No correlation with preference
Multicellular recording in IMHV	No correlation	Correlated

series of experiments were therefore conducted in which dark-reared chicks were presented with a choice between a stuffed hen and a variety of test stimuli created from cutting up and jumbling the pelt of a stuffed hen. Johnson and Horn (1988) concluded from these experiments that chicks have an untrained tendency, or predisposition, to attend toward features of the head and neck region of the hen. While this untrained preference seemed to be specific to the correct arrangement of features of the face/head, it was not specific to the species. For example, the head of a duck was as attractive as that of a hen.

The results of these and several other experiments led to the proposal that there are two independent brain systems that control filial preference in the chick (Horn, 1985; Johnson, Bolhuis, & Horn, 1985). The first of these controls a specific predisposition making newly hatched chicks orient toward objects resembling a mother hen. In contrast to non-specific color and size preferences in the chick (see Johnson & Bolhuis, 1991), this predisposition system appears to be specifically tuned to the correct spatial arrangement of elements of the head and neck region. While the stimulus configuration triggering the predisposition is not species- or genus-specific, it is sufficient to pick out the mother hen from other objects the chick is likely to be exposed to in the first few days after hatching. Although the neural basis for this predisposition is currently unknown, the optic tectum, the homolog of the mammalian superior colliculus, is one likely candidate.

The second brain system acquires information about the objects to which the young chick attends and is supported by the forebrain region IMHV. In the natural environment, it has been argued, the first brain system guides the second system to acquire information about the closest mother hen. Biochemical, electrophysiological, and lesion evidence all support the conclusion that these two brain systems have largely independent neural substrates (for review see Horn, 1985). For example, while selective lesions to IMHV impair preferences acquired through exposure to an object, they do not impair the specific predisposition (Johnson & Horn, 1986).

There are, of course, a number of different ways in which the predisposition could constrain the information acquired by the IMHV system. For example, the information in the predisposition could act as a sensory "filter" or template through which information had to pass before reaching the IMHV system. The evidence available at present is consistent with the view that the two systems influence the preference behavior of the chick independently, that is, there is no internal informational exchange between them. Instead, it appears that the input to the IMHV system is selected simply as a result of the predisposition biasing the chick to orient toward any hen-like objects in the environment. Given that the species-typical environment of the chick includes a mother hen in close proximity, and that the predisposition includes adequate information to pick the hen out from other objects in the early environment, the input to the learning system will be highly selected.

One benefit of this well-studied animal model for developmental cognitive neuro-science is that it allows us to examine the plausibility of the three perspectives on human functional brain development (while bearing in mind the possibility of species differences). The chick imprinting story is inconsistent with the skill learning view in that the predisposition is present without prior training, and the learning involves self-terminating plasticity. The chick model is also somewhat inconsistent with the maturational view in that the IMHV is relatively unconstrained in its learning, and appears to emerge from surrounding tissue as a result of experience. The evidence suggests that the emergence of a simple vertebrate social brain is consistent with the interactive specialization view as brain plasticity was constrained by simple biases, neural architecture, and the early environment.

5.4 BRAIN DEVELOPMENT AND FACE RECOGNITION

The other source of biological data that Johnson and Morton used to generate an account of human infant face recognition came from the postnatal development of the cerebral cortex. As previously mentioned (chapter 3), both neuroanatomical and neurophysiological data indicate that visually guided behavior in the newborn infant is largely (though not exclusively) controlled by subcortical structures such as the superior colliculus and pulvinar, and that it is not until several months of age that cortical circuitry comes to completely dominate subcortical control over behavior. Consistent with these arguments is the position that visually guided behavior in human infants, like that in domestic chicks, is based on activity in two or more distinct brain systems. If these systems have distinct developmental time courses, then they may differentially influence behavior in infants of different ages.

There is much evidence that the recognition of individual faces in adults involves cortical areas and pathways. This evidence comes from three main sources: (i) neuropsychological patients with brain damage who are unable to recognize faces (prosopagnosia); (ii) neuroimaging studies of face perception; and (iii) single- and multi-cellular recording studies with non-human primates. To briefly review this literature, prosopagnosia commonly results from damage to the region of cortex that lies between the temporal and occipital (visual) cortex, although the exact neuropathology required is still controversial and may vary between participants. Some cases have suggested that only a right-hemisphere lesion is necessary, while others suggest bilateral lesions are required (see Farah, 1990, for a review). The deficit resulting from these lesions can be fairly specific. Although prosopagnosic patients have difficulty recognizing individual faces, they sometimes seem to be able to identify other objects. Of course, exceptions to this have been noted, with some patients having difficulty identifying other complex objects. However, not all face processing is entirely abolished in these patients. For example, some prosopagnosic patients seem to have intact facial emotion processing (e.g. Bruyer et al., 1983), and many show "covert" recognition of familiar faces as indicated by sensitive measures such as galvanic skin responses (Tranel & Damasio, 1985).

Evidence from neuroimaging studies of human adults has demonstrated the involvement of a number of regions of cortex. A range of cortical regions within the social brain, including regions of the fusiform gyrus, lateral occipital area, and superior temporal sulcus, have all been implicated in neuroimaging studies as being face-specific regions involved in encoding or detecting facial information. The stimulus specificity of response has been most extensively studied for the "fusiform face area" (FFA), a region which is more activated by faces than by many other comparison stimuli, including houses, textures, and hands (Kanwisher et al., 1997). While the greater activation of the FFA to faces than other objects has led some to propose it is a face module (Kanwisher et al., 1997), others call this view into question. In particular, investigations demonstrating that (a) the distribution of response across the ventral cortex may be more stimulus-specific than the strength of response of a particular region such as FFA (Haxby et al., 2001; Ishai, Ungerleider, Martin, Schouten, & Haxby, 1999; but see Spiridon & Kanwisher, 2002), and (b) that activation of the FFA increases with increasing expertise in discriminating members of non-face categories (Gauthier et al., 1999), together suggest that the region may play a more general role in object processing. However, the observations do remain that faces more than any other object activate the FFA, and that the distribution of activity over the ventral cortex for faces differs from other objects in that it is more focal and less influenced by attention (Haxby et al., 2001).

Thus, there is considerable evidence for specific cortical involvement in face processing among adults. However, there is also evidence for a face preference in newborn infants, whose behavior, as discussed in the previous chapter, is thought to be guided largely by subcortical sensorimotor pathways. Consideration of this evidence led Morton and myself to propose a two-process theory of infant face preferences analogous to that in chicks. We argued that the first process consists of a system accessed via the subcortical visuomotor pathway (but possibly also involving some of the deeper, earlier developing, cortical layers) that is responsible for the preferential tracking of faces in newborns. However, the influence of this system over behavior declines (possibly due to inhibition by developing cortical circuits) during the second month of life. The second brain system depends upon cortical maturity, and exposure to faces over the first month or two, and begins to control infant orienting preferences from around 2 or 3 months of age. By extension with the evidence on chicks, we (Johnson & Morton, 1991) argued that the newborn preferential orienting system biases the input set to developing cortical circuitry. This circuitry is configured in response to a certain range of input, before it starts to gain control over the infant's behavior. Once this occurs, the cortical system has acquired sufficient information about the structure of faces to ensure that it continues to acquire further information about them. Like in the chick, the proposal is that a specific, early developing brain circuit acts in concert with the species-typical environment to bias the input to later developing brain circuitry. While this theory is far from proven, a number of strands of evidence are consistent with it. First, let us consider evidence about the neural basis of the face bias in newborns.

Johnson and Morton (1991) speculated that the face bias ("Conspec") was mediated largely, but not necessarily exclusively, by subcortical visuomotor pathways. This proposal was made for several reasons: (a) that the newborn preference declined at the same age as other newborn reflexes assumed to be under subcortical control; (b) evidence from the maturation of the visual system indicating later development of cortical visual processing, and (c) evidence from another species (the domestic chick). Owing to the continuing difficulty in successfully using functional imaging with healthy awake newborns, this hypothesis has, as yet, only been indirectly addressed. First, de Schonen and colleagues examined face preferences in a number of infants with perinatal damage to regions of cortex. Even in cases of damage to the visual cortex, the bias to orient to faces remained (Mancini et al., 1998). The second line of evidence used the fact that the nasal and temporal visual fields feed differentially into the cortical and subcortical visual pathways. Specifically, Simion and colleagues predicted that the face bias would be found in the temporal visual field, but not the nasal visual field. This prediction was confirmed (Simion, Valenza, Umilta, & Dalla Barba, 1998). A third line of indirect evidence comes from adult neuropsychological studies, and specifically evidence from adult patients with spatial neglect and extinction. Vuilleumier and colleagues (Vuilleumier, 2000; Vuilleumier et al., 2001) report that these patients extinguish (fail to detect) a face much less often than other stimuli. While a variety of explanations of this phenomena are possible, one view is that damage to cortical circuits in adults releases inhibition of a subcortical face bias. Finally, functional imaging studies in adults that include subcortical structures in their analysis have observed activation of a range of subcortical structures in addition to the well-known areas of cortical specialization (Adolphs, 2002).

While Johnson and Morton (1991) identified the superior colliculus as a major visuomotor structure that could be involved in determining Conspec preferences, another candidate structure is the pulvinar. Our knowledge of this brain structure has increased dramatically over the past decade, and the description of its function now makes it a candidate for involvement in newborn visual preferences. Specifically, portions of pulvinar receive input directly from the superior colliculus (as well as from the retina and, at least in adults, striate and extrastriate visual cortex). Additionally, in adults there are reciprocal connections to frontal, temporal, and parietal regions and to the anterior cingulate and amygdala. The advent of new technology suitable for studying the neural correlates of behavior in newborns may allow further investigation of this issue.

We now turn to the neurodevelopment of face processing during infancy and childhood. To re-cap, the three perspectives on human functional brain development discussed earlier make differing predictions about how this specialization arises. By a maturational view we expect to see the gradual addition of new brain modules relating to aspects of face processing ability. From a skill learning perspective, the fusiform face area should become active as the perceptual skill of face processing is acquired. From an interactive specialization view, we expect to observe the increasing neural specialization and more restricted localization of face processing with development. With these different predictions in mind, let us review some of the evidence from developmental cognitive neuroscience.

Several labs have examined changes in event-related potentials (ERPs) as adults view faces. In particular, interest has focused on an ERP component termed the "N170" (because it is a negative-going deflection that occurs after around 170 milliseconds), which has been strongly associated with face processing in a number of studies on adults (see de Haan, Johnson, & Halit, 2003, for review). Specifically, the amplitude and latency of this component vary according to whether or not faces are present in the visual field of the adult volunteer under study. An important aspect of the N170 in adults is that its response is highly selective. For example, the N170 shows a different response to human upright faces than to very closely related stimuli such as inverted human faces and upright monkey faces (de Haan et al., 2001). While the exact underlying neural generators of the N170 are currently still debated, the specificity of response of this component can be taken as an index of the degree of specialization of cortical processing for human upright faces. For this reason de Haan and colleagues undertook a series of studies on the development of the N170 over the first weeks and months of postnatal life.

The first issue addressed in these developmental ERP studies was when does the face-sensitive N170 emerge? In a series of experiments a component in the infant ERP that has many of the properties associated with the adult N170, but that is of a slightly longer latency, was identified (240–90 ms; de Haan, Pascalis, & Johnson, 2002; Halit, de Haan, & Johnson, 2003; Halit, Csibra, Volein, & Johnson, 2004). In studying the response properties of this component at 3, 6, and 12 months of age we have discovered that (1) the component is present from at least 3 months of age (although its development continues into middle childhood), and (2) the component becomes more specifically tuned to human upright faces with increasing age. To expand on the second point, we found that while 12-month-olds and adults showed different ERP responses to upright and inverted faces, 3- and 6-month-olds did not (de Haan et al., 2002; Halit et al., 2003). Thus, the study of this face-sensitive ERP component is consistent with the idea of increased specialization of cortical processing with age, a result also consistent with some behavioral results (see below).

While we still await definitive functional imaging studies on face processing in infants and young children, evidence for increased localization of cortical processing of faces comes from a recent fMRI study of the neural basis of face processing in children compared to adults (Passarotti et al., 2003). As illustrated in figure 5.6, in this study, even when children and adults were equated for behavioral ability (in a face-matching task), children activated a larger extent of cortex around face-sensitive areas than did adults. Similar conclusions can be drawn from a PET study conducted on 3-month-old infants, in which a large network of cortical areas were activated when infants viewed faces as compared to a moving dot array (Tzourio-Mazoyer et al., 2002). This study involved the "subtraction" of the activation resulting from a complex dynamic stimulus from that elicited by photographs of a female face. The resulting areas of activation corresponded to those regions activated by face processing in adults, namely bilateral activation of the superior and middle temporal gyrus (though the regions activated in infants may be more anterior than those in adults). Despite a low baseline of overall metabolic activity in the frontal lobes (in agreement with the Chugani et al. study [2002] reviewed in chapter 2), there was a significant increase in activity in the left orbito-frontal cortex and Broca's area in the face condition.

Converging evidence about the increasing specialization of face processing during development comes from a behavioral study that set out to test the intriguing idea that as processing "narrows" (Nelson, 2003) to human faces, then infants will lose their ability to discriminate non-human faces (Pascalis, de Haann, & Nelson, 2002). Pascalis and colleagues demonstrated that while 6-month-olds could discriminate between individual monkey faces as well as human faces, 9-month-olds and adults could only discriminate the human faces. These results are particularly compelling since they demonstrate a predicted competence in young infants that is not evident in adults.

The three lines of evidence reviewed above are hard to reconcile with a strictly maturational view that posits the addition of new components of processing with development. Rather, the evidence available to date suggests "shrinkage" of the cortical activity associated with face processing during development. While increased specialization and localization are specifically predicted by the interactive specialization view, these changes are not necessarily inconsistent with skill learning (Gauthier & Nelson, 2001). Thus, with regard to face perception, the available evidence from newborns allows us to rule out the skill learning hypothesis, while the evidence on the neurodevelopment of face processing over the first months and years of life is consistent with the kinds of dynamic changes in processing expected from the interactive specialization, and not the maturational, approach.

Before leaving the topic of face and individual face recognition, I should note that there is some evidence that infants in the first week of life are able to identify their mother (e.g. Pascalis, de Schonen, Morton, Deruelle, & Fabre-Grenet, 1995). At first sight this evidence seems to conflict with the view that cortical face

Figure 5.6 Face-matching task. (A) Significant clusters of functional activation in medio-lateral fusiform regions for the face-matching task, in 16 adults (left-hand side) and 12 children (right-hand side). (B) Significant clusters of functional activation in the middle temporal gyrus (BA 21) in adults (left-hand side) and children (right-hand side). Circled in yellow is the bilateral middle temporal gyrus activation, which is present only in children, not in adults. Note that posterior activation is within the middle (BA 19) and inferior (BA 18) occipital gyrus. The Z coordinates refer to the distance in mm of the axial slices (e.g. brain slices according to a superior-to-inferior axis) from the intercommissural (anterior commissure–posterior commissure) plane. The colored bar to the left represents the percent increase in intensity of activation in the experimental task, as compared to the control task. Note that according to the radiological convention the left side of the brain represents the right hemisphere (RH), and the right side of the brain represents the left hemisphere (LH). (See also colour plate.)

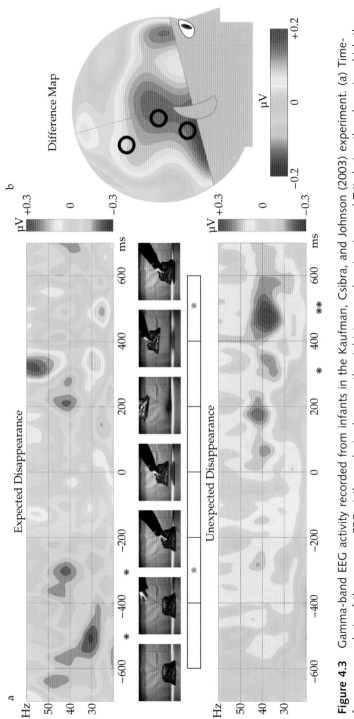

Figure 4.3 Gamma-band EEG activity recorded from infants in the Kaufman, Csibra, and Johnson (2003) experiment. (a) Time-frequency analysis of the average EEG at three electrodes over the right temporal cortex (around T4) during the phase in which the tunnel was lifted showed higher activations when the object should have been below the tunnel. Black asterisks below the maps indicate a significant difference from baseline; red asterisks indicate a significant difference between conditions in the average gamma activity in 200 ms-long bins. (b) A topographical map of the between-condition difference of Gamma-band (20–60 Hz) activity during the occlusion-related peak Gamma activity (from –400 to –200 ms) revealed a right-temporal focus. Circles signify right-temporal electrode sites.

Figure 5.6 Face-matching task. (A) Significant clusters of functional activation in medio-lateral fusiform regions for the face-matching task, in 16 adults (left-hand side) and 12 children (right-hand side). (B) Significant clusters of functional activation in the middle temporal gyrus (BA 21) in adults (left-hand side) and children (right-hand side). Circled in yellow is the bilateral middle temporal gyrus activation, which is present only in children, not in adults. Note that posterior activation is within the middle (BA 19) and inferior (BA 18) occipital gyrus. The Z coordinates refer to the distance in mm of the axial slices (e.g. brain slices according to a superior-to-inferior axis) from the intercommissural (anterior commissure–posterior commissure) plane. The colored bar to the left represents the percent increase in intensity of activation in the experimental task, as compared to the control task. Note that according to the radiological convention the left side of the brain represents the right hemisphere (RH), and the right side of the brain represents the left hemisphere (LH).

Figure 7.3 Covert language task: group average fMRI activation in the unaffected and affected members of the KE family. Activated regions are projected onto the surface rendering of a typical 3D individual brain, displayed at a statistical threshold of $p < .05$, corrected for multiple comparisons. L, left hemisphere; R, right hemisphere.

Figure 8.1 Interaction between wakefulness and the linguistic nature of the stimuli. This comparison isolated a right dorsolateral prefrontal region that showed greater activation by forward speech than by backward speech in awake infants, but not in sleeping infants.

processing does not emerge until at least the second month. However, this discriminative ability in newborns is based only on the general shape of the head and hair, and not on facial configuration or features. De Schonen and Mancini (1995) argue that this "third system" is a non-specific visual pattern learning ability which has also been evident from studies with visual patterns of many other kinds. Johnson and de Haan have modified the original two-process theory to take account of early hippocampal-based learning (see chapter 6).

FURTHER READING: DE HAAN, 2001

5.5 PERCEIVING AND ACTING ON THE EYES

Moving beyond the relatively simple perception of faces, a more complex attribute of the adult social brain is processing information about the eyes of other humans. There are two important aspects of processing information about the eyes. The first of these is being able to detect the direction of another person's gaze in order to direct your own attention to the same object or spatial location. Perception of averted gaze can elicit an automatic shift of attention in the same direction in adults (Driver et al., 1999), allowing the establishment of "joint attention" (Butterworth & Jarrett, 1991). Joint attention to objects is thought to be crucial for a number of aspects of cognitive and social development, including word learning. The second critical aspect of gaze perception is the detection of direct gaze, enabling mutual gaze with the viewer. Mutual gaze (eye contact) provides the main mode of establishing a communicative context between humans, and is believed to be important for normal social development (e.g. Kleinke, 1986; Symons, Hains, & Muir, 1998). It is commonly agreed that eye gaze perception is important for mother–infant interaction, and that it provides a vital foundation for social development (e.g. Jaffe, Stern, & Peery, 1973; Stern, 1977).

With regard to the social brain network, the superior temporal sulcus (STS) has been identified in several adult imaging studies of eye gaze perception and processing (for review see Adolphs, 2003). As with cortical face processing above, in adults the response properties of this region are highly tuned (specialized) in that the region responds only to non-biological motion (Puce, Allison, Bentin, Gore, & McCarthy, 1998). While we cannot directly capture the functioning of STS in infants, my colleagues and I have conducted a series of behavioral experiments to ascertain the specificity or otherwise of gaze cueing in infants.

Several studies have demonstrated that gaze cues are able to trigger an automatic and rapid shifting of the focus of the adult viewer's visual attention (Friesen & Kingstone, 1998; Driver et al., 1999; Langton & Bruce, 1999). All these studies used variants of the spatial cueing paradigm (see chapter 3), where a central or peripheral cue directs attention to one of the peripheral locations. When the target appears in the same location where the cue was directed (the congruent position), the participant is faster to look at that target compared to another target at an incongruent position relative to the previous cue. Human infants start to discriminate and follow adults' direction of attention at the age of 3 or 4 months (Vecera & Johnson, 1995; Hood, Willen, & Driver, 1998). In our studies we examined further the visual properties of the eyes that enable infants to follow the direction of the gaze. We tested 4-month-olds using a cueing paradigm adapted from Hood et al. (1998). Each trial began with the stimulus face eyes blinking (to attract attention), before the pupils shift to either the right or the left for a period of 1,500 ms (see figure 5.7). A target stimulus was then presented either in the same direction as the stimulus face eyes were looking (congruent position) or in a location incongruent with the direction of gaze. By measuring the saccadic reaction time of infants to orient to the target we demonstrated that the infants were faster to look at the location congruent with the direction of gaze of the face.

In a series of experiments using this basic paradigm, we have established that it is only following a period of mutual gaze with an upright face that cueing effects are observed. In other words, mutual gaze with an upright face may engage mechanisms of attention such that the viewer is more likely to be cued by subsequent motion. In summary, the critical features for eye gaze cueing in infants are (1) lateral motion of elements and (2) a brief preceding period of eye contact with an upright face.

Evidence from functional neuroimaging indicates that a network of cortical and subcortical regions are engaged in eye gaze processing in adults. This network of

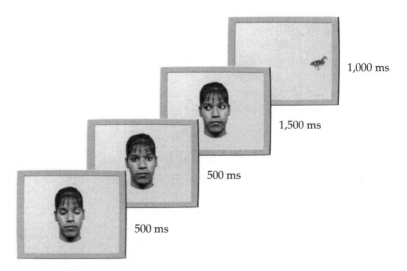

Figure 5.7 Example of the edited video image illustrating the stimulus for Experiment 1 in Farroni et al. (2000). In this trial the stimulus target (the duck) appears on the side incongruent with the direction of gaze.

structures overlaps with, but does not completely duplicate, the patterns of activation seen in the perception of motion, and the perception of faces in general. While it may be important to activate the whole network for eye gaze processing, one region in particular, the "eye area" of the superior temporal sulcus, appears to be critical. The finding that infants are as effectively cued by non-eye motion (Farroni, Johnson, Brockbank, & Simion, 2000) provides preliminary evidence that their STS may be less finely tuned than in adults.

Following the surprising observation that a period of direct gaze is required before cueing can be effective in infants, my colleagues and I investigated the developmental roots of eye contact detection. It is already known that human newborns have a bias to orient toward face-like stimuli (see earlier), prefer faces with eyes opened (Batki et al., 2001), and tend to imitate certain facial gestures (Meltzoff & Moore, 1977). Preferential attention to faces with direct gaze would provide the most compelling evidence to date that human newborns are born prepared to detect socially relevant information. For this reason we recently investigated eye gaze detection in humans from birth. We (Farroni et al., 2002) tested healthy human newborn infants by presenting them with a pair of stimuli, one a face with eye gaze directed straight at the newborns, and the other with averted gaze (see figure 5.8). Videotapes of the baby's eye movements throughout the trial were analyzed by the two recorders. The dependent variables we used

Figure 5.8 Results of the Farroni et al. (2000) preferential looking study with newborns. (a) Mean looking times (and Standard Error) spent at the two stimulus types. Newborns spent significantly more time looking at the face with direct gaze than at that with averted gaze. (b) Mean number of orientations toward each type of stimulus. (c) Filled triangles = reference scores for the direct gaze over the averted gaze for each individual newborn. Open triangles = average preference scores.

were the total fixation time and the number of orienting responses. Results showed that the fixation times were significantly longer for the face with the direct gaze. Further, the number of orientations was higher with the straight gaze than with the averted gaze.

In a second experiment, we attempted to gain converging evidence for the differential processing of direct gaze in infants, by recording event-related potentials (ERPs) from the scalp as infants viewed faces. We studied 4-month-old babies with the same stimuli as those used in the previous experiment with newborns, and found a difference between the two gaze directions at the face-sensitive component of the infant ERP discussed earlier (Farroni et al., 2002). Our conclusion from the second study is that direct eye contact enhances the perceptual processing of faces in 4-month-old infants.

The empirical evidence gathered on the development and neural basis of eye gaze processing in infants is consistent with the interactive specialization view. Specifically, the same primitive representation of high-contrast elements ("Conspec") as underlies the face bias in newborns may also be sufficient to direct them toward faces with direct eye contact. Therefore, the more frequent orienting to the direct gaze in newborns could be mediated by the same mechanism that underlies newborns' tendency to orient to faces in general. A face with direct gaze would better fit the spatial relation of elements in this template than one with gaze averted, suggesting that the functional role of this putative mechanism is more general than previously supposed. This primitive bias ensures a biased input of human faces with direct gaze to the infant over the first days and weeks of life.

According to the interactive specialization view, a network as a whole becomes specialized for a particular function. Therefore, I suggest that the "eye region" of the STS does not develop in isolation, or in a modular fashion, but that its functionality emerges within the context of interacting regions involved in either general face processing or in motion detection. Viewed from this perspective, STS may be a region that integrates motion information with the processing of faces (and other body parts). While STS may be active in infants, it may not yet efficiently integrate motion and face information. In other words, while the 4-month-old has good face processing and general motion perception, it has not yet integrated these two aspects of perception together into adult eye gaze perception. By this account, making eye contact with an upright face fully engages face processing, which then facilitates the orienting of attention by lateral motion. At older ages, eye gaze perception becomes a fully integrated function where even static presentations of averted eyes are sufficient to facilitate gaze.

5.6 THE ATYPICAL SOCIAL BRAIN

Beyond face processing and eye gaze detection there are many more complex aspects of the social brain such as the coherent perception of human action, and the appropriate attribution of intentions and goals to conspecifics. One way in which these issues have been addressed is through behavioral studies with infants, toddlers, and children. A second way is through studying developmental disorders in which aspects of social cognition are either apparently selectively impaired (autism) or selectively intact amidst otherwise impaired cognition (Williams syndrome).

Autism is a relatively rare developmental disorder (with an incidence of around 5 in 10,000 births, see appendix). While there is evidence for some genetic contribution to the disorder, there may be several possible genetic "routes" to autism, and there is also clearly an interaction with environmental factors (see Frith, 2003, for review). Most of the core deficits of the developmental disorder of autism lie in the domain of social relations with others, though there are many non-social cognitive deficits as well. Major behavioral symptoms include avoidance of eye contact, an apparent unawareness of the existence and thoughts of others, a reluctance to be held or touched by others, repetitive behaviors such as rocking or hand flapping, and commonly a fascination for certain objects or other inanimate aspects of their environment. Alongside these deviant behaviors are often deficits in other cognitive and language skills, such as echolalia (repeating words and sentences heard previously). A related disorder, which shares many of the same symptoms, is Asperger's syndrome, though these individuals have a normal verbal IQ (Happé, 1994; Pennington & Welsh, 1995).

Many different laboratories have attempted to locate specific brain deficits in autism. Applying the adult neuropsychology model (see the causal epigenesis view in chapter 1), it was initially assumed that there would be a focal structural deficit somewhere in the brain, and that this "hole" in the brain could be associated with a particular pattern of cognitive deficits. As we will see, although developmental deficits can result in seemingly quite specific profiles of cognitive deficit, the corresponding structural damage to the brain can be elusive, diffuse, and/or inconsistent across different individuals. In the case of autism, structural brain imaging and postmortem neuroanatomical studies have variously implicated the brain stem, cerebellum, limbic system, thalamus, and frontal lobes (for review see Happé & Frith, 1996). Several studies have reported enlargement of the ventricles, indicating atrophy in adjacent limbic and frontal structures (for review see Pennington & Welsh, 1995). However, like several of the brain atypicalities that have been reported in autism, ventricular enlargement is not specific to autism, since it is also observed in schizophrenia.

FURTHER READING: OZONOFF, 2001; TAGER-FLUSBERG, 2003

Another deficit observed in several studies on autism is in the cerebellum (e.g. Courchesne, Yeung-Courchesne, Press, Hesselink, & Jernigan, 1988). At present it is unclear whether this is a postnatal effect (recall from chapter 2 that cell migration in this region continues into postnatal life) or whether, as Courchesne et al. (1988) argue, it is caused by atypical cell migration between 3 and 5 months of gestation. Some evidence for migrational failures in cortex has also been observed, though these do not appear to be restricted to any particular area (Piven et al., 1990). One problem in determining developmental brain damage is that it is difficult to ascertain which atypicalities are the root cause, and which are subsequent consequences of earlier atypical development. In general, it is likely that structures and areas that develop latest are most likely to be affected by earlier deviations from the normal developmental trajectory. For example, in autism the atypicalities sometimes observed in the cortex, hippocampus, and cerebellum could all possibly be the consequences of a primary deficit in the thalamus.

The latest region of the cortex to show structural changes in postnatal development, the frontal cortex, has been a favorite region of focus for studies of autism and other developmental disorders such as phenylketonuria (see appendix and chapter 8). While atypicalities in this region may be responsible for some of the cognitive deficits observed, this does not mean that people with autism can be equated with patients with acquired prefrontal cortex damage.

While the brain damage that gives rise to autism may be diffuse and variable, the resulting cognitive profile presents a clearer picture. Many social processes observed in infancy appear to be intact in children with autism. However, they show clear deficits in a later developing aspect of social cognition called "theory of mind". Despite its grand title, theory of mind is a relatively basic and essential function for our understanding of, and interactions with, other people. Specifically, theory of mind refers to the ability most of us have to comprehend another person's thought processes, such as their feelings, beliefs, and knowledge. One type of task that can be used to study theory of mind abilities is the so-called "false-belief" task. For example, the following scenario can be demonstrated with dolls, puppets, or human actors (example of procedure taken from Wimmer & Perner, 1983).

> Sally has a marble that she puts in a basket. Sally then goes away for a walk. While Sally is away, Anne comes in and moves the marble from the basket to a box. The participant viewing this scenario is then asked "When Sally returns, where will she look for her marble?" If the participant simply tries to predict Sally's response on the basis of their own personal knowledge, then he or she will answer "the box". If, on the other hand, she predicts Sally's response on the basis of Sally's (false) belief, then the participant will correctly predict that Sally will look in the basket for the marble.

Another false-belief scenario involves showing the participant a container that normally holds candy well known to the child and asking the child what is in the container. The participant will reply with the name of the appropriate candy. The box is then opened and the child shown that it contains a pencil, and not candy. The child is then told that a friend will come in a moment and be shown the closed container and asked what is in it. The participant is asked what the friend will say. Once again, only if the child can infer the friend's inevitable false belief will he or she reply with the name of the candy rather than a pencil.

Baron-Cohen, Leslie, Frith and their collaborators have shown in a series of studies that most individuals with autism, unlike those with Down's syndrome, fail these and other theory of mind tasks (for reviews see Happé, 1994; Baron-Cohen, 1995; Frith, 2003), while they are relatively unimpaired (compared to mental-age-matched controls) on a variety of related tasks. This pattern of deficit would explain why people with autism often seem to regard others as little different from inanimate objects. Thus, many believe that a deficit in theory of mind is a central cognitive deficit in autism. While there is some agreement on the nature of this cognitive deficit, there are a number of detailed variants of this view that are currently being tested.

Other theoreticians have proposed more developmental accounts, arguing that a lack of theory of mind arises from deficits in precursors such as the infants' capacity for imitation (Rogers & Pennington, 1991) or the perception of emotion (Hobson, 1993). Thus, these authors believe that a social-cognitive deficit from birth, or very shortly thereafter, results in the later deficit of theory of mind. However, whether children subsequently diagnosed as autistic show clear abormalities before 18 months of age remains controversial. Recently, some laboratories have begun to use high-density ERPs to assess brain functioning in toddlers with a preliminary diagnosis of autism. For example, Dawson and colleagues studied effects of familiarity on face and object (toy) processing (Dawson, Carver, Meltzoff, McPartland, & Webb, 2002). While a control group of young children showed ERP evidence of recognition of both categories, the potentially autistic sample did not show evidence of recognizing the faces. This suggests some degree of specificity in their neural deficit. However, as the authors point out, this deficit is probably secondary to an earlier developmental cause such as failing to orient toward faces at birth. In a similar experiment, Grice and colleagues observed that the ERP correlates of eye gaze processing (as described earlier) appear to be developmentally delayed in young children with autism (Grice et al., in press).

Given the somewhat mixed structural neuroimaging and neuroanatomical evidence, some research teams have tried to use the pattern of cognitive deficits to infer which brain pathways and structures are damaged in autism. Perhaps the most commonly held neuropsychological view is that the pattern of cognitive deficits observed is consistent with damage to the frontal cortex (e.g. Damasio & Maurer, 1978; Pennington & Welsh, 1995). For example, even high-functioning people with autism fail on a number of "executive function" tasks thought to be markers for frontal lobe functioning, such as the Tower of Hanoi planning task and the Wisconsin card sorting task (Ozonoff, Pennington, & Rogers, 1991). At present it is unclear whether these deficits are primary to those in theory of mind, independent of theory of mind, or dependent on the same underlying computations (see Pennington & Welsh, 1995).

The view that the deficit in theory of mind is one of several cognitive deficits which share common underlying computations is also held by those who argue for the importance of the atypicalities observed in the cerebellum (e.g. Courchesne,

1991). By this view, theory of mind is disrupted because the cerebellum is important for the processing of complex context-dependent sequential information that
unfolds over time. It is likely that future studies involving functional neuroimaging
will allow the dissociation between these different neuropsychological hypotheses.

In contrast to the specific social deficit seen in autism, Williams syndrome
participants appear to have the putative "social module" intact. Williams syndrome (WS) (also known as infantile hypercalcemia) is a relatively rare disorder of
genetic origin effecting approximately 1 in 20,000 to 50,000 births (Greenberg,
1990) (see appendix). The disorder can now be diagnosed in early infancy through
genetic or metabolic markers, and is typified by a number of physical and cognitive characteristics.

Evidence from structural neuroimaging indicates that WS brains are only about
80–5 percent of the overall volume of typical brains, but there are no obvious gross
atypicalities or lesions (Jernigan & Bellugi, 1994). Currently, the only evidence for
a specific focus of damage is that they show a relative increase in volume in particular lobules on the cerebellum. This cerebellar atypicality contrasts with autism,
in which the same lobules are relatively smaller than normal (Jernigan & Bellugi,
1994). At the cytoarchitectonic level, a preliminary analysis by Galaburda, Wang,
Bellugi, and Rosen (1994) found disturbances within cortical layers and decreased
myelination. Given the lack of evidence for any discrete focal lesions, the specificity
of the neurocognitive profile that WS participants present is striking.

FURTHER READING: KARMILOFF-SMITH, 2002; TAGER-FLUSBERG, 2003

Alongside surprising linguistic abilities (see chapter 7), WS participants perform
as well as controls in a face discrimination task (the Benton test; Bellugi, Bihrle,
Neville, Jernigan, & Doherty, 1992), and better than typical adults on the face
recognition component of a standard memory test (the Rivermead Behavioral
Memory Test; Udwin & Yule, 1991). This pattern of spared abilities suggests
approximately the opposite of deficits described earlier for autism, and raised the
initial hypothesis that people with WS have intact a functional brain system
corresponding to a "social module." Specifically, one preliminary hypothesis is
that the social module remains intact in WS, while being specifically damaged in
autism. As discussed earlier, one prominent account of the cognitive deficit in
autism is that people with autism lack a theory of mind. Karmiloff-Smith and
colleagues carried out a series of experiments with WS participants to test the
hypothesis that there is "a broad cognitive module for representing and processing
stimuli relevant to other individuals, including face processing, language, and
theory of mind" (Karmiloff-Smith, Klima, Bellugi, Grant, & Baron-Cohen, 1995,
p. 197). While only about 20 percent of autistic participants pass theory of mind
tasks such as that described earlier, 94 percent of the WS participants passed these
tasks, indicating that theory of mind is intact alongside aspects of language and

face processing. From this result, along with some others, it is tempting to portray WS as showing approximately the opposite neurocognitive profile to autism (while acknowledging that both groups may show some general retardation). This hypothesis is enhanced by the differential cerebellar atypicalities.

However, Karmiloff-Smith et al. (1995) cite evidence from other developmental disorders that is contrary to the simplest view of an impaired or intact prespecified module. For example, in Down's syndrome, a serious deficit in face processing and in the use of morphology in language can co-occur with relatively good performance on theory of mind tasks (Baron-Cohen, Leslie, & Frith, 1985, 1986). Conversely, in an individual with hydrocephalus with associated myelomeningocele, very competent language output co-exists with serious deficits in face processing and theory of mind (Cromer, 1992; Karmiloff-Smith, 1992). These different patterns of dissociation clearly challenge the notion of a predetermined social module in the brain.

An alternative view (Karmiloff-Smith, 2002) is that some degree of modularization is a result of postnatal development, and not a precursor to it (see also chapter 10). Specifically, domain-specific biases in the newborn (such as the face preference discussed earlier in this chapter and the speech discrimination abilities discussed in chapter 7) ensure that cortical circuits are preferentially exposed to socially relevant stimuli like language and faces. With prolonged exposure to such stimuli, plastic cortical circuits develop representations appropriate for processing these inputs, eventually giving rise to an emergent superordinate system for the pragmatics of social interaction in general.

FURTHER READING: KARMILOFF-SMITH, 2002

If this general view of the emergence of the social brain is correct, it implies that early sensory or social deprivation may have long-term consequences. Two lines of research have pursued this issue. In the first, Maurer and colleagues have studied people who suffered visual deprivation for varying periods of time following birth due to uni- or bilateral cataracts. These dense cataracts prevent structured visual input until they are reversed by surgery, usually within the first year. By studying aspects of face processing in this clinical population, this research group showed that even after years of normal experience of faces some deficits remained (Le Grand, Mondloch, Maurer, & Brent, 2001). In other words, visual deprivation over the first months has detectable life-long effects on face processing. Further, by examining cases of unilateral deprivation it has recently been shown that these effects are more due to right hemisphere (left eye) deprivation. Data such as these present a severe challenge for the "skill learning" approach to human functional brain development, and suggest propensity of the right hemisphere for face processing from the first months.

While the cataract population can inform us about sensory deprivation, other populations have been studied that suffered from social deprivation. For example, samples of children raised in orphanages (e.g. during the Romanian communist regime) can subsequently have multiple social, cognitive, and sensorimotor problems (for review see Gunnar, 2001). While orphanage rearing can be variable in general care quality, at a minimum, stable long-term relationships with caregivers are missing (Rutter, 1998). The outcome from "good" orphanages can include problems with executive functions (see chapter 8) and social cognition, while other aspects of sensorimotor, cognitive, and linguistic development can recover well. At the other extreme, in a sample of children raised in Romanian orphanages for at least the first 12 months, 12 percent exhibited features of autism, although even here these symptoms tended to diminish over time (Rutter et al., 1999).

FURTHER READING: GUNNAR, 2001

5.7 GENERAL SUMMARY AND CONCLUSIONS

As discussed at the beginning of this chapter, the three viewpoints on functional brain development make different predictions about the development of the social brain. Evidence reviewed from the neurodevelopment of face processing appeared inconsistent with a maturational account. The long-term effects of early deprivation and the presence of face and eye gaze biases in the newborn discourage a strictly skill learning perspective. Thus, there is probably neither an innate module for social cognition, nor innate representations relating to these functions that "mature" in the cortex during postnatal life. Rather, complex representations for processing information about other people, their probable thoughts, and likely future actions emerge in the brain as a result of at least three sets of factors: initial biases to attend to socially relevant stimuli such as faces and language; complex interactions with other people; and the basic architecture of the cortex and relevant subcortical structures. Atypicalities in any of these factors could send the infant into a deviant path in which only components of normal social cognitive abilities develop.

A challenge for this interactive specialization view of the emerging social brain will be to generate hypotheses about the consequences of the network of social processing areas being initially intermixed with other cortical networks. Behavioral studies with infants have demonstrated that, from at least 9 months of age, they attribute goals to appropriately moving objects even when these objects do not physically resemble biological forms (see Csibra, 2003, for review). Indeed, some have suggested that infants and toddlers may over-extend their social cognitive abilities to physical objects that adults would not (Csibra, 2003). Whether this blurring of the boundary between social and non-social perception is a by-product of a social brain that has not yet fully emerged from the rest of the brain remains an interesting topic for future research.

6 MEMORY AND LEARNING

A distinction has been made between two types of memory, a cognitive, declarative, or explicit form of memory system, and a procedural or habit memory system. An initial hypothesis was that while the latter system was present from birth, the former took longer to develop due to its dependency on the development of the limbic system, and particularly the hippocampus. However, recent evidence favors the view that (i) there is a more graded development of explicit memory, and (ii) there are a variety of different implicit learning systems. One proposal is that there is a gradual expansion from a hippocampally mediated pre-explicit memory system present shortly after birth, to an adult-like explicit memory system toward the end of the first year of life. The expansion of cortical involvement in the neural basis of explicit memory may be due to an experience-dependent increasing specialization of cortical regions related to the hippocampus. A further similarity with the domains reviewed in other chapters is that several brain systems may be engaged by most memory tasks.

Learning is clearly a fundamental aspect of human cognitive development, and is represented in many of the other chapters in this book, especially with regard to the development of face recognition, object properties, and language acquisition. Learning is often contrasted with maturation in cognitive development, but the boundary between what is learning and what is development, and between different learning and memory systems, can be somewhat unclear. A number of authors have, however, taken a cognitive neuroscience approach to the development of memory systems that are assumed to be dissociable from the plasticity of developing neural circuitry. These authors have utilized the wealth of data from animal and human adult cognitive neuroscience studies on the neural bases of different learning and memory systems in the brain (for reviews see Murray, 2000; Squire

& Knowlton, 2000). Nevertheless, this developmental cognitive neuroscience approach to memory faces a number of challenges:

• Behavioral development in a memory task may be due to the emergence of function in non-memory-related brain systems. Further, at the molecular and cellular level, development and learning often share common mechanisms, making the distinction between them unclear.
• Behavioral neuroscience and neuropsychological investigations have revealed that there are multiple brain systems supporting different types of memory. Even in the adult these various systems have proved difficult to disentangle.
• Some forms of "explicit" memory in human adults involve conscious awareness of information, something that is difficult to ascertain in pre-verbal infants.

Despite these difficulties, in this chapter we will see that considerable progress has been made by adopting a cognitive neuroscience approach to the development of memory. As a starting point, most researchers have turned to studies of the neural basis of various memory systems in adults and animals. They have then attempted to develop marker tasks for the functioning of these systems, often speculating that deficits in memory abilities in young infants and children may be due to the differential development of neural systems supporting particular types of memory function.

There have been a number of attempts to characterize a dissociation between two types of memory systems, one of which is variously described as "explicit", "declarative," or "cognitive," and the other of which is termed "implicit," "procedural," or "habit" memory. Explicit, declarative, or cognitive memory refers to memory that can be brought to mind as an image or proposition, whereas implicit or procedural memory refers to memory that is embedded in a skill or procedure and of which the subject is not consciously aware (Squire, 1986). One source of data that provides the impetus for this dissociation comes from the much studied adult neuropsychological patient called H.M. To cure severe seizures, H.M. had surgery to remove the anterior part of both his temporal lobes (including the hippocampus and amygdala – see figure 6.1). While the seizures were much reduced by this operation, he suffered from a severe memory impairment in which he was unable to form new explicit or declarative memories, while being relatively unimpaired in procedural or implicit memory tasks (Scoville & Milner, 1957; Squire, 1986). Thus, memory for information which involves conscious recall or recognition of previously learned material requires the limbic temporal lobe, including the hippocampus. These structures are not essential for information acquired through skilled motor activity. This commonly accepted dissociation into two systems is sometimes subdivided further. Table 6.1 shows one classification of memory systems based on the analysis of Nelson and Webb (2003), which I will use to structure this review.

One of the first cognitive neuroscience hypotheses about memory development was put forward by Schacter and Moscovitch (1984), who speculated that the

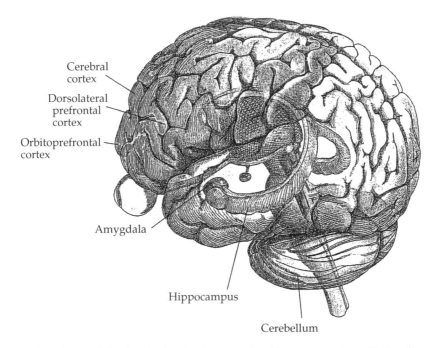

Cerebral
cortex

Dorsolateral
prefrontal
cortex

Orbitoprefrontal
cortex

Amygdala

Hippocampus

Cerebellum

Figure 6.1 Some of the key brain structures involved in memory, in particular the dorsolateral prefrontal cortex and the hippocampus.

brain mechanisms necessary for the long-term storage of information, most probably in the limbic system, are not functional for the first year or two of life. A related hypothesis was put forward by Bachevalier and Mishkin (1984), who pointed out similarities between the amnesic syndrome, in which limbic system damage in adults results in deficits in recognition memory but no deficits in learning stimulus–response "habits," and the profile of memory abilities in infants (for a more recent version of this account see Bachevalier, 2001). Mishkin and colleagues had earlier demonstrated that a similar pattern of deficits to that observed in human amnesic syndrome patients could be seen in adult monkeys following surgical lesions to portions of the limbic system. These observations led to the proposal that infant memory abilities reflected the more delayed postnatal maturation of limbic circuits.

FURTHER READING: BACHEVALIER, 2001; NELSON, 2002; NELSON & WEBB, 2003

To test the hypothesis that the putative "cognitive memory" and "habit" systems show a different ontogenetic timetable, Bachevalier and Mishkin (1984) tested

Table 6.1 The major memory systems and developmental tasks

General system	Subsystems	Tasks	Neural systems related to tasks
Implicit memory (non-declarative memory)	Procedural learning	Serial reaction time (SRT) task	Striatum, supplementary motor association, motor cortex, frontal cortex
		Visual expectation paradigm (VExP)	Frontal cortex, motor areas
	Conditioning	Conditioning	Cerebellum, basal ganglia
	Perceptual representation system	Perceptual priming paradigms	Modality-dependent: parietal cortex, occipital cortex, inferior temporal cortex, auditory cortex
Explicit memory	Pre-explicit memory	Novelty detection in habituation and paired comparison tasks	Hippocampus
	Semantic (generic knowledge)	Semantic retrieval, word priming, and associative priming	Left prefrontal cortex, anterior cingulate hippocampal cortex
	Episodic (autobiographical)	Episodic encoding	Left prefrontal cortex, left orbitoprefrontal cortex
		Recall and recognition	Right prefrontal, anterior cingulate, parietal, cerebellum, hippocampal cortex

infant monkeys aged 3, 6, and 12 months on two types of tasks. The first task was a visual recognition task that involved the infant monkey learning to identify the novel object of a pair following the earlier presentation of the familiar one (delayed-non match to sample – DNMS). This task was thought to require a "cognitive memory" system. In the second task, a visual discrimination habit task, the infant monkey was sequentially exposed to 20 pairs of objects every day. Every day the same object of each pair was baited with a food reward, even though their relative positions were varied. The monkeys had to learn to displace the correct object in each pair.

Infant monkeys failed to learn the "cognitive memory" task until they were approximately 4 months old, and did not reach adult levels of proficiency even by the end of the first year. In contrast, infant monkeys of 3 or 4 months old were able to learn the visual "habit" as easily as adults. Bachevalier and Mishkin suggested that this dissociation in memory abilities in infant monkeys is due to the prolonged postnatal development of the limbic system delaying the ability of recognition and association ("cognitive") memory relative to sensorimotor habit formation. This explanation could be extended to human infants since they are also unable to acquire the delayed non-match to sample task in early infancy (until around 15 months), and still have not reached adult levels of performance at 6 years old (Overman, Bachevalier, Turner, & Peuster, 1992).

More recent evidence from both cognitive and neuroscience studies has indicated that this initial two-systems view of the ontogeny of memory is not sufficient to explain the data. The cognitive evidence comes from studies indicating that human infants can recall experiences from the first year of life several years later (for review see Rovee-Collier 1993). These findings suggest some continuity of memory mechanisms from early infancy to later life. Further, other behavioral experiments on memory processes in infants suggest that differences between infant and adult memory processes are quantitative (retrieval time, memory span) rather than qualitative (see Rovee-Collier 1993). Thus, at least some prominent researchers believe that there is not a transition from one form of memory to another during infancy, but rather just a change in the characteristics of memory storage.

Another issue is that human infants are successful at the DNMS task at much younger ages if the response required is for the subject to merely *look* at the novel stimulus, rather than manually displacing it (to obtain the reward). This suggests that the standard reaching version of DNMS requires some additional ability, such as the ability to inhibit a previously rewarded action (Diamond, Werker, & Lalonde, 1994; see chapter 8). Consequently, other tasks which tap into "cognitive" or "explicit" memory need to be studied in infants.

FURTHER READING: DIAMOND, 2001, 2002

Even more damaging for Bachevalier and Mishkin's original hypotheses is evidence that lesions to the limbic system impair recognition memory abilities in infant monkeys in the first month of life (Bachevalier, Brickson, & Hagger, 1993), indicating that even from this early age the limbic system plays some role in memory processes. Bachevalier and colleagues measured recognition memory by a paired comparison preferential looking task similar to one used with human infants. In this task the subject is shown an object for 30 seconds. After a short delay the subject is presented with a pair of objects, one of which is novel, and their extent of looking at each of the objects is recorded. Between 15 and 30 days of age, normal infant rhesus monkeys develop a strong preference for looking toward the novel stimulus, indicating recognition of the familiar one. This preference was not found in monkeys that received medial temporal lobe lesions including the hippocampus in early infancy. These surprising results suggest that limbic structures make a significant contribution to visual recognition memory even at this very early age, and that other neurocognitive systems that mature more slowly may be responsible for the developments in memory ability observed in other tasks. More recent animal and adult neuroimaging studies are consistent with the view that the hippocampus supports recognition memory via responses to novelty, but that the detection of novelty itself may require additional structures (see Nelson, 2002; Nelson & Webb, 2003).

To summarize so far, the original two-systems view argued that deficiencies in infants' memory were due to the lack of a cognitive or explicit memory system mediated by the limbic/hippocampal system. However, this account is not adequate because (i) cognitive evidence suggests that the development of memory involves the graded increase of existing systems, rather than the maturation of independent systems (implying that memory development entails overlapping, as opposed to dissociable, systems), (ii) when direction of looking rather than a manual reaching measure is used, there is evidence of a form of explicit memory from shortly after birth, and (iii) the hippocampus seems to play a role in this form of explicit memory from birth or shortly after.

After reviewing much of this literature, Nelson proposed that there are more than two types of memory system that develop from infancy (see table 6.1). Further, he views the development of some memory systems in terms of the expansion of a neural system to include additional structures and capacities, as opposed to the *de novo* appearance of a new system(s) dissociable from others. The systems outlined by Nelson (2002; Nelson & Webb, 2003) are as follows:

- An implicit memory system involved in visual expectations, such as the tasks used by Haith and colleagues and described in chapter 3. This type of procedural memory is dependent on the striatum, and not the temporal lobe or cerebellum. Visual expectancies can be readily elicited from the human infant by at least 3 months of age.
- An implicit memory system involved in tasks that require conditioning, such as the contingent leg-kicking response studied by Rovee-Collier (1993) and colleagues (see below). Nelson suggests that this system may depend on the cerebellum and deep nuclei of the brain stem, and possibly also the hippocampus, in tasks that require retrieval or visual recognition. Evidence suggests that conditioning can be acquired by at least 3 months of age in the human infant.
- A pre-explicit memory system that is responsible for infants showing novelty preferences in paired comparison tests with short delays (see chapter 1). Nelson suggests that the hippocampus is critical for this behavior, and that it is present from birth or shortly thereafter.
- An explicit memory system that is involved in a variety of tasks involving recognition memory, the coordination of information across different sensory modalities, including the "self" in memories, and the generation of action schemes based on prior information. This memory system involves an expansion of the neural substrate of the pre-explicit memory system with the additional involvement of the entorhinal cortex, and inferior temporal cortex (e.g. area

TE). This "adult" form of explicit memory becomes functional around the end of the first year of life, although it continues to develop into the teenage years associated with prefrontal cortical development. Explicit memory may be further divided into semantic memory (e.g. remembering one's name) and episodic memory (e.g. remembering the first time one went to the beach) (Tulving, 1983; Drummey & Newcombe, 2002).

- A working memory system which starts to develop between 6 and 12 months of age, but which shows a protracted development throughout childhood. The dorsolateral prefrontal cortex is a critical component of the neural substrate for this form of memory, and is discussed further in chapter 8.

Nelson's view that there is a graded development from a pre-explicit to an "adult" explicit memory system can account for most of the findings that are problematic for the original two-process account. The notion of the expanding involvement of brain structures involved in explicit memory is more consistent with the cognitive data implying a graded change in memory abilities, rather than the appearance of a dissociable new system(s). Nelson's graded account of the development of an explicit memory system implies that successful performance on looking versions of the DNMS task can be obtained from infants in the first few months of life due to the pre-explicit memory systems being able to support novelty preference when no action planning (reaching) is required. Between 8 and 18 months of age infants become able to perform DNMS and other tasks that serve as markers for explicit or cognitive memory. This form of "explicit" memory is dependent upon adequate development of the hippocampus and also related cortical areas, such as area TE. However, apparently successful performance can be elicited from infants younger than 8 months in tasks that depend solely on them showing a novelty preference, and do not require them to dissociate how often events were presented or do not involve a delay before the response is required. Nelson (2002) hypothesizes that this "pre-explicit" memory requires only the functioning of the hippocampus, and not related temporal cortex structures (although other structures may be required for the original detection of novelty). Around 8 months of age the development of temporal cortical areas, or their integration with the hippocampus, correlates with a transition from pre-explicit to explicit memory.

One form of explicit memory that has recently become a topic for investigation in developmental cognitive neuroscience is source or "autobiographical" memory. Source memory refers to recall of the context (place, time, etc.) for a remembered event (Johnson, Hashtroudi, & Lindsay, 1993). Autobiographical memories relate an experience to one's own personal past, including any emotions or perceptual details (Tulving, 1983). Drummey and Newcombe (2002) tested children of 4, 6, and 8 years old in a source memory paradigm adapted from those previously used with adults. In this task the children were first presented with ten facts (on a variety of topics) by either an experimenter or a puppet. After a delay of one week the children were asked questions on the facts, and also asked to identify the source of the fact (experimenter, puppet, teacher, or parent). Children showed a steady improvement with age in their ability to remember the facts, but showed an abrupt improvement between 4 and 6 years in their ability to monitor the source of those facts. In particular, the 4-year-olds made many errors in identifying the source of the facts. Since this kind of "source amnesia" is characteristic of adult populations with frontal cortex disruption, it was intriguing that the changes in the children were in some case related to behavioral measures of prefrontal cortex function (see chapter 8).

In some of the explicit tasks, as outlined above, infants have been tested in behavioral tasks that are close analogs of the monkey and adult tasks. In contrast, with the implicit forms of memory there has been little attempt to develop marker tasks for infants that closely correspond to tasks used with animals, neuro-psychological patients, or functional brain imaging. One exception to this is the conditioned eye blink, a paradigm in which a harmless puff of air blown on to the eye, or a gentle tap on the forehead, causes the infant (or animal) to blink. In a conditioning procedure, the forehead tap, or airpuff can come to be predicted by an unrelated sensory stimulus such as auditory tone. The early development of the cerebellum may be responsible for the fact that between 10 and 30 days the human infant starts to show the conditioned eyeblink response (see Lipsitt, 1990; Dziurawiec, 1996).

For other forms of implicit memory, Nelson (2002, 2003) has suggested some similarities between types of learning that have been studied in infants, and cognitive neuroscience tasks. For example, the visual expectancies paradigm (discussed in chapter 3), in which infants of 3 months and older start to anticipate the location where the next target in a fixed sequence will appear, resembles some sequence learning tasks thought to involve the striatum. While there is little evidence on the development of human striatum, it seems likely from the evidence reviewed in chapter 2 that this structure is functional by around birth. A further constraint on the emergence of infant visual expectation abilities, however, may be the control of eye movements by the frontal eye fields (see chapter 3). However, the ability to learn auditory sequences of tones can provide converging evidence. For example, Saffran, Johnson, Aslin, and Newport (1999; see Aslin & Hunt, 2001) examined the response of 8-month-olds to sequences of pure tones, and showed that the infants could group these tones based solely on their distributional properties within a sequence. Whether such abilities are present nearer to birth is currently unknown.

FURTHER READING: ASLIN & HUNT, 2001

Another example of implicit learning present from early infancy is contingent leg-kicking, mentioned above (Rovee-Collier, 1993). In this procedure infants lie on their backs and watch a mobile suspended above them. A ribbon is attached to the mobile at one end and to one of the infant's legs at the other. Thus, by kicking the relevant leg the infant can animate the mobile. Infants as young as 3 months will readily learn to associate their leg movement with the movement of the mobile, and will increase their leg movement to well above baseline levels. The infant is then removed from the test situation. After a time interval (which, in different studies, varies from minutes to weeks) the infant is returned to the experiment. When returned to the test a variety of things can be varied, such as the nature of the mobile, the context of the crib, and so on. In many of the variants of this procedure, young infants show evidence of learning retained over periods of weeks or months.

Nelson (2002; Nelson & Webb, 2003) suggest that a possible analogy to contingent leg-kicking in infants is the instrumentally conditioned limb flexion response in which animals learn to flex their legs when a tone predicts a shock. Lesions to parts of the cerebellum disrupt this form of learning, suggesting that the same brain structure may be critical for contingent leg-kicking in infants. However, the additional complexities of the infant leg-kicking task, such as the need to recognize the mobile and task context, make it likely that other memory circuits will also be engaged. While further research is needed, some PET and myelination evidence indicates that the human cerebellum approximates its adult state shortly after birth.

A final aspect of implicit memory involves the changed response of the brain to a sensory stimulus that is repeated several times. Priming involves the improvements in detecting and processing a perceptual object based on recent experience, while habituation refers to the decrement of responses to a frequently repeated stimulus. Given the large literature on the neural basis of sensory habituation in animals, and the prevalence of habituation methods in infancy research, it is initially surprising that very little research has been done on the neural basis of habituation in infants. However, several laboratories have conducted ERP studies with infants using habituation paradigms (in which the subject is familiarized by repeated presentations of one stimulus prior to the introduction of a novel stimulus) and related paradigms, such as the "oddball" paradigm (in which an infrequent novel stimulus appears amidst repeated exposures to a familiar one). In a review of this literature, Nelson (1994) draws the conclusion that there are three major components of the ERP signal which emerge as important in these studies. These three components probably reflect distinct cognitive processes with different neural bases.

First, when infants are presented with a visual stimulus, even when it is repeated many times, a well-defined negative component of the ERP is observed. This negative component occurs regardless of whether the stimulus is familiar or novel, and Nelson (1994) suggests that it probably reflects an attentional process (and may be related to a negative-going deflection that occurs around 400 ms after stimulus onset, known as N400, which is linked to attention in older subjects). A variable that influences the latency of this negative component is the age of the subjects, with it having a longer latency in younger infants (around 800 ms after stimulus onset in 4-month-olds) than in older infants (around 400 ms in 12-month-olds).

Second, following this negative peak there is often a sustained negative slow wave that Nelson suggests reflects the detection of novel stimuli. It generally occurs when an unfamiliar stimulus is detected after a sequence of familiar ones. In contrast, when a familiar stimulus is repeated, the initial negative peak discussed above quickly returns to baseline. This peak may reflect "attention load." The third component is a late positive component that may be invoked by stimuli that are only partially encoded and require further processing or updating. In infants it can be invoked by novel or rarely encountered stimuli (see Nelson & Collins, 1992; Pascalis, de Haan, Nelson, & de Schonen, 1998). This component has not been observed in infants under 6 months. This wave may be related in some respects to P300, the positive-going deflection that occurs around 300 ms after stimulus onset, which is observed in adults and suggested to mark the updating of working memory (Nelson, Thomas, de Haan, & Wewerka, 1998).

While these components of ERPs in infants have not been related to particular brain structures, Nelson speculates that the late positive component may be due to medial temporal lobe activity. Possibly the emergence of this component of the ERP corresponds to development of cortical regions related to the hippocampus (such as area TE), and the transition from "pre-explicit" to explicit memory systems.

From the discussion above it is evident that most memory tasks likely engage multiple memory systems, in a similar way to the partially independent brain pathways that are engaged in eye movement control and attention shifts. A lack of maturity in one or other pathway may be masked in some tasks due to compensatory activity in other pathways. Possibly it is the extent of integration between different memory pathways that is the most significant change with postnatal development. If this is the case, it is not until we have a more integrative account of the relations between different brain memory pathways that we will be able to make sense of the developmental data.

Moving from habituation to priming, Webb and Nelson (2001) showed 6-month-old infants brief presentations of upright and inverted faces, some of which were repeated 8 to 12 images later. When they compared the first (novel) presentation to the repeated (primed) presentation they observed a difference in the ERP at the mid-latency negative component (Nc). There was no difference at the later components associated with explicit memory, suggesting that implicit memory processes were differentially activated.

Another source of evidence on the development of memory systems comes from rare cases of children who, as infants, suffer damage to the hippocampus. Vargha-Khadem and colleagues have reported that such children, termed "developmental amnesics," grow up with persisting deficits in episodic memory, but show relative sparing of semantic memory (table 6.1; Gadian et al., 2000, Vargha-Khadem et al., 1997; Varga-Khadem, Gadian, & Mishkin, 2001). For example, Vargha-Khadem et al. (2001) report on eleven amnesic patients known to have suffered perinatal or early childhood hypoxic ischaemic (lowered blood oxygen) damage to the hippocampus. In all cases there was a dissociation between severely impaired episodic memory and relatively spared semantic memory. In general, however, these children grow up to be surprisingly typical in their cognitive abilities, including near-normal language ability and IQ. One reason for the relative sparing of aspects of explicit memory in these children might be that the perirhinal, entorhinal, and parahippocampal areas are relatively spared (Maguire, Varga-Khadem, & Mishkin, 2001; Schoppik et al., 2001). However, it is also likely that other regions and pathways involved in learning and memory adjust their functionality in an activity-dependent way to at least partially compensate for the missing components.

 GENERAL SUMMARY AND CONCLUSIONS

It is clear that several types of procedural or habit memory, probably dependent on subcortical structures such as the cerebellum and hippocampus, are present from birth or shortly thereafter. There are currently few marker tasks that allow the direct comparison of cognitive neuroscience data to developmental findings, but this seems a promising area for future research. While there is some capacity for explicit memory in the newborn, this expands over the first year of life. At the neural level this expansion may involve regions of the temporal cortex becoming coordinated with the hippocampus, possibly through a process of input-dependent increasing specialization. This graded development of explicit memory may be able to account for some of the previously discrepant findings in the field.

7 LANGUAGE

This chapter starts with the question of whether language is "biologically special." This issue refers to the extent to which the human infant's brain is predisposed to learn about language. Cognitive neuroscience approaches to this question are outlined. First, studies from early brain damage indicate that different regions of cortex are capable of supporting nearly normal language acquisition. Second, ERP studies with congenitally deaf participants show that regions which normally support oral language can also support other functions. While these two lines of evidence indicate that there are no innate language representations in the cortex, there is strong functional neuroimaging evidence that the left temporal lobe is efficient at processing speech input from shortly after birth.

The ability to process the rapid temporal transitions that discriminate phonemes may be essential for normal language acquisition. In addition to the ERP work with neonates, some children with specific language impairment (SLI) show deficits in rapid temporal processing. In some cases this may lead to reading problems like those observed in dyslexia.

A number of neural correlates of stages of normal language acquisition are outlined. In some developmental disorders, such as Williams syndrome, language can be relatively proficient as compared to other domains of cognition. In others, such as SLI, language appears to be deficient alongside normal scores in other domains. While these apparent dissociations have sometimes been characterized as evidence for an "innate language module," they are also consistent with an interactive specialization view.

7.1 INTRODUCTION

Speech and language processing has been one of the most actively researched areas of adult cognitive neuroscience and neuropsychology. A network of regions of the adult cortex has been typically associated with language functions, and this network is illustrated along with the putative functions of each region in figure 7.1. It is important to distinguish between speech perception, which refers to the complex sensory processing required to discriminate between and analyze the sound patterns of an incoming speech stream, and language processing, which refers to a variety of hypothesized mechanisms, including the meaning and application of rules for grammar. While some theorists believe that speech and language share common mechanisms, the majority assume merely a developmental relation between the two, in that early speech perception abilities may be vital for later

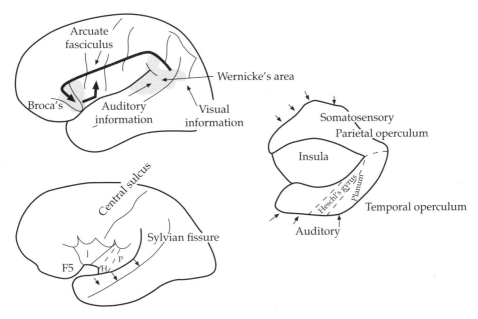

Figure 7.1 Some of the key structures involved in language processing. Top left: Schematic view of information flow from posterior sensory areas to frontal response areas through the inferior temporofrontal loop. The dotted regions show where brain damage causes fluent (Wernicke's) and non-fluent (Broca's) aphasia. These regions are conceptual rather than anatomical. Bottom left: The Sylvian fissure has been pulled out and down in the direction of the arrows to reveal the insula (I) and the auditory cortex (H, P) on the superior surface of the temporal lobe. The region of the frontal operculum indicated as F5 contains mirror neurons in the monkey. It is thought that these neurons play a crucial role in imitation learning. Right: Enlarged view of Heschl's gyrus and planum temporal.

construction of successful language processing (e.g. Benasich, Thomas, Choudhury, & Leppaenen, 2002).

A general problem with studying language acquisition in developmental cognitive neuroscience is that it is not possible to use animal models to study an aspect of cognition unique to humans (although some work has been done on the auditory aspects of language such as speech perception in other species, e.g. chinchillas, and song learning in birds – see, e.g., Marler, 2002). However, a number of other approaches have been taken such as functional neuroimaging, studies of infants with focal brain damage, studies of congenital atypicalities, and correlations between phases of language acquisition and neuroanatomical development. An implicit or explicit motivating question for many researchers in this field has been the extent to which language is "biologically special." This issue refers to the extent to which the human child is predisposed to learn language. To translate this question into the framework presented in chapter 1, does a region of the cortex have innate representations for language, or are language representations the emergent result of a variety of constraints, including the basic architecture of the cortex?

FURTHER READING: WERKER & VOULOUMANOS, 2001; MARLER, 2002

Two cognitive neuroscience approaches to this question have been pursued. The first of these has been to investigate whether there are particular parts of the cortex critical for language processing or acquisition. If particular parts of the cortex are critical for language, some assume that this region(s) contains innate language-specific representations. In contrast, if several regions of cortex can support language acquisition, this suggests that the representations involved will emerge given the combination of language input and basic cortical architecture. The second cognitive neuroscience approach has been to attempt to identify neural correlates of language-related processing abilities very early in life. I start by reviewing evidence relevant to the first of these approaches.

7.2 ARE SOME PARTS OF CORTEX CRITICAL FOR LANGUAGE ACQUISITION?

Language acquisition has become a focal point for studies designed to investigate the extent to which particular cortical areas are prespecified to support specific functions. Two complementary directions have been taken, with one set of studies examining the extent to which language functions can be supported by other regions of the cortex, and another group of studies concerned with whether other functions can "occupy" regions that normally support language. The first of these lines of research has asked whether children suffering from perinatal lesions to "language areas" can still acquire language. The second line of research has involved testing congenitally deaf children to see what functions occupy regions of cortex that are normally (spoken) language areas, and also by studying the consequences of brain damage on the ability to produce sign language in a previously fluent signer.

If particular cortical regions are uniquely prespecified to support language, then it is reasonable to assume that early damage to such regions will impair the acquisition of language. This implicit hypothesis has motivated a large body of research, the conclusions of which still remain somewhat controversial. In an influential book, Lenneberg (1967) argued persuasively that if localized left-hemisphere damage occurred early in life, it had little or no effect on subsequent language acquisition. This contrasted both with the effect of similar lesions in adults or older children, and with several congenital atypicalities in which language is delayed or never emerges (see appendix). Lenneberg's view lost adherents in the 1970s, as evidence accumulated from studies of children with hemispherectomies suggesting that left-hemisphere removal always leads to selective subtle deficits in language, especially for syntactic and phonological tasks (e.g. Dennis & Whitaker, 1976). Similar results were also reported for children with early focal brain injury due to strokes (Vargha-Khadem, Isaacs, & Muter, 1994). These findings were compatible with studies of normal infants indicating a left hemisphere bias at birth in processing speech and other complex sounds (see below), and led some researchers to the conclusion that functional asymmetries for language in the human brain are established at birth, and cannot be reversed. Unfortunately, some of the secondary sources that summarized the work on hemispherectomies and/or early focal injury failed to note that the deficits shown by these children are far more subtle than the frank aphasias displayed by adults with homologous forms of brain damage (see Bishop, 1983, for a critique of the Dennis & Whitaker, 1976, study). Indeed, most of the children with left-hemisphere injury who have been studied to date fall within the normal range, attend normal age-appropriate schools (Stiles, Bates, Thal, Trauner, & Reilly, 2002), and do far better than adults with equivalent damage.

While most studies to date have involved assessing language competence in children who acquired perinatal lesions many years beforehand, Bates, Stiles and their colleagues have, over the past fifteen years, carried out *prospective* studies of language and spatial cognition in children who have suffered a single unilateral injury to either the right or the left hemisphere, prenatally or before 6 months, confirmed by at least one radiological technique (Bates & Roe, 2001; Stiles & Thal, 1993; Stiles et al., 2002). Children in these studies were identified prior to the onset of measurable language skills and were examined longitudinally. This team has now studied more than twenty cases between 8 and 31 months of age, all with unilateral lesions that occurred before language development would normally begin. Regardless of the lesion site, infants with focal brain lesions were delayed, suggesting, not surprisingly, that there is a general non-specific cost to early brain injury. However, the prospective study of these infants also produced a number of rather surprising results. Based on the adult aphasia literature, delays in word comprehension would be expected to be most severe in children with damage to left posterior sites. In contrast to this, it appears that comprehension deficits are actually more common in the right-hemisphere infant group. Such a deficit is rarely reported in adults with right-hemisphere damage. This and other findings led these authors to suggest that the regions responsible for first-language learning in children are not necessarily the regions responsible for language use and maintenance in the adult.

FURTHER READING: BATES & ROE, 2001; STILES ET AL., 2002; LEONARD, 2003

Another complicating factor revealed by prospective studies of infants with focal lesions came from a study of language production by Reilly, Bates and Marchman (1998). This study used the same population with pre- or perinatal lesions just discussed. Reilly and colleagues looked at many different aspects of lexical, grammatical, and discourse structure in a storytelling task, in children with focal lesions and typically developing controls between 3 and 8 years of age. In this study (like many others within this age range), there were no significant differences between the left- and right-hemisphere groups on any of the language measures. However, the infants with focal lesions as a whole performed worse than typically developing controls on several measures of morphology, syntax, and narrative structure. Each of these disadvantages appears to resolve over time in the children with focal lesions group, but each time the child moves on to the next level of development (in language acquisition), differences between the infants with focal lesions and typically developing infants reappear. Thus, functional recovery does not appear to be a one-off event, but rather may re-occur at several critical points during acquisition.

To summarize, the effects of early focal lesions on language acquisition are complex. However, in general the evidence supports the following conclusions:

1 Most children with early left-hemisphere damage go on to acquire language abilities within the normal range (although often at the lower end).
2 In general, there is no significant difference in language outcomes when direct comparisons are made between children with early left- versus right-hemisphere damage.
3 Different regions of the cortex may be involved in the actual acquisition of language from those that are important for language use in adults.
4 Functional compensation may have to re-occur at several points in language acquisition, and is not a one-off event.

Another approach to studying the extent to which the cortical areas supporting language are prespecified is to ascertain whether other functions can occupy the cortical regions that normally support aspects of language. Such experiments would be analogous in logic to the neurobiological studies mentioned in chapter 2 in which input to a developing region of cortex was "re-wired" such that representations generated from a new sensory modality were produced.

Neville and colleagues (see Neville, 1991, for review) have used ERPs (chapter 2) to examine cortical plasticity related to inter-sensory competition. Evidence from visual and spatial tasks in deaf participants suggests that visual processing in the cortex is different in individuals reared in the absence of auditory input. Specifically, the congenitally deaf seem more sensitive to events in the peripheral visual field than are hearing participants. ERPs recorded over classical auditory regions, such as portions of the temporal lobe, are two or three times larger for deaf than for hearing participants following peripheral visual field stimulation. Thus, the lack of auditory input has resulted in a normally auditory area becoming at least partially allocated to visual functions.

FURTHER READING: NEVILLE & BAVELIER, 2002

Thus, the evidence described so far indicates that regions of the cortex are not prespecified for language processing, and that other functions may be able to "capture" areas that normally end up processing language. However, it is still possible that small variations on the basic architecture of the cortex may be sufficient to "attract" language processing to some regions during normal functional brain development.

Some evidence for this view comes from studies of deaf signers with acquired focal brain lesions. After reviewing evidence that sign language has most of the same formal properties as spoken languages, Bellugi, Poizner, and Klima (1989) found that deaf signers with left-hemisphere lesions acquired in adulthood were aphasic for sign language, while showing intact performance on several visuospatial tasks. Adult patients with recently acquired right-hemisphere lesions, on the other hand, showed the reciprocal pattern of performance. In this latter group, signing was fluent even to the extent of being able to sign fluently about the contents of their room while showing gross spatial distortion in their description of its contents! This, and other evidence, led Bellugi and colleagues to propose that it is the computations required for linguistic processing, rather than its modality, that determine cortical localization.

This conclusion received partial support from a more recent fMRI study in which hearing and deaf participants were scanned while reading sentences in either English or American Sign Language (ASL) (Neville et al., 1998; see Neville & Bavelier, 2002). The top of figure 7.2 shows patterns of cortical activation when hearing adults read English. Consistent with previous research, there was robust activation within some classical left-hemisphere language areas, such as Broca's area. No such activation was observed in the right hemisphere. When deaf people

Figure 7.2 Cortical areas showing increases in blood oxygenation on fMRI when normal hearing adults read English sentences (top), when congenitally deaf native signers read English sentences (middle), and when congenitally deaf native signers view sentences in their native sign language (American Sign Language).

viewed an ASL signer performing the same sentences (bottom of figure), they showed activation of most of the left-hemisphere regions identified for the hearing participants. Since ASL is not sound-based, but does have all of the other characteristics of language, including a complex grammar (Klima & Bellugi, 1979), these data suggest that some of the neural systems that mediate language can do so regardless of the modality and structure of the language acquired. Having said this, there were also some clear differences between the hearing and deaf activations, with the deaf group activating some similar regions in the right hemisphere. One interpretation of the right-hemisphere activation is that it is evoked by the biological motion inherent in sign, but not spoken, language. A third condition addressed the issue of whether there is a sensitive period for the establishment of left-hemisphere language. In this condition, deaf people read English (their second language, learned late), and did not show activation of the classical left-hemisphere language regions, suggesting that if a language is not acquired within the appropriate developmental time window, the typical pattern of adult activation does not occur.

7.3 NEURAL BASIS OF SPEECH PROCESSING IN INFANTS

The second general approach to investigating the extent to which language is "biologically special" involves attempting to identify speech-processing-relevant processes in the brains of very young infants. A further question then concerns how specific to speech these correlates are. The logic here is that if there are specific neural correlates of speech processing observable very early in life, this may indicate language-related neural processing prior to significant experience.

One example of this approach concerns the ability to discriminate speech-relevant sounds such as phonemes. Behavioral experiments have revealed that young infants show enhanced (categorical) discrimination at phonetic boundaries used in speech such as /ba/, /pa/. That is, a graded phonetic transition from /ba/ to /pa/ is perceived as a sudden categorical shift by infants. These observations initially caused excitement as evidence for a speech-perception-specific detection mechanism in humans. However, over the past decade it has become clear that other species, such as chinchillas, show similar acoustical discrimination abilities, indicating that this ability may merely reflect general characteristics of the mammalian auditory processing system, and not an initial spoken-language-specific mechanism (see Werker & Vouloumanos, 2001). However, Werker and Polka (1993) have reported that while young human infants can discriminate between a very wide range of phonetic constructs, including those not found in the native language (e.g. Japanese infants, but not Japanese adults, can discriminate between "r" and "l" sounds), this ability becomes restricted to the phonetic constructs of the native language around 10 months of age.

> FURTHER READING: ASLIN & HUNT, 2001; WERKER & VOULOUMANOS, 2001

If brain correlates of this process could be identified, it may be possible to study the mechanisms underlying this speech-specific selective decrease of sensitivity.

As mentioned in chapter 1, ERPs offer a good opportunity to study the neural correlates of cognition in normal infants in a non-invasive manner. The excellent temporal resolution of ERPs can be complemented by some spatial resolution through the use of high-density ERPs (HD-ERP). When components of ERP differ in both latency (following the event) and spatial resolution, we may be confident that different neural circuitry is being activated. An example of this approach comes from a HD-ERP study of phonetic discrimination in 3-month-old infants.

Dehaene-Lambertz and Dehaene (1994) presented their participants with trials in which a series of four identical syllables (the standard) was followed by a fifth that was either identical or phonetically different (deviant). They time-locked the ERP to the onset of the syllable and observed two peaks with different scalp locations. The first peak occurred around 220 ms after stimulus onset and did not habituate to repeated presentations (except after the first presentation) or dishabituate to the novel syllable. Thus the generators of this peak, probably primary and secondary auditory areas in the temporal lobe, did not appear to be sensitive to the subtle acoustical differences that encoded phonetic information.

The second peak reached its maximum around 390 ms after stimulus onset and again did not habituate to repetitions of the same syllable, except after the first presentation. However, when the deviant syllable was introduced, the peak recovered to at least its original level. Thus, the neural generators of the second peak, also in the temporal lobe but in a distinct and more posterior location, are sensitive to phonetic information. Further studies need to be carried out to ascertain whether the recovery of the second peak is due to the categorical perception of phonemes, or whether it would be elicited by any acoustical change. A later peak was observed over frontal regions following the deviant stimuli, a finding common to many paradigms with unexpected auditory or visual stimuli. This peak probably represents detection of novelty regardless of the input modality and, as discussed earlier, may reflect the updating of working memory. Similar ERP measures may be useful for the early detection of infants at risk for later language disorder (Benasich & Tallal, 2002).

Recently, researchers have used two methods with better spatial resolution to investigate early correlates of speech perception. Dehaene-Lambertz, Dehaene, and Hertz-Pannier (2002) measured brain activation with fMRI in awake and sleeping healthy 3-month-olds while they listened to forwards and backwards speech in their native tongue (French). The authors assumed that forward speech would elicit stronger activation than backward speech in areas related to the segmental and suprasegmental processing of language, while both stimuli would activate mechanisms for processing fast temporal auditory transitions (see Werker & Vouloumanos, 2001, for a discussion of the appropriate control stimuli for human speech). Compared to silence, both forward and backward speech activated widespread areas of the left temporal lobe, which was greater than the equivalent activation on the right for some areas (planum temporale). This activation pattern is consistent with the ERP experiment described above. However, forward speech activated some areas that backward speech did not, including the angular gyrus and mesial parietal lobe (precuneus) in the left hemisphere. The authors suggest that these findings demonstrate an early functional asymmetry between the two hemispheres. However, they acknowledge that their results cannot discriminate between an early bias for speech perception, or a greater responsivity of the left temporal lobe for processing auditory stimuli with rapid temporal changes (both of which could start during the final trimester in uterus). Further, in awake infants only, the right dorsolateral prefrontal cortex showed greater activation to forwards speech, an observation that we will return to in chapter 8.

The general conclusions from the above studies are reinforced by converging results from a new methodology – near infra-red spectroscopy (NIRS; chapter 1). In this experiment, Mehler and colleagues (2003) played normal infant-directed speech or the same utterances played in reverse while they measured changes in the concentration of total hemoglobin over the right and left hemisphere. They observed that left temporal areas showed significantly more activation when infants were exposed to normal speech than to backwards speech or silence, leading them to conclude that neonates are born with a left-hemisphere bias for speech processing.

Taken together, the experiments on speech perception just described provide perhaps the best example in developmental cognitive neuroscience of the power of converging methodology. It is encouraging that similar conclusions can be drawn from experiments using behavioral, ERP, fMRI, and NIRS methods.

7.4 DYSLEXIA

Dyslexia was one of the first developmental disorders to be associated with a particular underlying neural atypicality. In 1907, Hinshelwood postulated that it was a developmental version of alexia (failure to recognize words) and associated it with atypicality of the left angular gyrus of the cortex. Key symptoms of dyslexia are difficulties in learning to read and spell, sometimes with letter and number reversals, and unusual errors. These correlated deficits (such as in naming, and verbal short-term memory) are thought to be due to primary cognitive deficit in the phonological coding of spoken language. There is both structural and physiological evidence from the brains of people with dyslexia consistent with Hinshelwood's original proposal that developmental atypicalities in the left hemisphere are important.

The structural evidence comes from the work of Galaburda and colleages (e.g. Galaburda, Sherman, Rosen, Aboititz, & Geschwind, 1985), who conducted autopsies on the brains of several individuals with dyslexia. They observed symmetry (between the right and left side) of a particular part of the temporal lobe of the cortex, the planum temporale (see figure 7.1). This region is part of the so-called Wernicke's area, which has been implicated in phonological processing. Galaburda and colleages also observed malformations in the clustering of neurons in this region and, to a lesser extent elsewhere in the cortex of these individuals. These cellular atypicalities are not evident in structural MRI or CT scanning, indicating that developmental atypicalities at the cellular or molecular level will not always be evident in terms of gross brain structure.

Turning to functional studies of the brain of this group, Wood, Flowers, Buchsbaum, and Tallal (1991) described studies from blood flow, PET, and scalp-recorded evoked responses. Consistent with the postmortem studies, they concluded that people with dyslexia showed atypical processing in the left temporal lobe in both phonemic discrimination and orthographic tasks. Similar conclusions were reached by Paulesu and colleagues (Paulesu et al., 1996), who compared people with dyslexia to a control group during a rhyming task and a short-term memory (for visually presented letters) task. The results showed that only a subset of the regions normally active during these tasks were activated in the individuals with dyslexia. Specifically, unlike in the control group, Broca's area and Wernicke's area were never activated together, possibly because they were not functionally connected via the insula.

Research by Tallal and colleagues has suggested that the ability to process the rapid temporal information necessary for phonemic discrimination (see previous section) may be critical for normal language acquisition (e.g. Tallal & Stark, 1980; see Merzenich et al., 2002). Specifically, children with oral language delay often, but not always, have deficits in the perception and discrimination of rapidly changing acoustic information (Tallal, Stark, Clayton, & Mellits, 1980). The inability to discriminate some phonemes with rapid temporal transitions, such as /ba/ and /da/, may have consequences for oral speech recognition. Tallal, Merzenich and colleagues have produced preliminary evidence that the inability to process rapid temporal transitions in children with language delay can be rectified by training with adapted speech in which the temporal transitions are extended (Tallal et al., 1996; Merzenich et al., 2002). Whether such remediation can be successfully extended to a wider range of language and reading disorders remains to be seen. However, some reports have indicated that children with language delay frequently develop reading problems symptomatic of some types of dyslexia.

FURTHER READING: MERZENICH ET AL., 2002

The above studies are all broadly consistent with involvement of the left temporal lobe in both phonemic discrimination and dyslexia. However, it is important to stress that there is considerable controversy about the exact nature of the cognitive deficits observed in dyslexia (e.g. Pennington & Welsh, 1995) and that there is also evidence for atypicalities elsewhere in the brain (e.g. Livingstone, Rosen, Drislane, & Galaburda, 1991). Further, the putative involvement of the left temporal lobe in this disorder need not be interpreted in terms of a causal epigenesis pathway. It is tempting to infer that a neural deficit or atypicality in the left temporal lobe gives rise to a failure to process the rapid temporal transitions necessary for phonemic discrimination, and that in some cases this might be related to subtypes of dyslexia. However, the evidence on cortical development and plasticity discussed in chapter 2, and the apparent initial success of the training studies by Merzenich et al. (2002), suggest a more probabilistic epigenetic view.

Roughly speaking, this view is that regions of the left temporal lobe are engaged by inputs that require rapid temporal processing. This is due to having an architecture slightly different from the basic structure common to the rest of the cortex. This makes this region the best, but not the only, possible "home" for speech processing. If this region is damaged, other parts of cortex can also support these representations, though perhaps not quite as efficiently. Processing speech within this region influences its synaptic and dendritic microstructure through some of the mechanisms discussed in chapter 2. Through interaction with a certain type of input it thus becomes increasingly specialized and different from other regions. Some degree of plasticity may remain during development, resulting in a reconfiguration of the microcircuitry of the region following specific training. Differences in neural structure between this region in adults with dyslexia and controls would reflect this deviant developmental pathway, much of which may have occurred postnatally. Thus, a slight initial bias can be enhanced through development into greater anatomical and functional specialization.

7.5 NEURAL CORRELATES OF TYPICAL AND ATYPICAL LANGUAGE ACQUISITION

Bates, Thal, and Janowsky (1992) reviewed and identified a number of correlations between neuroanatomical developments in the human cerebral cortex and "landmarks" in language acquisition. Such correlations cannot be used to establish firm links between neural events and cognitive ones. However, the approach is useful for identifying specific hypotheses that can then be tested with more direct methodologies.

Consistent with the findings reviewed so far in this chapter, Bates et al. (1992) suggested that the evidence for some neuroanatomical differences between the right and left hemispheres at birth may set up computational differences that "bias" language toward the left hemisphere. As discussed in chapter 2, it is likely that these differences between the hemispheres are due to differential timing of development, rather than a genetic encoding of a specific architecture. Bates et al. (1992) identify a peak transition in both behavioral and neural development at around 8–9 months after birth. They discuss the establishment of long-range connections (especially from the frontal cortex) and the onset of an adult distribution of metabolic activity (from the PET study of Chugani, 1994, reviewed in chapter 2) at this age, and suggest that these neural developments enable the onset of a number of language-related skills such as word comprehension, and the inhibition of non-native speech contrasts.

Around 16–24 months there is a "burst" in vocabulary and grammar, and Bates and colleagues argue that this correlates with a steep increase in synaptic density in many relevant cortical regions. The increased synaptic density, they speculate, enables a larger capacity for storage and information processing. At around 4 years of age most normal children have acquired the basic morphological and syntactic structures of their native language, and thus have reached the end of the "grammar burst." Bates and colleagues point out that this "stabilization" of language coincides with the decline in overall brain metabolism and synaptic density (although, as mentioned in chapter 2, the peaks of these two measures may not coincide exactly).

Developmental disorders involving language can also be informative about the neurodevelopmental basis of these abilities. Some authors have argued that developmental disorders in which language is relatively deficient, despite a lack of problems in other domains, constitute evidence for an innate language module. Conversely, cases where language is supposedly intact, despite impairment in other domains, could provide powerful converging evidence. An example of the former kind that has attracted much scientific and media interest in recent years concerns three generations of the KE family and the "FOXP2" gene. Initial reports suggested that about half of the members of this unfortunate family had an inherited specific impairment in grammar (Gopnik, 1990), and excitement surrounded the identification of a specific gene, "FOXP2," associated with this disorder (Lai, Fisher, Hurst, Vargha-Khadem, & Monaco, 2001). However, claims for a "grammer gene" have been diluted by the finding that the deficits in the affected family members are much broader than grammer alone. Varghha-Khadem and colleagues have conducted extensive work on the family and found deficits in coordinating complex mouth movements (orofacial dyspraxia), timing of rhythmic motor movements, various aspects of language outside grammar (e.g. lexical decision), with IQ scores 18–19 points below unaffected members of the same family (Vargha-Khadem, Watkins, Alcock, Fletcher, & Passingham, 1995). Nevertheless, the relatively simple single-gene basis of the condition, and its association with language, make it worthy of further study (see Marcus & Fisher, 2003, for further discussion). One such study has involved fMRI during verb generation and repetition tasks (Liégeois et al., 2003). This study demonstrated that affected members of the family showed significant underactivation mainly in two regions: Broca's area and the putamen. However, as can been in figure 7.3, the affected members also showed greater activation than did controls in a variety of other cortical regions, suggesting widespread adjustment of cortical networks in response to the aberrant gene.

While the KE family may not have turned out to have the specific deficits initially hypothesized, similar claims about the specificity of language deficits have been made for so-called "specific language impairment" (SLI). While there is much controversy about the behavioral specificity or otherwise of this condition (see Bishop, 1997), most neuroanatomical studies have tended to focus on the particular regions thought to be important for language as discussed above. Thus, it is difficult to know whether or not regions outside the adult classical language

Figure 7.3 Covert language task: group average fMRI activation in the unaffected and affected members of the KE family. Activated regions are projected onto the surface rendering of a typical 3D individual brain, displayed at a statistical threshold of $p < .05$, corrected for multiple comparisons. L, left hemisphere; R, right hemisphere. (See also colour plate.)

regions are atypical as well. However, a recent study set out to examine the whole brain of "SLI" participants with MRI (Herbert et al., 2003). Compared to controls, these children showed a substantial increase (more than 10 per cent) in cerebral white matter throughout the brain. This atypical pattern was no more severe in the classical language areas than anywhere else in the brain, suggesting to the authors that the population they studied had a "generalized systems impairment" that differentially affected language.

A case where language is supposedly spared relative to other domains of impairment is Williams syndrome. In Williams syndrome (WS) (see chapter 5 and appendix), language can be strikingly proficient, despite severe deficits in other domains. Several studies have demonstrated that linguistic and face-processing skills are surprisingly good in WS participants, despite low IQs (typically in the 50s–60s) and serious deficits on visuospatial, number, motor, planning, and problem-solving tasks (see Karmiloff-Smith et al., 1995, for review). The linguistic ability of these participants is not just superficial (such as repetition of previously heard sentences), but is generative in the sense that they can create new sentences with appropriate grammatical structure. The depth of this linguistic knowledge is currently the subject of debate. In certain cases the dissociation between linguistic ability and other abilities can be very marked. For example, the following is the spontaneous speech of a 21-year-old WS participant (studied by Annette Karmiloff-Smith and colleagues) with performance equivalent to a mental age of $5^1/_2$ years as assessed on a standardized spatial cognition task (Ravens Matrices):

> [*talking about her job at the hospital where she helps with the catering staff*]
> Well sometimes I do and sometimes I don't. They just tell you how many cups you put on the tray and the saucers and how many (um) spoons and sugars and creams you put on the tray and how many sandwiches they want for how many people.
>
> [*Experimenter*: But do you count them yourself, the cups?]
> No, they count them and I just put them on the trays. So, I put them in with clingfilm on top so they don't get wet.

In this example, while this participant is unable to count relatively small numbers (the number of cups on a tray), she is able to express herself grammatically and has a fairly wide vocabulary. While it seems initially attractive to account for such cases of isolated proficient language in terms of innate representations for language, the evidence on cortical development in chapter 2 should make us wary of jumping to this conclusion. A better way to view such cases is that some deviation from the normal trajectory of brain development results in a slightly maladaptive architecture in some structures (Karmiloff-Smith, 2002). This slightly deviant aspect of neural architecture has much more effect on some domains of processing than others. Once early postnatal development deviates from the normal trajectory, then it is likely that this deviation will be amplified by atypical interactions with the environment.

7.6 GENERAL SUMMARY AND CONCLUSIONS

The degree to which the acquisition of language is "biologically special" has been hotly contested on the basis of linguistic and behavioral data. While the addition of cognitive neuroscience data has not resolved this debate, it has illuminated some of the constraints and biases that ensure that most adults acquire a specialized brain network for the production and processing of language. For example, converging evidence from several cognitive neuroscience methods indicates that, from birth or even earlier, regions of the left temporal lobe are engaged by, and process, auditory inputs that require rapid temporal processing. While these regions may be the ideal "home" for speech processing, if they are damaged early in life then other parts of cortex can also support this function, though perhaps not quite as efficiently. In accord with the interactive specialization view, it is likely that processing speech within this region from early in life influences its synaptic and dendritic microstructure, resulting in it becoming increasingly specialized and different from other regions. Some degree of plasticity may remain during development, resulting in a reconfiguration of the microcircuitry of the region following specific training.

Developmental disorders in which language functions are supposedly selectively impaired, or remain "intact" in the face of other deficits, have been used as examples in support of claims for an "innate language module." Closer examination of such cases reveals that they are better viewed as deviations from the typical trajectory of brain development that have more effect on some domains of processing than others. Once early postnatal development deviates from the typical trajectory, then it is likely that this deviation will be amplified by atypical interactions with the environment.

Language acquisition and speech perception have been some of the most active areas of developmental cognitive neuroscience. The use of converging methodologies, and frequent comparisons between typical and atypical trajectories of development, make it the general domain most likely to see major breakthroughs over the next decade.

8 FRONTAL CORTEX, OBJECT PERMANENCE, AND PLANNING

The frontal cortex shows the most prolonged development of any region of cortex. This chapter outlines two approaches to understanding the role of this part of cortex in cognitive development. The first approach has entailed associating the perseverative errors of young infants on object permanence and retrieval tasks with maturation of the dorsolateral prefrontal cortex by means of data from human infants, infant monkeys, and adult prefrontal-cortex-lesioned monkeys. These data support the view that maturation of this region of cortex allows integration of information across space and time, and the inhibition of prepotent responses. This maturational account will require some modification in the light of recent evidence from marker tasks with younger infants involving looking, rather than reaching, as the relevant response, and in the light of recent neuroimaging data. A second view of the role of the prefrontal cortex in cognitive development is that it is needed for skill learning and plays an important and early role in brain organization. Studies of EEG coherence suggest a role for prefrontal regions in the cyclical reorganization of cortical representations during cognitive development. Some of the problems with this approach are outlined. It is concluded that the specificity of prefrontal cortex functioning probably arises from a combination of initial neurochemical and connectivity biases, and the relatively protracted plasticity of the region.

8.1 INTRODUCTION

As discussed in chapter 2, the frontal cortex shows the most prolonged period of postnatal development of any region of the human brain, with detectable changes in synaptic density and myelination even into the teenage years (Huttenlocher, 1990; Giedd et al., 1999). For this reason, it has been the part of the brain most commonly associated with developments in cognitive abilities during childhood.

Furthermore, several different developmental disorders present with behavioral symptoms said to resemble those of adult patients with acquired damage to the prefrontal cortex. Two major unresolved issues concerning frontal cortex development are as follows:

- Are the specialized computations performed by the frontal cortex due to a unique neuroanatomy/neurochemistry, or to other factors?
- How are we to align evidence for prefrontal cortex functioning within the first 6 months of life, with evidence for the continuing neuroanatomical development of the region until the teenage years?

We will return to these issues at the end of the chapter. Initially, however, we will explore two alternative views that have been taken of the relation between frontal cortex structural development and increases in cognitive ability in childhood. The first of these is that structural developments in the frontal cortex occur at a particular age, allowing certain increases in cognitive ability (a recent refinement of this general view is that the frontal lobes are composed of a number of regions which subserve different functions and show differential rates of maturation, e.g. Diamond, 1991). This view is in line with the maturational perspective outlined in chapter 1. The alternative view is that the frontal cortex is consistently involved in acquisition of new skills and knowledge from very early in life, and that it may also play a role in organizing other parts of cortex (e.g. Thatcher, 1992). By this second view, regions of frontal cortex play a fundamental role in cognitive transitions primarily because of the region's involvement in the acquisition of *any* new skill or knowledge. A corollary of this hypothesis is that frontal involvement in a particular task or situation may decrease with experience of the task. This perspective on frontal cortex development is inspired by the skill learning model of functional brain development outlined in chapter 1. With regard to frontal cortex development, many of the predictions from this view model overlap with those from the interactive specialization view. Consequently, I will not attempt to differentiate these two perspectives until the end of the chapter. I begin by reviewing attempts to relate the maturation of particular regions of prefrontal cortex to aspects of cognitive development.

 ## 8.2 PREFRONTAL CORTEX, ACTION PLANNING, AND WORKING MEMORY

One of the most comprehensive attempts to relate a cognitive change to underlying brain development has concerned the emergence of object permanence in infants. In particular, Diamond, Goldman-Rakic, and colleagues (Goldman-Rakic, 1987; Diamond & Goldman-Rakic, 1989; Diamond, 1991) have argued that the maturation of prefrontal cortex during the last half of the human infant's first

year of life accounts for both Piaget's (1954) observations about object permanence and a variety of other transitions in related tasks which involve working
memory and the inhibition of prepotent responses (e.g. Diamond et al., 1994).

The region of the frontal lobe anterior to the primary motor and premotor
cortex, commonly called the prefrontal cortex, accounts for almost one-third of
the total cortical surface in humans (Brodmann, 1909, 1912; see figure 6.1 in
chapter 6) and is considered by most investigators to be the locus of control for
many abilities central to higher level cognition. Extensive clinical (Milner, 1982)
and experimental observations of the effects of injury to this region have also
supported the notion that the prefrontal cortex supports important aspects of
cognition (for reviews see Owen, 1997; Duncan, 2001). While there are no univer-
sally accepted theories of frontal cortex functioning, the particular forms of
cognitive processing that have been consistently linked to the frontal cortex in
adults pertain to the planning or carrying out of sequences of action, the maintenance of information "on-line" during short temporal delays, and the ability to
inhibit a set of responses that are appropriate in one context but not another.

It was Piaget who first observed that infants younger than around 7 months fail
to accurately retrieve a hidden object after a short delay period if the object's
location is changed from one where it was previously and successfully retrieved.
In particular, infants of this age make a particular preservative error. That is, they
often reach to the hiding location where the object was found on the immediately
preceding trial. This characteristic pattern of error, called "A not B," was cited by
Piaget (1954) as evidence for the failure of infants to understand that objects
retain their existence or permanence when moved from view. Between $7^1/_2$ and
9 months, infants begin to succeed in the task at successively longer delays of
1 to 5 seconds (Diamond, 1985, 2001). However, their performance is unreliable:
infants continue to make the AB error up to about 12 months if the delay between
hiding and retrieval is incremented as the infants age increases (Diamond, 1985).

FURTHER READING: BENES, 2001; DIAMOND, 2001, 2002

Diamond and Goldman-Rakic (1989) tested monkeys in a version of Piaget's
object permanence task. In the object permanence task, participants are shown an
object hidden at location A and are permitted to retrieve it. After a predetermined
number of successful retrievals at location A (usually three), the object is then
hidden at location B. Infant monkeys failed to retrieve the hidden object at
location B when the delay between hiding and retrieval was 2 seconds or more.
Diamond and Goldman-Rakic (1989) found that animals with lesions to the parietal cortex, a brain region closely associated with spatial processing, did not show
this performance deficit; nor did lesions to the hippocampal formation, a region
known to be crucial for other memory-related tasks, impair monkey performance
on A not B (Diamond, Zola-Morgan, & Squire, 1989). However, lesions to the

dorsolateral prefrontal cortex severely impaired the adult monkeys' performance, indicating that this region plays a central role in delayed response tasks that require the maintenance of spatial information over temporal delays.

Developmental evidence that links maturation in frontal cortical regions to the emergence of working memory abilities comes from studies (Diamond & Goldman-Rakic, 1986, 1989) that showed that infant monkeys failed the A not B task and failed an object retrieval task (in which the participant has to retrieve an object from behind a barrier) in ways similar to monkeys with frontal cortex damage. By contrast, older, unlesioned monkeys succeeded in these tasks and showed an ability to withstand longer delays. Evidence linking this change in behavior to brain maturation comes from studies which show that prefrontal afferents and efferents myelinate later than other cortical areas (Yakovlev & Lecours, 1967). Furthermore, in a series of EEG studies with normal human infants (Fox & Bell, 1990; Bell, 1992a, 1992b; Bell & Fox, 1992), increases in frontal EEG responses have been shown to correlate with the ability to respond successfully over longer delays in delayed response tasks. Most recently, an optical imaging study with infants has revealed a correlation between behavioral success in the AB task and blood oxygenation in the prefrontal cortex (Baird et al., 2002).

Converging evidence for the importance of frontal cortex maturation comes from studies on children with a neurochemical deficit in the prefrontal cortex resulting from phenylketonuria (PKU) (Welsh, Pennington, Ozonoff, Rouse, & McCabe, 1990; Diamond, 2001; see appendix). Even when treated, this metabolic disorder can have the specific consequence of reducing the levels of a neuro-transmitter, dopamine, in the dorsolateral prefrontal cortex (see chapter 2). These reductions in dopamine levels in the dorsolateral prefrontal cortex result in these infants and children being impaired on tasks thought to involve the prefrontal cortex such as the object permanence and object retrieval tasks, and being relatively normal in tasks thought to be dependent on other regions of cortex such as delayed non-matching to sample (Welsh et al., 1990; Diamond, 2001).

In Diamond's (1991) view, the emergence of the ability to demonstrate know-ledge about an object's permanence results from the maturation of prefrontal cortical regions between the ages of 5 and 12 months. Diamond proposed that this region of the cortex is important when a participant has to both retain informa-tion over spatial delays and inhibit prepotent (previously reinforced) responses. Let me briefly review the evidence for this position. Infants younger than $7^1/_2$ months fail to retrieve hidden objects when any delay is imposed between hiding and retrieval. In this sense, human infants behave like the adult monkeys with prefrontal lesions and infant monkeys, as discussed previously. Human infants of this age make similar retrieval errors in both the A not B task, in which the side of hiding is switched after several repeated hidings on one side, and in an object retrieval task when the side of hiding is varied randomly (Diamond & Doar, 1989). This suggests that Piaget's observations about object permanence reflect the state of development of one or more underlying neural mechanisms common to per-formance on both the object permanence and retrieval tasks. Since successful performance on these tasks requires both memory for the most recently hidden location and the inhibition of an incorrect reach to the last rewarded location, the underlying neural mechanism must subserve both behaviors. Extensive neurobiological evidence implicates the prefrontal cortex in spatial working memory performance, and lesions of this region frequently reveal patterns of behavior in which the inhibition of inappropriate responses is impaired. Consequently, Diamond and colleagues have presented a strong case for the importance of dorsolateral prefrontal cortex development.

FURTHER READING: DIAMOND, 2001, 2002

Two recent lines of evidence suggest that the prefrontal cortex maturation hypothesis is not the whole story, and that some modification or elaboration of the original account will be required. The first of these lines of evidence concerns a different marker task for the dorsolateral prefrontal cortex that was discussed in chapter 3, the oculomotor delayed response task. Gilmore and Johnson (1995) found that infants can succeed on this task at a much younger age than is indicated by the object retrieval tasks, even though it also requires the participant to maintain spatial information over a delay and inhibition of a prepotent response (to make a saccade to the cue when it appears). One explanation of the discrepancy between performance in Piaget's object permanence task and the results of Gilmore and Johnson (1995, 1997) is that tasks in which the response is an eye movement (looking) are easier since oculomotor planning develops more rapidly than other forms of motor output such as reaching. This proposal is consistent with several studies showing that infants can perform successfully in analogous object permanence tasks as young as 4 or 5 months of age if looking rather than reaching performance is measured (Lecuyer, Abgueguen, & Lemarie, 1992). Further, in chapter 4 evidence was reviewed that infants as young as 4 months look longer at the impossible events, indicating that they have an internal representation of the occluded object.

In order to account for the apparent discrepancy between these results, and those with the reaching measures, some have provided "means–ends" explanations, arguing that infants do not know how to coordinate the necessary sequence of motor behaviors to retrieve a hidden object (Diamond, 1991; Baillargeon, 1993). To test this idea, Munakata, McClelland, Johnson, and Siegler (1994) trained 7-month-olds to pull on a towel or press a button in order to retrieve objects placed at a distance from them. Infants retrieved objects when a transparent screen was interposed between them and the toy, but not if the screen was sufficiently opaque to make the object invisible. Since the same means–ends planning is required whether the screen is transparent or opaque, it was concluded that this cannot account for the discrepancy between the looking and the reaching tasks. Munakata et al. (1994) proposed an alternative "graded" view of the discrepancy implemented as a connectionist model. This model illustrates how weak internal representations of a stimulus can be sufficient to drive a simple output, such as an eye movement, but may be insufficient to initiate a more complex motor output, such as reaching.

The maturational approach to prefrontal cortex development has also been extended to later childhood and adolescence. The results from a variety of behavioral tasks designed to tap into advanced prefrontal cortex functions have demonstrated that adult levels of performance are not reached until adolescence or later (see Fabiani & Wee, 2001; Luciana, 2003). For example, participants from 3 to 25 years old were tested on the CANTAB (Cambridge Neuropsychological Testing Automated Battery), a well-established and validated battery of tests previously used on adult human and animal lesion populations (Fray, Robbins, & Sahakian, 1996). This battery assesses several measures, including working memory skills, self-guided visual search, and planning. Importantly for developmental studies, the battery is administered with touch-screen computer technology, and does not require any verbal or complex manual responses. Using the CANTAB, Luciana and Nelson (1998, 2000; Luciana, 2003) found that while measures that depend on posterior brain regions (such as recognition memory) were stable by 8 years, measures of planning and working memory had not yet reached adult levels by age 12.

FURTHER READING: LUCIANA, 2003

While such behavioral measures are useful as marker tasks, it is even better to use functional imaging while children perform tasks likely to engage prefrontal cortical regions. This strategy has been adopted by Casey and colleagues, who use fMRI to compare children and adults in working memory and inhibition tasks. In one experiment they used event-related fMRI while children and adults were engaged in a "go–no go" task (Durston et al., 2002). In this task, participants had to suppress their response when presented with a particular visual item within an ongoing sequence of stimulus presentations (e.g. one Pokemon character within a sequence of other Pokemon characters). The difficulty of the task was increased by increasing the number of "go" items that preceded the "no go" character. Successful response inhibition was associated with stronger activation of prefrontal regions for children than for adults. Also, while in adults the activation of some prefrontal regions increased with increasing numbers of preceding "go" trials (consistent with increasing need for inhibition), in children the circuit appeared to be maximally active for all trial types. Along with the poorer behavioral performance of children in this and other inhibitory tasks, these findings suggest that the functional development of some prefrontal cortical regions is important for the mature ability to inhibit prepotent tendencies. The greater activation seen in children will be discussed further below.

FURTHER READING: CASEY ET AL., 2001

8.3 PREFRONTAL CORTEX, SKILL LEARNING, AND INTERACTIVE SPECIALIZATION

An alternative approach to understanding the role of the prefrontal cortex in cognitive development has been advanced by several authors who have suggested that the region plays a critical role in the *acquisition* of new information and tasks. From this perspective, the challenge to the infant brain in, for example, learning to reach for an object is equivalent in some respects to that of the adult's brain when facing complex motor skills like learning to drive a car. Three concomitants of this general view are that (i) the cortical regions crucial for a particular task will change with the stage of acquisition, (ii) the prefrontal cortex plays a role in organizing information within or allocating it to other regions of cortex, and (iii) that development involves the establishment of hierarchical control structures, with the frontal cortex maintaining the currently highest level of control. Three recent lines of evidence indicating the importance of prefrontal cortical activation early in infancy have given further credence to this view: (1) fMRI and PET studies, (2) psychophysiological evidence, and (3) the long-term effects of perinatal damage to the prefrontal cortex.

The limited number of fMRI and PET studies that have been conducted with infants have often surprisingly revealed functional activation in the prefrontal cortex, even when this would not be predicted from adult studies. For example, in an fMRI study of speech perception in 3-month-olds, Dehaene-Lambertz and colleagues (2002) observed a right dorsolateral prefrontal cortex activation that discriminated (forward) speech in awake, but not sleeping, infants (see figure 8.1 and also previous chapter). Similar activation of DLPC was found in response to faces at the same age (Tzourio-Mazoyer et al., 2002). While this is evidence for activation of at least some of the prefrontal cortex in the first few months, it remains possible that this activation is passive as it does not play any role in directing the behavior of the infant. Two other recent lines of evidence, however, suggest that this is not the case.

Developmental ERP studies have often recorded activity changes over frontal leads in infants, and some recent experiments suggest that this activity has important consequences for behavioral output. These experiments involve examining patterns of activation that precede the onset of a saccade (chapter 3). In one example, Csibra and colleagues (1998, 2001) observed that pre-saccadic potentials that are usually recorded over more posterior scalp sites in adults are observed in frontal channels in 6-month-old infants. Since these potentials are time-locked to the onset of an action, it is reasonable to infer that they are the consequence of computations necessary for the planning or execution of the action.

Figure 8.1 Interaction between wakefulness and the linguistic nature of the stimuli. This comparison isolated a right dorsolateral prefrontal region that showed greater activation by forward speech than by backward speech in awake infants, but not in sleeping infants. (See also colour plate.)

Further evidence for the developmental importance of the prefrontal cortex from early infancy comes from studies of the long-term and widespread effects of perinatal damage to the area. In several of the previous chapters we have seen how selective perinatal damage to the relevant regions activated in adults often has, at worst, mild effects on infants, with subsequently almost complete recovery of function. In contrast, perinatal damage to frontal and prefrontal cortical regions often results in both immediate and long-term difficulties. This generalization from several domains suggests that the prefrontal cortex plays an important structuring or enabling role from very early in postnatal development. One example of this theoretical approach to functional prefrontal cortex development has been advanced by Thatcher (1992) and Case (1992) (for another, related approach see Stuss, 1992).

Thatcher (1992) and colleagues have analyzed EEG data from a large number of participants at various ages between 2 months and 18 years. During recording, the participants sat quietly and, as far as can be ascertained, were not responding to any stimuli. From 16 leads placed evenly across the scalp the spontaneous EEG rhythms of the brain were recorded before being subjected to a complex analysis that ascertained the extent to which the recordings from each lead "cohered" (roughly speaking, correlated in their activity) with other leads. From the large amount of raw data that such an analysis generates, the major factors (i.e. which leads cohere) could be adduced for each age group, and the age "peaks" of rate of increase in coherence for these leads could be computed. Thatcher then added two working assumptions to this data, namely that scalp electrode locations provide reasonable indications of underlying cortical activity, and that the extent of correlation between the activity of regions (leads) reflects the strength of neural connections between them. The result was a hypothesis about recurring cycles of cortical re-organization orchestrated by the frontal cortex.

Figure 8.2 illustrates the hypothesis put forward by Thatcher on the basis of a complex analysis of a subset of his data. The lines in between points indicate the leads that show the greatest rate of increase in cohesion at that age. Thatcher's claim is that there are cycles of cortical re-organization which begin with microcycles involving re-organization of short-range connections in the left hemisphere. Following this, longer-range frontal connections become important, at first only on the left side, but then bilaterally. The cycle is then completed by re-organization of short-range connections on the right-hand side. According to Thatcher, a complete cycle of this kind takes approximately four years, though subcycles and microcycles provide the basis for shorter-term periods of stability and transition. By virtue of the longer-range connections related to the frontal cortex, Thatcher suggests that this part of cortex plays an integral role in the re-organization of the cortex as a whole.

Case (1992) attempted to use these EEG findings to relate brain re-organizations to cognitive change by arguing (i) that cognitive change has a similarly "recursive" character, and (ii) that many limitations on cognitive performance are due to functions such as working memory commonly associated with the frontal cortex. One example used to illustrate that neural and cognitive changes may both be manifestations of a common underlying process is the rate of change in EEG coherence between a particular pair of leads (frontal and parietal) and the rate of growth in working memory span during the same ages (see figure 8.3). While the change in the rate of growth in the two variables may seem compelling at first glance, there are a number of reasons why it cannot be regarded as more than suggestive at present. One of these is that there is no clear rationale for choosing

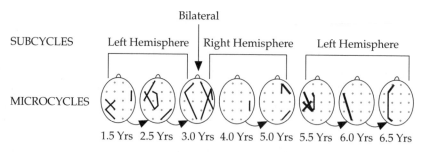

Figure 8.2 Summary of the sequence and anatomical distribution of the coherence patterns reported by Thatcher (1992). Lines connecting electrode locations indicate a measure of strong coherence. "Microcycles" are a developmental sequence that involves a lateral-medial rotation that cycles from the left hemisphere to bilateral to right hemisphere in approximately four years. Note the hypothesized involvement of the frontal cortex in the "bilateral" subcycle.

A

B

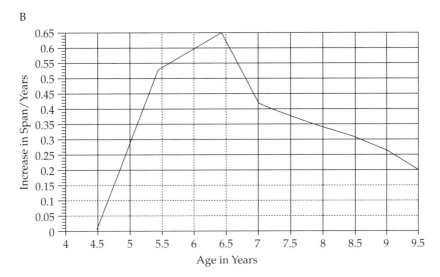

Figure 8.3 (A) Rate of growth of EEG coherence between frontal and posterior lobes during middle childhood (F 7–P 3). (Thatcher, 1992). (B) Rate of growth of working memory (counting span and spatial span) during the same age range.

the particular pair of electrodes presented – there are, after all, 56 possible pairs to select from, and there are always likely to be a few that show peaks in growth at similar ages to some developing cognitive function.

Even assuming that watertight correlations between the peaks in rates of increase in cognitive abilities and EEG coherence could be obtained, this association between brain and cognition would still be based only on temporal correlation, a form of evidence which, when take in isolation, is not very compelling. Hopefully, in the future this approach will attempt to consider the fact that EEG coherence shows phases of significant decreases of coherence as well as increases, which may be associated with "dips" in performance at the behavioral level, and more dynamic, as opposed to stage-based, accounts of cognitive change.

8.4 GENERAL SUMMARY AND CONCLUSIONS

Two different viewpoints on the development of the prefrontal cortex have been reviewed in this chapter. The view that the maturation of regions of the prefrontal cortex enables particular cognitive functions is, of course, a *causal epigenesis* type of account (maturational view, chapter 1), and such accounts will always be vulnerable to demonstrations of partial functioning of the region in question at earlier ages. On the other hand, the second approach discussed, in which the frontal lobes are a critical part of the cyclical self-organization of cortex, still remains relatively unspecified, with only preliminary evidence to support it at the moment. Nevertheless, bearing in mind the evidence for these two approaches, we can return to the unresolved issues raised at the start of the chapter.

The first of these issues concerned whether the specialized computations performed by the frontal cortex are due to a unique neuroanatomy and/or neurochemistry, or to other factors. The view put forward in chapter 2 was that while the cerebral cortex provides architectural constraints on the representations that emerge during ontogeny, there are no innate representations. However, it seems likely that graded differences in neurotransmitter densities, and differences in patterns of interconnectivity to other regions of cortex, will provide initial biases that may subsequently lead to some regional differences in microcircuitry. In addition, however, the relatively delayed developmental trajectory of the frontal cortex means that it is likely to develop representations which capture invariances in the structure of the external world, and interactions with the external environment, at greater spatial and temporal distances than other regions of cortex. In other words, it will tend to integrate information over larger time and space intervals than will other regions of cortex. Thus, a combination of small intrinsic biases and relatively delayed development may give rise to the unique information-processing properties of this region of cortex. Whether this region plays a role in orchestrating the specialization of other regions of cortex, as Thatcher claims, is an exciting topic for research in the future.

The second unresolved issue concerned how to reconcile evidence for continuing neuroanatomical development in the frontal cortex until the teenage years, on the one hand, and evidence for some functioning in the region as early as the first few months of age, on the other. The evidence for early functioning of the prefrontal cortex provides perhaps the biggest challenge to the maturational approach. One possible resolution to this issue is that representations that emerge within this region of cortex are initially weak, and sufficient only to control some types of output, such as saccades, but not others, such as reaching (Munakata et al., 1994). Other plausible resolutions of this issue come from Diamond's (1991) proposal that different regions of frontal cortex are differentially delayed in their development, and Thatcher's (1992) suggestion that prefrontal regions may have a continuing role in the cyclical re-organization of the rest of cortex. Whether these hypotheses work out or not, there is good reason why some degree of prefrontal cortical functioning is vital from the first weeks of postnatal life, or even earlier (Hykin et al., 1999; Moore et al., 2001; Fulford et al., 2003). The ability to form and retain goals, albeit for short periods, is vital for generating efforts to perform actions such as reaching for objects. Early, and often initially unsuccessful, attempts to perform motor actions provide the essential experience necessary for subsequent development.

9 CEREBRAL LATERALIZATION

A major feature of human brain function is the differential specialization of the two cerebral hemispheres. Three developmental models of hemispheric specialization of function are presented: "biased gene" models, "biased brain" models, and "biased head/uterus" models. Some of these models also address the relation between manual lateralization and hemispheric specialization for cognitive functions. A variety of genetic models of handedness and laterality have been put forward. While these models are increasing in their complexity, none of them have yet achieved universal acceptance, and there are remaining doubts about the heritability of handedness. Biased brain models are designed to account for neuroanatomical evidence of hemispheric specialization in newborns. Consequently, no firm conclusions can be drawn about prespecified computational properties of the two hemispheres. Biased head models argue that motor biases in the newborn, such as the tendency to turn the head to the right when lying on their backs, result in some visual inputs being biased to one visual field. Thus motor lateralization may indirectly initiate hemispheric specialization.

Within the first year of life, hemispheric specialization emerges for cognitive functions such as language and face processing. Several authors have proposed that these specializations are not due to prespecified computations (innate representations), but rather due to an initial difference in developmental timing between the two hemispheres. Such an initial difference in developmental state could result in certain types of inputs being more readily processed by one hemisphere. Subsequent dynamic inhibition between the hemispheres could increase this functional lateralization to such an extent that the other hemisphere can no longer take over processing the inputs in question following damage to the opposite side. Thus, slight differences in timing between the hemispheres may mean that the detailed architecture of one side is engaged more readily by certain inputs. Processing these inputs increases the specialization of these circuits to the extent that other cortical regions eventually cannot replace them.

A major feature of biological organisms is symmetry around a central axis (e.g. we have two hands, two eyes, two lungs). In their general morphology, the two cerebral hemispheres of the brain are very similar, and initially appear to be symmetric. However, a number of domains of adult cognition seem to be differentially processed in the two hemispheres, such as face recognition, language, and spatial cognition. In developmental neuropsychology debate has ensued about the extent to which such hemispheric specialization is prespecified (generally equated with being present from birth), as opposed to it being an emergent product of differential timing of development. This debate has been further complicated by the fact that empirical studies of hemispheric functional and structural specialization during postnatal development have sometimes produced apparently contradictory results, with the left hemisphere appearing to be more mature at some points of development and the right at others (Thatcher, Walker, & Giudice, 1987; Spreen et al., 1995). A further source of difficulty has concerned the extent of the interrelationship (if any) between the hemispheric specialization of cognitive functions and the lateralization of motor functions (such as handedness).

It is now generally agreed that there is some degree of neuroanatomical hemispheric lateralization present from shortly after birth in the human infant. However, there is still considerable disagreement about how this laterality arises and its relation to subsequent adult hemispheric specialization. Hopkins and Rönnqvist (1998) have discussed a number of hypotheses about the developmental origins of handedness and hemispheric laterality. They divided the range of theories into a number of types, including "biased gene" models, "biased brain" models, and "biased head/uterus" models.

"Biased gene" models provide genetic accounts of laterality. Among the most prominent of these is the "right shift theory" of Annett (1985) and the model of McManus and Bryden (1993). Briefly, the right shift theory states that the majority of individuals inherit a gene which predisposes them to left-hemisphere control of speech as a by-product of right-handedness. The minority of individuals that do not have this "right shift gene" have their laterality determined by environmental factors. Specifically, this model accounts for the high percentage of right-handedness observed in the children of two left-handed parents. McManus and Bryden (1993) have pointed out a number of problems with the right shift theory, and proposed a more complicated alternative that incorporates the influence of a second, sex-linked, modifier gene. This modifier gene allows them to account for some of the sex differences observed (left-handedness being more common in males, and left-handed mothers giving rise to more left-handed offspring than left-handed fathers). The increasingly complex genetic models of laterality reflect the fact that the heritability of handedness remains controversial, and the effects that have been reported are subtle and interact with other factors such as sex and early experience. A further problem is that the relation between handedness and cognitive lateralization remains unclear (see below). Additionally, until the ontogenetic function of the putative genes in question is known, the behavior genetic approach is necessarily limited in its explanatory value. Finally, we need not assume that these putative gene(s) have their effect in the central nervous system. Instead they may bias some other factor that indirectly influences brain development.

The "biased brain" models refer to neuroanatomical observations of hemispheric differences around the time of birth. A number of neuroanatomical studies have shown differences between parts of left and right cerebral cortex in adults. For example, Geschwind and Levitsky (1968) reported that the left planum temporale, an area thought to be involved in language (see chapter 7), was larger than the right in 65 percent of adult brains studied. A number of groups have looked for similar differences in infant brains. Chi, Gooling, and Gilles (1977) investigated the timing of gyral and sulcal development in the fetus. In certain cases these developed earlier on the right than on the left. In particular, a region of the temporal lobe thought to be important for language decoding and comprehension, Heschl's gyrus, was found to develop a little earlier on the right than on the left. In apparent contradiction to this finding of earlier development of the right hemisphere are several studies that report that as early as the 29th week of gestation the left planum temporale is usually larger on the left than on the right (Teszner, Tzavaras, Gruner, & Hecaen, 1972; Witelson & Pallie, 1973; Wada, Clark, & Hamm, 1975). It is important to remember, however, that these measures refer simply to the extent of folding in the cortex. As reviewed in chapter 2, the cerebral cortex is a thin flat sheet that becomes convluted as it grows within the skull. Gyral and sucal measures can therefore only tell us about the quantity of cortical tissue within a region (roughly speaking, the more tissue, the more folding) and cannot be used to argue for architectural prespecification. The latter can only be established by examining the detailed cytoarchitecture of the regions concerned. Until such studies are conducted with postmortem tissue from newborn infants, no definite conclusions can be reached about different computational properties of the left and right cerebral hemispheres at birth.

Even if empirical evidence for the "biased brain" hypothesis was obtained, the question of the factors responsible for this bias remains. The model of Geschwind, Behan, and Galaburda (GBG) (Geschwind & Behan, 1982; Geschwind & Galaburda, 1987) provided a causal account of how some of these neuroanatomical differences may arise and their consequences for later life. Briefly, these authors argued for a causal relationship between hormone levels in the uterus and the development of cerebral dominance, and a further relationship between the former and the immune syndrome. More specifically, they argued that higher or lower levels of the hormone testosterone *in utero* can slow down or accelerate the embryological migration of neurons from the neural crest into the cortex. Raised testosterone levels, more commonly found in males, are said to delay migration specifically in the left hemisphere, resulting in "anomalous dominance" in which a reduced degree of hemispheric specialization is observed. A characterisation of the GBG hypothesis is illustrated in figure 9.1.

A number of theoretical and empirical problems with this theory have been reviewed by McManus and Bryden (1993) and Previc (1994). Among the more serious problems with the theory are that it posits that those who are not right-handed

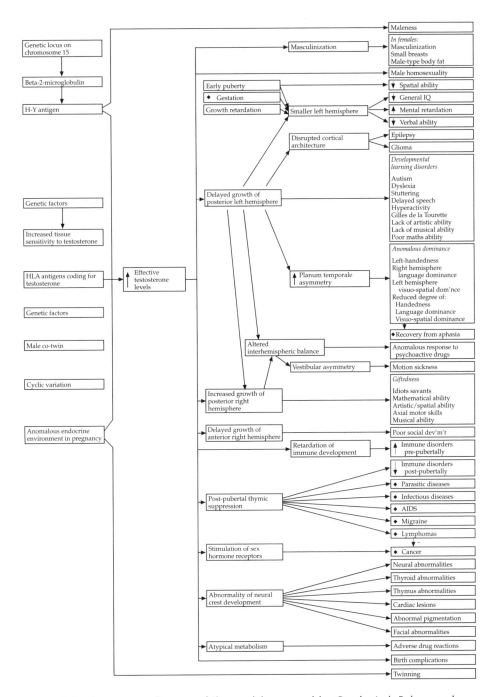

Figure 9.1 A summary diagram of the model proposed by Geschwind, Behan, and Galaburda. Arrows between boxes indicate direct causal link.

are part of the "abnormal dominance" population, and such an over-inclusive category does not seem likely to be clinically useful. Another problem is that the theory does not differentiate between a number of possible outcomes: for example, why does elevated testosterone sometimes lead to autism and sometimes to dyslexia? Despite these problems, recent evidence has led to a resurgence of interest in the more general claims of the GBG model.

In one set of studies, fetal testosterone levels (as measured in amniotic fluid) have been shown to correlate strongly with social-cognitive assessments in toddlers. For example, there is a strong inverse correlation between fetal testosterone and amount of eye contact (a risk factor for autism) at 12 and 24 months, and between the size of vocabulary at 18 and 24 months postnatally (Lutchmaya, Baron-Cohen, & Raggatt, 2002a, 2002b). These studies demonstrate a prospective relationship between fetal testosterone and aspects of typical social-cognitive development.

FURTHER READING: CAMERON, 2001; BERENBAUM ET AL., 2003

The third class of model Hopkins and Rönnqvist (1998) refer to as the "biased head" or uterus models. These models share the assumption that laterality, and possibly also hemispheric specialization, results from a strong tendency for young infants to angle their head to one side. A number of researchers have noted that when lying on their back newborn infants commonly orient their head toward the right side (though a minority orient strongly to the left). This can be demonstrated both in spontaneous behavior and after a period in which the head is held at the midline (e.g. Turkewitz & Kenny, 1982). This head bias may be caused by the most common position in the uterus restricting the extent of possible head and hand movement to one side (Michel, 1981). These restrictions, in turn, are imposed by asymmetries in the shape of the uterus. A consequence of a bias to turn the head to one side when supine are that one hand (most commonly the right) falls into view more frequently, generating a preference for use of that hand for subsequent visually guided reaching. Alternatively, head turning preference and manual handedness may share a common neural basis. While full-term newborns have been shown to have a preference for turning and maintaining the head to the right (Hopkins, Lems, Janssen, & Butterworth, 1987), the findings of a longitudinal study from 12 weeks gestational age to term indicate that a predominant head position to the right was not achieved until 36 to 38 weeks (Verver, de Vries, van Geijn, & Hopkins, 1994). Thus, the attainment of a biased head position is a late-occurring event in human pregnancy, but one that is sustained for some 2 to 3 months after birth (Hopkins et al., 1990).

Whichever of the above models of laterality turns out be most correct, it is clear that by a few months after birth infants start to show behavioral evidence for some hemispheric specialization for cognitive functions. For example, in adults the right hemisphere shows an advantage in certain kinds of face processing tasks. De Schonen and Mathivet (1989) reviewed a number of studies indicating that the right hemisphere (left visual field) has an advantage for the recognition of faces in the human infant by 4 or 5 months of age. One way to interpret these findings is that the right hemisphere has innate representations for face processing. However, de Schonen and colleagues (de Schonen & Mathivet, 1989; de Schonen & Mancini, 1995) believe that this emergent right-hemisphere specialization for face processing is a product of small biases in the detailed architecture of this hemisphere relative to the left, since other (abstract) patterns also differentially engage processing in the two hemipheres. The architectural differences are argued by these authors to arise from slightly different timing of development in the two hemispheres, with the right temporal lobe being a little ahead of its counterpart on the left. This differential timing means that the right temporal lobe processes the low spatial frequency input that carries most of the information about facial identity. Thus, by this view, differential timing of development between the two hemispheres in early infancy may be sufficient to bias each of them to process particular types of inputs.

Similar views have been expressed with regard to hemispheric specialization for language (see chapter 7). For example, Bullock, Liederman, and Todorovic (1987) argued against Witelson's (1987) view that the left hemisphere is innately prespecified to process language, and that the ability of the right hemisphere to support language following early damage to the left is due to specialized trauma-induced plasticity mechanisms. Bullock et al. argued instead that developmental timing differences cause an initial small bias for language to be processed on the left. This initial bias, when combined with dynamic inhibition between the hemispheres, leads to increasing lateralization of cognitive function with development. By this view, the end of the "sensitive period" within which the right hemisphere can compensate for damage to the left is a function of the extent of hemispheric specialization for language that had occurred prior to the damage.

GENERAL SUMMARY AND CONCLUSIONS

It is difficult to directly align the three theories of laterality presented in this chapter with the three perspectives of functional brain development discussed in earlier chapters. However, the dynamic probabilistic epigenesis view of hemispheric specialization of function can also potentially explain data from recovery of function following early unilateral damage. Nevertheless, it has to be acknowledged that one of the major contributions of functional imaging in infants has been to demonstrate a surprising degree of lateralization function within the first few months (see chapter 7). An exciting decade lies ahead in which functional imaging measures of lateralization could be associated with behavioral, hormonal, and genetic information.

INTERACTIVE SPECIALIZATION

In this chapter we return to the three viewpoints on human functional brain development raised in chapter 1. It is suggested that interactive specialization can best account for the majority of data currently available. Interactive specialization provides an account of developmental changes in two of the major issues in cognitive neuroscience: localization (the extent of cortex activated in a given task situation) and specialization (how finely tuned the functionality of a given cortical area is). Mechanisms underlying interactive specialization are reviewed, and some of their functional consequences are explored in more detail. A variety of types of selectionist theories are outlined, but all share the common belief that the loss of synapses and circuits during postnatal development increases the specificity of neural and cognitive functioning. The loss of synaptic contacts and circuits is also invoked in a developmental mechanism called "parcellation." Parcellation is the increasing encapsulation (informational isolation) of neural circuits. This process is argued to have a number of computational consequences such as a reduction in interference, and a reduction in informational exchange, between neural systems.

10.1 THREE VIEWPOINTS ON HUMAN FUNCTIONAL BRAIN DEVELOPMENT

In chapter 1 we discussed three different perspectives on human functional brain development: the maturational view, the skill learning view, and interactive specialization. In later chapters, a number of themes emerged from our review of several domains of cognitive development. From our review of the available evidence on cortical development in chapter 2 we concluded that while large-scale regions of cerebral cortex show graded differential patterns of gene expression, the small-scale functional areas of interest to the cognitive neuroscientist require activity-dependent processes for their specialization. In other words, most of the areal divisions of cortex arise from a combination of intrinsic spatial and timing factors and extrinsic input. However, the laminar structure of the cortex, and the particular connectional and neurochemical properties of the general region, impose architectural constraints on the representations that can emerge within these areas.

In several of the other chapters evidence from human infants and children was consistent with the general viewpoint outlined above. In most of the domains examined there was evidence that cortical representations for cognitive functions emerged postnatally, and partially under the influence of the informational structure of the input in question. In some cases where there was evidence of specific information about the world in the newborn, such as the preferential responses to face patterns (chapter 5), subcortical circuits appeared to play an important contributory role in controlling the behavior. Thus, while the current state of the evidence does not allow definitive conclusions, of the three perspectives on functional brain development discussed in this book, I suggest that the interactive specialization (IS) approach is most consistent with the majority of data available.

Table 10.1 illustrates some of the assumptions that underlie the three approaches outlined earlier. It is a defining feature of the maturational approach that it assumes deterministic epigenesis; region-specific gene expression is assumed to effect changes in intra-regional connectivity that, in turn, allow new functions to

Table 10.1 Three viewpoints on human functional brain development

	Brain-cognitive mapping	Primary locale of changes	Plasticity	Cause
Maturational	One-to-one mapping Static over development	Intra-region connectivity matures	A specialized mechanism invoked by stroke or injury	Brain changes cause cognitive development
Skill learning	Changes during acquisition of skill		Life-long; no clear sensitive period	
Interactive specialization	Networks/neural systems Dynamic changes during development	Inter-regional connectivity changes and shapes intra-regional connectivity	An inherent property – the state of having not yet specialized Sensitive – period determined by state of specialization	Bi-directional relations between structure and function

emerge. A related assumption commonly made within the maturational approach is that there is a one-to-one mapping between brain and cortical regions and particular cognitive functions, such that specific computations come "on-line" following that maturation of circuitry intrinsic to the corresponding cortical region. In some respects, this view parallels "mosaic" development at the cellular level in which simple organisms (such as *C. elegans*) are constructed through cell lineages that are largely independent of each other (Elman et al., 1996). Similarly, different cortical regions are assumed to have different maturational timetables, thus enabling new cognitive functions to emerge at different ages.

In contrast to the maturational approach, IS (Johnson, 2001, 2002) has a number of different underlying assumptions. Specifically, a probabilistic epigenesis assumption is coupled with the view that cognitive functions are the emergent product of interactions between different brain regions. With regard to the latter of these assumptions, IS follows recent trends in adult functional neuroimaging. For example, Friston and Price (2001) point out that it may be an error to assume that particular functions can be localized within a certain cortical region. Rather, they suggest, the response properties of a region are determined by its patterns of connectivity to other regions as well as by their current activity states. By this view, "the cortical infrastructure supporting a single function may involve many specialized areas whose union is mediated by the functional integration among them" (Friston & Price, 2001: 276). Similarly, in discussing the design and interpretation of adult fMRI studies, Carpenter and collaborators have argued that: "In contrast to a localist assumption of a one-to-one mapping between cortical regions and cognitive operations, an alternative view is that cognitive task performance is subserved by large-scale cortical networks that consist of spatially separate computational components, each with its own set of relative specializations, that collaborate extensively to accomplish cognitive functions" (Carpenter et al., 2001: 360). Extending these ideas to development, the IS approach emphasizes changes in *inter-regional* connectivity, as opposed to the maturation of *intra-regional* circuitry. Specifically, inter-regional connectivity influences intra-regional connectivity, including the shaping of smaller-scale areas. While the maturational approach may be analogous to mosaic cellular development, the IS view corresponds to the "regulatory" development seen in higher organisms in which cell–cell interactions are critical in determining developmental fate. While mosaic development can be faster than regulatory, the latter has several advantages. Namely, regulatory development is more flexible and better able to respond to damage, and it is more efficient in terms of genetic coding. In regulatory development genes need only orchestrate cellular-level interactions to yield more complex structures (see Elman et al., 1996).

As well as the mapping between structure and function at one age, we can also consider how this mapping might change during development. When discussing functional imaging of developmental disorders, many researchers have assumed that the relation between brain structure and cognitive function is unchanging during development. Specifically, in accordance with a maturational view, when new structures come on-line, the existing (already mature) regions continue to support the same functions that they did at earlier developmental stages. The "static assumption" is partly why it is acceptable to study developmental disorders in adulthood and then extrapolate back in time to early development. Contrary to this view, the IS viewpoint suggests that when a new computation or skill is acquired, there is a re-organization of interactions between different brain structures and regions (Johnson, 2001). This re-organization process could even change how previously acquired cognitive functions are represented in the brain. Thus, the same behavior could potentially be supported by different neural substrates at different ages during development.

Stating that structure–function relations can change with development is all very well, but it lacks the specificity required to make all but the most general predictions. Fortunately, the view that there is competitive specialization of regions during development gives rise to expectations about the types of changes in structure–function relations that should be observed. Specifically, as regions become increasingly selective in their response properties during infancy, patterns of cortical activation during behavioral tasks may therefore be more extensive than those observed in adults, and involve different patterns of activation.

The basic assumption underlying the skill learning approach is that there is a continuity of the circuitry underlying skill acquisition from birth through to adulthood. This circuit is likely to involve a network of structures that retains the same basic function across developmental time (a static brain-cognition mapping). However, other brain regions may respond to training with dynamic changes in functionality similar or identical to those hypothesized within the IS framework. Another way in which the skill learning view differs from the other perspectives is with regard to the notion of "plasticity."

Plasticity in brain development is a phenomenon that has generated much controversy, with several different conceptions and definitions having been presented (Elbert, Heim, & Rockstroh, 2001; Kolb & Gibb, 2001). The three perspectives we have discussed provide different viewpoints on plasticity. According to the maturational framework, plasticity is a specialized mechanism that is activated following brain injury. According to the IS approach, plasticity is simply the state during which a region's function is not yet fully specialized. That is, there is still remaining scope for developing more finely tuned responses. This definition corresponds well to the view of developmental biologists that development involves the increasing "restriction of fate." Finally, according to the skill learning hypothesis, plasticity is at least the result of specific circuitry that remains in place throughout the life span. This hypothesis, unlike the IS approach, does not claim that plasticity necessarily reduces during development.

10.2 INTERACTIVE SPECIALIZATION (IS)

IS specifically addresses two of the most fundamental issues in cognitive neuroscience: *localization* and *specialization*. In this context, localization refers to the extent to which a given computational function can be associated with a region or area of cortex. Specifically, the extent of cortex activated following the presentation of a given task or perceptual stimulus may change during development. Specialization refers to the degree of specificity of function of a given region or area of cortex. Functions may be finely tuned, such as an area that is activated only by a restricted category of visual objects or under a very narrow range of task circumstances, or broadly tuned, in that they are activated under a wide range of circumstances. According to the IS view, the issues of localization and specialization are two sides of the same coin, and are both consequences of the same common underlying mechanisms. These mechanisms are explored in later sections of this chapter.

To re-cap on the basis of the IS view, it argues that early in postnatal development many areas begin with poorly defined functions, and consequently can be partially activated by a wide variety of sensory inputs and tasks. During development, activity-dependent interactions between regions result in modifications of the intra-regional connectivity such that the activity of a given area becomes restricted to a narrower range of circumstances. As a result of becoming more finely tuned, small-scale functional areas become increasingly distinct from their surrounding cortical tissue, and this will be evident in functional imaging studies as increasing localization of function.

To briefly review some of the evidence consistent with this approach, in the development of face processing (chapter 5) we discussed ERP and behavioral evidence consistent with the idea of increasingly finely tuned cortical processing of faces (also referred to by Nelson [2003, see chapter 5] as "perceptual narrowing"). For example, this narrowing process resulted in better recognition of non-human faces by younger infants (Pascalis et al., 2002). Along with these changes in specialization, fMRI work showed increasingly restricted localization of face processing when children were compared to adults in a face-matching task. Some similar findings were reported for language acquisition in chapter 7. In chapter 3 we discussed evidence that changes in visual orienting abilities as assessed by fMRI revealed multiple sites of change throughout a network of different pathways involved in oculomotor control, and not just the activation of one or two "new" functional areas. This evidence is consistent with adjustments throughout a network of regions as it accommodates to a new function. In atypical development resulting from genetic disorders, structural and functional imaging has usually revealed widespread atypical patterns of activation, and changes in the extent of white matter (connectivity) (Johnson, Halit, Grice, & Karmiloff-Smith, 2002). These latter findings are consistent with processes of interactive specialization that have gone awry, or specialized differently in an attempt to compensate for an earlier deviation or deficit.

In summary, according to the IS view, small-scale areas of cortex become tuned for certain functions as a result of a combination of factors, including (i) the suitability or otherwise of the biases within the large-scale region (e.g. transmitter types and levels, synaptic density, etc.), (ii) the information within the sensory inputs (sometimes partly determined by other brain systems), and (iii) competitive interactions with neighboring regions (so that functions are not duplicated). In the following sections we explore in more detail the neurocomputational mechanisms that may underlie interactive specialization.

 ## 10.3 SELECTIVE PRUNING

In chapter 2 the marked postnatal loss of synaptic contacts within the cerebral cortex was reviewed. This ubiquitous observation has led some authors to specu-late on the functional consequence of this selective loss process (Changeux, Courrege, & Danchin, 1973; Ebbesson, 1980; Gazzaniga, 1983; Changeux, 1985; Edelman, 1987). One of the best known "selectionist" accounts has been provided by Changeux and his collaborators. They argue that connections between classes of cells are prespecified, but are initially labile. Synapses in their labile state may either become stabilized or regress, depending on the total activity of the post-synaptic cell. The activity of the post-synaptic cell is, in turn, dependent upon its input. Initially, this input may be the result of spontaneous activity in the network, but rapidly it is evoked by input to the circuit. The critical concept here is that of *selective stabilization*. In short, Changeux and colleagues propose that "to learn is to eliminate," as opposed to learning taking place by instruction, or new growth.

Changeux and Dehaene (1989) extended and generalized the earlier neuro-computational account of selective loss. Specifically, they argued that there are definable biological levels in the brain (molecular, circuit level, and cognitive), and that selectionist theory can be used to bridge these levels. They then intro-duced a "Darwinian" version of selectionism. By their view, a "Darwinian" change has two stages. The first of these is a constructive process that generates a range of possible options, while the second is a mechanism for selecting among these options. At the neural level, these two stages are implemented as an exuberance of connections specified within a particular genetic envelope, followed by the selec-tion of particular synapses, or groups of synapses, selected either as a result of patterns of spontaneous activity within neural circuitry, and/or as a result of the information structure of sensory input. Changeux and Dehaene (1989) then out-lined how an analogous mechanism might operate at the cognitive level. The initial step, the generation of options, they suggest, is achieved by the presence of "prerepresentations." Prerepresentations are described as transient, dynamic, "privileged" spontaneous activity states in neural circuits. The selection process is achieved by particular prerepresentations from the set available "resonating" with particular sensory inputs. This process probably takes place in seconds or less, whereas a more prolonged time course may be necessary for the process of attrition at the neural level.

Selectionist-type mechanisms of functional brain development vary along a number of dimensions. One of these dimensions is the scale of the unit selected.

For example, Edelman (1987) has proposed a similar selectionist account to that outlined above except that particular "neuronal groups" are the unit of selection rather than single synapses. (Crick, 1989, suggests that such neuronal groups will be composed of around 200–1,000 neurons, or a "mini-column.") Possibly the cognitive level of selection posited by Changeux and Dehaene (1989) could be implemented as the dynamic selection of large-scale neural circuits or pathways according to particular task demands. Most likely, selection occurs at multiple scales and time courses.

Another dimension along which selectionist theories can vary is the extent to which the selective loss is responsive to sensory input, as opposed to being determined by intrinsic factors. In the model of Changeux and colleagues, sensory input or spontaneous activity determines both the pattern and the timing of the loss. Ebbesson (1988) discussed some examples in which both the pattern and timing of connection loss is insensitive to experience, such as when it occurs prenatally. That is, not only is the initial excess of connections genetically specified, but so is the extent and pattern of loss of connectivity. This difference between the Changeux and Ebbesson selection mechanisms is not trivial, and has implications for how plasticity in a developing neural system is terminated. For Changeux the process is self-terminating, with only connections that are actively employed remaining. For Ebbesson, the end of plasticity is more rigidly determined: that is, by a given developmental stage, a certain proportion of connections *must* be lost, regardless of experience. A "hybrid" selectionist account of postnatal neural development which draws on aspects of both the Changeux and Ebbesson accounts has also been advanced (see Johnson & Karmiloff-Smith, 1992). The emphasis in this account is on a distinction between *timing* and *patterning* of loss. The hypothesis put forward was that whilst the timing and extent of loss of connections or neurons may be a product of interactions intrinsic to the organism (innate, by the definition in chapter 1), the specificity or particular pattern of that loss is partly determined by interactions with the extrinsic environment. By this view there can be an intrinsically determined termination of the phase of selective loss, while the pattern of loss within the "sensitive period" may be determined by experience-driven neural activity. These different possibilities will require systematic investigation in real developing nervous systems, and their different effects at the computational level will need to be assessed through neural network modeling.

As discussed in the previous section, a number of modelers have investigated the functional consequences of different variations of link loss (Barto, Sutton, & Anderson, 1983; Kerszberg, Dehaene, & Changeux, 1992; Jacobs, 2002), including the interaction between activity-dependent link loss and overall network decreases in "trophic" factors (Shrager & Johnson, 1995). However, it is important to note that selective loss is only one of several aspects of postnatal neural development (see Purves, 1994), and so a selectionist account alone can never provide a complete account of neurocognitive development.

In an influential article, Quartz and Sejnowski (1997) criticized selectionist theories, and instead proposed that the specificity of neural connections can arise from directed dendritic growth. These authors suggest that by utilizing a constructive process of growth, as opposed to synaptic loss, development has more flexibility. Similar arguments have been made with regard to computational models of cognitive development by Shultz (2003). Quartz and Sejnowski's mechanism for directed dendritic growth involves a variation of Hebbian associative learning in which a small volume of neural tissue attracts dendritic growth by passive diffusion (possibly of nitric oxide) and without synaptic contacts. While this is a plausible computational mechanism for directed dendritic growth, there is, as yet, no compelling neurobiological evidence to support it. In addition, directed dendritic growth should be seen as an additional, rather than an alternative, mechanism for increasing the specificity of neural connections. Specifically, synaptic (connection) loss in brain development is part of a dynamic ongoing process of synaptic turn-over, with new synapses being generated at almost the same rate as they disappear.

FURTHER READING: BOURGEOIS, 2001; GREENOUGH ET AL., 2002

 10.4 PARCELLATION AND EMERGENT MODULARITY

As discussed above, the IS view predicts that cortical areas will gain increasing functional specialization during development. Another facet of this specialization may be that processing in any given area becomes increasingly separated from that of neighboring regions, a process sometimes referred to as "parcellation."

On the basis of evidence from a variety of species and neural systems, Ebbesson (1984) argued that the increasing differentiation of the brain into separate processing streams and structures during both phylogeny and ontogeny occurs as a result of the selective loss of synapses and dendrites. The result of this parcellation process is the creation of informationally encapsulated processing streams and structures. At the cognitive level, such systems may correspond to "modules" in the adult mind/brain (Fodor, 1983). While some authors have viewed parcellation as comparatively insensitive to the effects of experience (Ebbesson, 1984), others have viewed the process as being at least partially experience-dependent (O'Leary, 1989; Killackey, 1990). Johnson and Vecera (1996) hypothesized that certain behavioral and cognitive changes may be directly related to the increasing segregation of streams of information (i.e. parcellation) at the neuronal level. Clearly, neural parcellation occurs at a number of different levels, and both within and between cortical regions. However, Johnson and Vecera argued that in all these cases differentiation by selective loss at the neuronal level gives rise to increasingly modular information processing. (Modular here was used in its most general sense, to refer to information-processing systems that are isolated from others.) Specifically, they argued that evidence is consistent with the following consequences of a developmental increase in the extent of cortical modularization:

- less informational exchange between certain brain systems with development;
- less interference between certain brain systems with development;
- increased specificity in sensory detection.

One example of parcellation is the emergence of ocular dominance columns, discussed in chapter 3. Recall that ocular dominance columns that received inputs exclusively from one eye emerged from a situation in which most layer 4 cells (in the primary visual cortex) received afferents from both eyes. The parcellation process would lead us to expect that the selective loss of afferents will result in components of the network becoming increasingly encapsulated and inaccessible to other parts. Held and his colleagues (see Held, 1993) tested this idea with the experiment described earlier in which they demonstrated that infants under 4 months had a form of integration between the two eyes not observed in older infants. The older infants did not show this integration between the eyes because by this age neurons in cortical layer 4 of primary visual cortex only receive inputs from one eye.

The example of ocular dominance column formation also demonstrates that parcellation (or segregation) at one level of processing can allow for more adaptive or accurate recombination at another level of processing. Thus, while parcellation may result in a loss of a certain level of integration between systems (e.g. binocular summation in the case of ocular dominance columns), it may be followed by the acquisition of a new level of integration (e.g. binocular vision, as in the current example).

A more recent example of increased segregation with development comes from the separation of color- and motion-processing channels in adult primates (Dobkins & Anderson, 2002). Specifically, in adults, brain pathways that encode direction of object motion do not also process color (e.g. Merigan & Maunsell, 1993). This dissociation of processing means that in psychophysical experiments adults are very poor at detecting the direction of motion (as measured by directionally appropriate eye movements) of red- and green-striped color gratings. In contrast, infants of 2, 3, and 4 months were much better at detection than adults, suggesting that color input to motion processing is relatively stronger in the immature visual system. Furthermore, younger infants showed more evidence of this integration than did older ones, demonstrating a dynamic process of increasing segregation of these streams of information (Dobkins & Anderson, 2002).

Another domain in which parcellation processes were described by Johnson and Vecera (1996) was cross-modal integration (see also Maurer, 1993). While the example of ocular dominance columns concerned increasing differentiation *within* a sensory projection, it is possible that a similar process may occur *between* sensory modalities. Many mammals appear to have transient connections between different sensory cortices early in life. For example, Dehay et al. (Dehay, Bullier, &

Kennedy, 1984; Dehay et al., 1988) have reported transient connections between visual, auditory, somatosensory, and motor cortices in the kitten. The loss of the connections through parcellation would presumably result in less cross-talk between sensory modalities at the level of primary sensory representations. Two consequences of increasing parcellation between sensory modalities were discussed by Johnson and Vecera: (i) sensory input should provide a broader pattern of activation across the cortex prior to parcellation, and (ii) there will be more "cross-talk" between sensory modalities prior to parcellation.

With regard to the first of these predictions, Wolff, Matsumiya, Abroms, Van Velzar, and Lombroso (1974) investigated the cortical evoked response of 3- and 4-day-old infants to somatosensory and auditory stimulation. Their evidence suggested that auditory input (white noise) had a modulating effect on the somatosensory evoked responses in these very young infants. However, when a similar experiment was run with adults, no effects of auditory input on somatosensory responses was found. One interpretation of these results is that there is less inter-sensory integration at this level in adults as a result of parcellation between the auditory and somatosensory modalities.

With regard to the second prediction, it should be noted that there are likely to be multiple levels of information exchange between sensory modalities. This fact means that an infant is likely to go through a sequence of developmental stages in which he or she integrates increasingly specific forms of information across the sensory modalities. Considering this, the prediction from parcellation is that infants will go through developmental periods in which they show an apparent loss of inter-sensory integration within a particular cross-modal task. This may then be followed by subsequent re-integration between modalities of a more specific kind, resulting in some cases in an apparent U-shaped pattern of developmental change.

Lewkowicz (1991), when reviewing the development of inter-sensory functions in human infants, argues that there is strong evidence for non-specific cross-modal influences early in life. For example, Lewkowicz and Turkewitz (1981) established that the looking preferences of newborn infants for bright or dim stimuli were affected by prior exposure to auditory stimuli. Infants tested in silence looked longer at intermediate-intensity lights, whereas infants exposed to an auditory tone looked longest at the dimmest light.

Other cross-modal experiments with infants have been concerned with apparently more complex types of stimuli, such as the matching of numerical quantity (Starkey & Cooper, 1980; Starkey, Spelke, & Gelman, 1983, 1990). When infants succeed in these tasks at a young age, the results can be interpreted in one of two ways. One explanation is that infants have "intelligently" matched input in one sensory modality to input in another. The other explanation is that infants are unable to discriminate the sensory modality of the input and merely respond to some non-specific aspect of the stimulus such as intensity or quantity. In the first case the infant is viewed as having separate representations of the visual and auditory input, and then actively extracting the similarity between them. In the second case the representations from the two sensory modalities are blended within the cortex such that infants cannot discriminate between them. Rather, they just perceive a certain stimulus intensity. The parcellation conjecture predicts an initial state in which there are non-specific connections between primary sensory representations. These connections will then be pruned, resulting in the apparent loss of cross-modal influence. Subsequently, more specific cross-modal matching may emerge. This account of the development of cross-modal effects makes the counterintuitive prediction that early cross-modal influences should decline with development, a surprising prediction for which there is in fact some evidence.

Streri (1987) and Streri and Pecheux (1986) investigated whether there is intermodal transfer of shape from touch to vision (and vice versa) in infants from 2 to 5 months old. Infants were familiarized with an object visually or tactually (hand) until they habituated to it. Subsequently, the infant was presented with the same shape in the other modality and the duration of look or grasp was recorded. If the infants were capable of cross-modal habituation, then they should remain habituated to that shape and show little interest in it. Streri found no evidence for cross-modal transfer from touch to vision in 5-month-old infants, but strong evidence for such transfer in 2- and 3-month-olds. Older infants have yet to be tested in this experiment.

Meltzoff and Borton (1979) conducted a cross-modal "matching" experiment with 1-month-old infants. These authors reported cross-modal matching between the infant mouthing nubby or smooth pacifiers for 90 seconds and whether they subsequently looked more toward a picture of a nubby or smooth pacifier when presented side by side. Maurer and Stager (reported in Maurer 1993) also found an effect with 1-month-old infants, but failed to find any effects in a group of 3-month-olds in the same experiment. This pattern of loss is consistent with the increasing parcellation of cortical sensory inputs.

Johnson and Vecera (1996) also speculated that since developmental atypicalities may have failed or deviant patterns of parcellation in the cortex, they may also have symptoms of inappropriate cross-modal integration. They then note reports of synaesthesia, or multi-channel sensory experiences, in adults with autism (Cesaroni & Garber, 1991). Another area in which parcellation processes may be speculatively applied is in particular aspects of language acquisition. Johnson and Karmiloff-Smith (1992) discuss some examples on language acquisition from Karmiloff-Smith's earlier work, in which some components of the language system appear to become modularized as a result of development, in the sense that other information-processing streams no longer have access to its contents. One example of this occurs in a study of awareness of linguistic repairs within a narrative. Younger participants (11-year-olds) were able to detect one type of linguistic repair, "discourse cohesion" repairs, more frequently than were adults. Discourse cohesion repairs involved either a change from noun-phrase to pronoun (e.g. then the girl/then she), or a change from pronoun to noun-phrase (e.g. he's got/the man's got), depending on whether the expression referred to the main or to the subsidiary character in the story, according to the "thematic participant constraint" (Karmiloff-Smith, 1985). The results showed that whilst participants of all ages were successful in detecting all categories of repair and could easily furnish explanations of lexical and referential repairs, they were remarkably poor at providing metalinguistic explanations of discourse cohesion repairs. Although there was some increase in correct responses between 7 and 11 years, this was followed by a decline by adulthood. Karmiloff-Smith and colleagues suggest that discourse cohesion rules can be accessed at some points in development, whereas in adulthood that access is lost. The discourse cohesion system becomes progressively more modular and cognitively impenetrable and begins to operate automatically (thereby allowing for focus on propositional content) (Karmiloff-Smith, 1985).

While I believe that the association between neural parcellation and increasing cognitive encapsulation may be a fruitful one for further research, there are a number of limitations and complicating factors that must be acknowledged. The first of these is that refinement of neural connections also occurs at subcortical levels in structures such as the superior colliculus (Stein, 1984) and the hippocampus (Duffy & Rakic, 1983). While parcellation at the subcortical level could also have behavioral consequences, much of the parcellation in these structures appears to occur prenatally. The second caveat is that some aspects of behavioral development that Johnson and Vecera (1996) attributed to cortical-level parcellation could also be attributed to a shift from subcortical to cortical processing. For example, in the cross-modal integration studies, it is known that the superior colliculus contains many multisensory neurons and plays an important role in attending to and orienting toward such stimuli (e.g. Stein, 1984). Whether the superior colliculus could support the cross-modal abilities observed in human infants is not known, but this is certainly a possibility that cannot be excluded. Third, the most compelling evidence for cognitive encapsulation comes from apparent decrements in performance during development. Arguably, however, development would not involve these processes unless they led to some eventual computational benefit to the organism. Presumably, a partially modular brain is more efficient in generating behavior in some respects. Finally, the increasing encapsulation of neural systems within a brain could also involve the strengthening of connections within a system, possibly by dendritic growth mechanisms similar to that outlined by Quartz and Sejnowski (1997).

10.5 MODELING INTERACTIVE SPECIALIZATION

The mechanisms underlying interactive specialization can also be investigated through computational neural network modeling. For example, several groups have used simple "cortical matrix" models to investigate the factors and mechanisms responsible for cortical specialization (e.g. Kerszberg et al., 1992; Shrager & Johnson,

1995; Oliver, Johnson, Karmiloff-Smith, & Pennington, 2000). In these artificial neural networks connections between nodes are pruned according to variations of Hebbian learning: links between nodes that are often active together are strengthened, whereas links between nodes that are not often co-active get weaker and are pruned. In some of these models, the degree of pruning of connections during learning approximately matches that seen during the course of human brain development. During exposure to patterned input (roughly equivalent to sensory stimulation), nodes become more selective in their response properties, and under certain conditions clusters of nodes with similar response properties emerge. Thus, in these computational models selective pruning plays a role in the emergence of clusters of nodes (localization) that share common specific response properties (specialization) (see figure 10.1).

Another aspect of interactive specialization that may be important for development concerns the role of top-down feedback on earlier stages of sensory processing. In much the same way as we hypothesized that lateral inter-regional interactions help shape the intrinsic connectivity of areas to result in functional specialization, interactions between regions connected by feedback and feedforward connections may also help shape the specialization of the areas involved. Top-down effects play an important role in sensory information processing in the adult brain (e.g. Siegel, Körding, & König, 2000). For example, during perception, information propagates through the visual processing hierarchy from primary sensory areas to higher cortical regions, while feedback connections convey information in the reverse direction. In a neurocomputational model of feedback in visual processing in the adult brain, Spratling and Johnson (2004) demonstrated that a number of different phenomena associated with visual attention, figure/ground segmentation, and contextual cueing could all be accounted for by a common mechanism underlying cortical feedback. Extending these ideas to development, there are potentially two important implications of feedback that will benefit from future exploration. The first of these will be to examine how the specialization of early sensory areas is shaped by top-down feedback, and vice versa, during development. The second topic for investigation will be to examine the consequences of relatively poor or diffuse cortical feedback in the immature cortex. For example, possibly some of the failures in object processing in infants can be explained by a lack of adequate top-down feedback.

10.6 GENERAL SUMMARY AND CONCLUSIONS

In this chapter we focused on the interactive specialization view of human functional brain development. Interactive specialization provides an account of developmental changes in two of the major issues in cognitive neuroscience: localization (the extent of cortex activated in a given task situation) and specialization (how finely tuned the functionality of a given cortical area is). Mechanisms of selective

(a) Condition A   Time=0   (b) Condition B

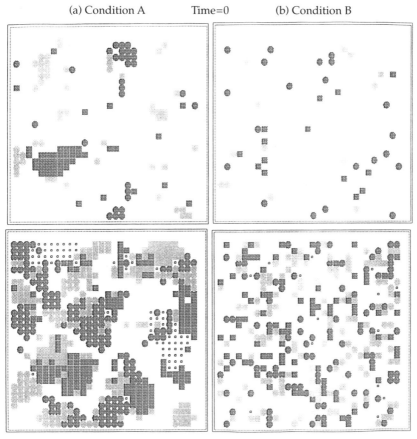

Time=1344

Figure 10.1 The formation of representations in the cortical matrix model under two different architectural conditions. The left upper panel shows the starting state and the left lower the final state. In the final state, "structured" representations emerge in which stimuli that have features in common tend to be clustered together (spatially aligned). With just a minor change in the architecture of the network (changing the relevant average lengths of intrinsic excitatory and inhibitory links: the right-hand side), nodes in the network fail to form structured clustered representations.

pruning underlying interactive specialization were reviewed, and some of their functional consequences were explored in more detail. The loss of synaptic contacts and circuits was also invoked in parcellation (the increasing encapsulation of neural circuits). This process was argued to have a number of computational consequences, such as a reduction in interference, and a reduction in informational exchange, between neural systems. Finally, some preliminary attempts to build computational models of interactive specialization were mentioned.

11 TOWARD AN INTEGRATED DEVELOPMENTAL COGNITIVE NEUROSCIENCE

This final chapter attempts to tie together some themes of the book, and points out some future directions. The first issue discussed is the value of the molecular genetic analysis of cognitive development. While this approach is likely to prove powerful over the next decade, some reasons for caution about the interpretation of findings are outlined. It is suggested that the role of genes in functional development can only be interpreted from within a developmental cognitive neuroscience approach. Next, I expound the value of a level of neural network modeling that can make contact with both neural and cognitive data. I suggest that this approach can also be extended to developmental disorders, and to assessing the effects of developmental changes in levels of neuromodulators. Finally, I stress the need for applying multiple methods to cognitive transitions, and for training a future generation of developmental cognitive neuroscientists.

11.1 INTRODUCTION

The earlier chapters of this book have introduced the reader to the newly emerging field of developmental cognitive neuroscience (or at least one person's perspective on it). No doubt it is evident that there is a long way to go before it becomes a cohesive and well-integrated field of inquiry. However, the extent to which previously disparate fragments of information are coming together encourages optimism for the future. In this final chapter some conclusions and recommendations are presented which may facilitate further progress in the field.

11.2 GENES AND COGNITIVE DEVELOPMENT

The first issue concerns the relation between genes and cognition. Molecular biological techniques are unquestionably going to have a major impact on our understanding of genetic contributions to cognitive change. However, it is important to bear in mind that genes do not "code for" functional components of cognition in any direct sense. We are never likely to discover a "gene for language" for the same reason as there is not a gene for the big toe. Both language and big toes are the result of complex interactions between many genes, their products, and multiple levels of environments. Similarly, with regard to brain structure it is likely that most relevant genes have widespread effects throughout several or all brain regions, and commonly other organs (such as the heart). As attractive as the notion may seem at first sight, patterns of gene expression do not neatly localize to small-scale areas of cerebral cortex. Since brain structure is not directly "coded for" in genes, but rather is the product of complex self-organizing interactive processes, providing causal accounts of cognitive change purely in terms of gene action is certain to be inadequate. Rather, expression of particular genes will have to be located within a developmental cognitive neuroscience framework that includes some account of the interactions at molecular, cellular, and organism–environment levels. Ultimately, development is the path from genotype to phenotype, and no cognitive "function" for a gene can be attributed without some account of this mapping. In other words, attempting to "explain" a cognitive developmental change purely in terms of gene expression will miss out much that should be of core interest to the developmental cognitive neuroscientist.

Despite the above caveats, it is clear that understanding the roles of genes in human brain function is one of the major challenges for developmental cognitive neuroscience (see Pennington, 2001, 2002). Broadly speaking, there are two strategies that are being taken to understand this mapping. The first of these is to begin with identified genes (or genetic defects that involve single genes) and to try to assess the cognitive and behavioral concomitants. Examples of this approach include the developmental disorders Fragile-X and PKU, and the use of "knockout" rodent models (see Tager-Flusberg, 2003). The alternative strategy is to study the genetic basis of syndromes with uneven cognitive profiles. Examples of this approach include the search for a genetic basis for autism and dyslexia. While these approaches have been successful in some cases, it may be that a closer two-way interaction between geneticists and psychologists that focuses on cases at the fringes of a disorder group will be most successful. For example, Williams syndrome (WS) results from a microdeletion (on the long arm of chromosome 7) that typically involves at least 19 genes. People with this microdeletion normally show the full Williams syndrome physical and cognitive phenotype, including relative strengths in the domains of language and face recognition and extreme impairments in visuo-spatial construction and number (see appendix; Tager-Flusberg,

2003). A recent thrust in WS research has been the investigation of cases in which not all of the 19 genes are deleted: partial deletions. Some of these cases have the full WS phenotype, some show only some of the atypicalities, and others show none. By studying the cognitive abilities of such cases in detail, a closer under-standing can be reached of the combinations of genes that contribute to a behavioral phenotype (Karmiloff-Smith et al., 2003).

FURTHER READING: PENNINGTON, 2001, 2002; KARMILOFF-SMITH, 2002; TAGER-FLUSBERG, 2003

Another direction for the future of gene–behavior mapping is to consider special cases that reduce the length of the complex explanatory pathway between the two. One way to do this is to consider potential mappings between genes and brain function, since this avoids the further complicating factor of how brain function relates to cognition and behavior. In this respect it seems worthwhile to investigate correlations between gene measures and activations revealed by func-tional neuroimaging (Fan, Fossella, Sommer, Wu, & Posner, 2003). Further, study-ing the effects of neurotransmitters will be beneficial since these are closer to gene products than are neuronal structures.

Ironically, it is the genes that play a role in synaptic plasticity and transmission that perhaps offer the best hope for our understanding of their computational consequences. In these cases we can study changes due to gene expression that take place sometimes even in the adult animal. The action of specific genes on the formation of representations could be monitored by regulation of synaptic density and activity through neuromodulators. Another fruitful area for further investiga-tion is the expression of genes involved in synaptic plasticity, so-called "immediate early" genes. This special class of genes is involved in rapid plastic changes in cortex and other regions, and are probably also involved in developmental plasticity. It may be, therefore, that there are a limited number of genes which are critical for maintaining or terminating plasticity in neural circuits. In addition to molecular biological studies of these types of genes, one approach to understand-ing the contribution of the expression of the genes may be in detailed cellular neural network modeling in which the effects of gene expression can be simu-lated, and then compared to real neurobiological systems.

A related side-issue is that it is not sufficient for understanding the role of a gene(s) in a developmental sequence to demonstrate that knocking out the gene in question eliminates a particular behavior in later life. In these experimental cases, and in human developmental disorders with an identifiable genetic atypicality, we may say that the gene defect *causes* the behavioral deficit. However, this does not allow the inference that the gene codes for the aspect of behavior which is disrupted, or that this aspect of behavior is the "function" of the gene, for the reasons discussed above.

11.3 RELATIONS BETWEEN BRAIN STRUCTURE AND FUNCTION IN DEVELOPMENT

Another issue that surfaced in several of the preceding chapters was the apparent discrepancy between structural and functional development. For example, with regard to the prefrontal cortex, there is evidence of neuroanatomical changes occurring until the teenage years, yet infants as young as 6 months appear to pass some behavioral marker tasks of prefrontal cortex functioning and show activation in functional imaging experiments. These findings are, however, only a problem for a causal epigenesis (maturational) view (chapter 1) in which cause operates in a single direction from brain development to cognitive change. The data can be resolved by taking a probablistic epigenesis view, in which there are two-way interactions between brain and cognitive development. In fact, there are several ways that they can be reconciled. One way is to invoke the graded development of representations in which input helps to tune the fine structure of a network over time (chapter 10). Another is the view advanced by Thatcher (1992) and others that there are dynamic changes in the connectivity between cortical regions which lead to a re-organization of representations at several points in development. Finally, the interactive specialization view predicts that detailed structural changes in postnatal development will be a consequence of increasing functional specialization.

Throughout this book I have made use of comparisons to connectionist-style neural network models (see also Elman et al., 1996). The use of these models does not necessarily commit one to an empiricist (behaviorist) viewpoint on development, as some critics have suggested. Rather, as we have seen in this book, these models are excellent research tools for exploring interactions between intrinsic and extrinsic information during the emergence of representations, and interpreting the functional consequence of partial or weak representations. When information about brain structure is added to the network architecture, neural network models can potentially provide a theoretical bridge between neurobiology and cognitive psychology.

Combining these two applications of connectionist modeling, we can devise models in which aspects of postnatal developmental neuroanatomy can be simulated, such as the selective loss of synapses, and the interacting effects of different variables studied. In my opinion, for such models to be useful they need to be pitched at an appropriately abstract level to make contact with both neural and cognitive data. Such models are only just beginning to be developed. Similarly, some network models of neural development are pitched at a detailed cellular level and thus do not allow any inferences about cognitive representations. In order to study the possible functional consequence of developments in neural structure, we need models that make contact with both sets of data. Other types of non-linear models, such as those derived from dynamic systems theory (Thelen & Smith, 1994), may be useful in certain contexts, such as motor development.

However, while these models tend to give good descriptions of the shape of development change in a given task or behavior, they do not address the fundamental (in my view) issue of representational transformation (see Karmiloff-Smith & Johnson, 1994). Consequently, they may as yet be of limited utility for studying some types of cognitive transitions during development (see Developmental Science, 2003).

One of the general assumptions that pervades this book is that an understanding of cognitive change during ontogeny will be best achieved at a neurocomputational level. Looking for mechanisms of cognitive change at this level does not imply a maturationist, empiricist, or reductionist viewpoint. It does, however, require a belief that a level of explanation closer to neural mechanisms will bring benefits. While this belief remains largely untested, it is no less plausible than the widely held assumption that cognitive models, unconstrained by neural evidence, can provide the best explanation of behavioral change.

11.4 NEUROCONSTRUCTIVISM

In the previous chapter I suggested that the interactive specialization (IS) approach to human functional brain development is likely to be more productive than the maturational or skill learning views. IS is a specific example of a broader approach to brain and cognitive development sometimes called neuroconstructivism (Mareschal et al., in press). Neuroconstructivism differs in several ways from more traditional unidisciplinary approaches to behavioral and cognitive development. One difference is that the organism's interaction with its current external environment is taken into account. Taking this more "ethological" view of cognitive development changes the types of representations we consider in our models of cognitive development in two ways. First, it inclines the researcher to consider the entire neurocognitive path from input to output. This is done because the nature of the input representations, and the nature of the representations necessary for certain outputs, severely restrict the possible intermediate representations. In other words, there is a need for models that, while less detailed, attempt to capture the functioning of several brain systems within a given domain. The second, and related, difference in an ethological approach is that taking into account the structure of the external environment in which the organism develops means that the information contained in mental representations can be relatively impoverished, but still be adaptive. In other words, the representation need only be as detailed as that which is sufficient for adaptive behavior in a given context. For example, in chapter 5 I reviewed the hypothesis that the face representation possessed by newborn infants is merely a primitive "sketch" of the face (something like three blobs corresponding to the eyes and mouth) (Johnson & Morton, 1991). This somewhat impoverished representation is sufficient for adaptive behavior, however, given that faces engage this representation, and that the early environment of the infant is guaranteed to have faces present. Few naturally occurring stimuli (other than those generated by developmental psychologists for experiments!) are likely to engage the same representation.

Neuroconstructivism also has implications for developmental disorders. The developmental disorders discussed in this book are those in which the most research has been done in attempting to link cognitive and neural deficits (see appendix). However, even in these cases the mapping from neural to cognitive remains far from clear. In some cases multiple brain regions have been implicated despite apparently focal cognitive deficits. In my opinion, a number of factors contribute to the complexity of this mapping:

- If a region that develops relatively early in the course of brain development is atypical, then this is likely to have knock-on consequences for later developing regions. For example, if the projections from the thalamus to the cortex are atypical, then the subsequent parcellation of the cortex into areas will be disturbed. Further, it is likely that cognitive deficits result from a combination of primary and secondary neural atypicalities. Indeed, it is possible that the primary cognitive deficits arise from secondary neural effects.
- It is likely that the most devastating forms of brain injury in development are those that affect a major brain system, rather than, for example, a particular cortical area. In most cases of genetic atypicality, or insult early in gestation, the neural consequences are likely to be widespread. Thus they are more likely to disturb whole brain systems than are focal lesions acquired in later life. Focal lesions commonly result in compensation at neural and cognitive levels in primate infants.
- It is possible that a number of different types of developmental brain damage can result in the same cognitive profiles. This could be because the same brain system is ultimately affected, and/or because the self-organizing and adaptive nature of brain development channels deviant developmental trajectories to one of a small number of adaptive outcomes. This consideration highlights the importance of taking an "emergent" as opposed to a "static" approach to developmental disorders (see chapter 1). Developmental disorders are unlikely to yield to the same types of neuropsychological analysis as applied to adults with acquired brain damage (Karmiloff-Smith, 1998).

Given that conventional "static" neuropsychological analysis can only provide, at best, a preliminary analysis of the neural basis of developmental disorders, what could the constructivist approach provide? At present there are still few attempts at computational modeling of developmental trajectories (but see Thomas & Karmiloff-Smith, 2003). As a preliminary attempt to study the ways in which the "normal" formation of structured representations in the cortex can go wrong, Oliver et al. (2000) developed simulations with a simple cortical matrix model (see chapter 10) in which one or other of the parameters known to be important was deliberately changed. The results of one such simulation are illustrated in figure 10.1. In this case, when we manipulated an aspect of the intrinsic structure of the network, the relative length of excitatory and inhibitory links, we totally disrupted the formation of structured representations. In other simulations, representations can emerge, but distorted in different ways relative to the "normal" case. By developing a taxonomy of the ways that structured representations can go awry, we hope to be able to shed light on some developmental disorders.

Within the same general constructivist viewpoint we can also consider developmental disorders in terms of Waddington's intuitive conceptualization of developmental trajectories in the form of an epigenetic landscape (see chapter 1; figure 1.3). In the epigenetic landscape, a perturbation to the trajectory early in development (possibly corresponding to prenatal) will lead to an entirely different pathway (valley) being taken. However, a variety of different sources of perturbation could lead to the same alternative path being taken, and therefore the same behavioral phenotype could result. This corresponds to the fact that there are probably several sources of perturbation that can result in autistic symptoms, for example. Waddington's analysis would, however, predict that these perturbations occur around the same developmental stage. Perturbations to development that occur later in development when the organism is in a chreod (possibly corresponding to perinatal or early postnatal) are compensated for by self-regulatory (adaptive) processes which ensure that the same behavioral phenotype results. I suggest that this corresponds to the effects of perinatal and early postnatal acquired cortical damage. As we have seen, if perinatal damage is limited to regions of the cortex, there is often a degree of functional compensation not seen in adults and older children. For example, lesions to the left temporal lobe early in life do not have a devastating effect on language acquisition (chapter 7). The effects are subtle and affect other domains of cognition also. Thus, in these cases the injured brain adapts to preserve the patterns of specialization which results from normal development. Obviously, major perturbations, such as the loss of most of the cortex, or prolonged rearing in darkness or social isolation, are likely to push the child into a different phenotype.

11.5 CONCLUDING REMARKS

The past decade has seen developmental cognitive neuroscience grow from newborn to toddler. The next steps will be dependent on successful collaboration between developmental neuroscientists, cognitive developmentalists, and computational modelers. New methods and new theoretical approaches will be equally important. In the longer term we will depend on the next generation, who will need some familiarity with all of these fields, and will become developmental cognitive neuroscientists.

APPENDIX
ATYPICALLY DEVELOPING BRAINS

While this book has focused primarily on the typical trajectory of development of the human brain, we have alluded to a number of different developmental disorders. Most of these disorders are assumed to begin with a genetic deviation of some kind. Genetic deviations can involve mutations of single genes (such as Fragile-X and phenylketonuria), atypicalities in chromosomal structure (such as Down's syndrome), and microdeletions that involve several genes from one part of a chromosome (such as Prader–Willi and Williams syndrome). There are also several developmental disorders that are believed to have complex genetic bases that have not yet yielded to molecular analysis (e.g. autism, ADHD).

When considering the brain consequences of these disorders, there are at least four levels at which they can be described: (1) gross brain anatomy, (2) individual "deficit" areas, (3) functional neural systems and pathways, and (4) neurochemistry and microcircuitry. As described in this book and elsewhere (Johnson et al., 2002), the initial search for discrete localized cortical or subcortical "lesions" resulting from genetic disorders has largely proved fruitless. Rather, genetic disorder results in an atypically developing brain often with widespread unusual features in gross, systems level, and detailed neuroanatomy. To take the case of autism, Rumsey and Ernst (2000) summarize their review of functional imaging of autistic disorders as "studies of brain metabolism and blood flow thus far have yet to yield consistent findings, but suggest considerable variability in regional patterns of cerebral synaptic activity" (p. 171). Other authors reviewing work on autism concur with this conclusion. Deb and Thompson (1998) state that "Various abnormalities of brain structure and function have been proposed, but no focal defect has been reliably demonstrated" (p. 299), and Chugani (2000) concludes that "data from the various imaging modalities have not yet converged to provide a unifying hypothesis of brain mechanisms" (p. 183) with a range of cortical (frontal, medial prefrontal, temporal, anterior cingulate) and subcortical (basal ganglia, thalamus, cerebellum) structures implicated in different studies. According to Filipek (1999), a similar situation obtains with respect to attention deficit/hyperactivity disorder.

She concludes that neuroimaging studies "have, in fact, confirmed the lack of consistent gross neuroanatomical lesions or other abnormalities in Attention Deficit Disorder" (Filipek, 1999, p. 117). For ADHD, there are atypicalities in widespread cortical areas including, at a minimum, the frontostriatal, cingulate, and parietal regions. In sum, for at least these two disorders there is little support for the notion that discrete lesions to functional cortical areas can be observed in developmental disorders.

Another important point to note is that the majority of brain atypicalities associated with developmental disorders are *not* specific to one disorder. For example, an atypical cerebellum has been reported for autism, Fragile-X, Williams syndrome, and dyslexia. In my view, these atypicalities that are shared across several developmental disorders are no less interesting, but they do raise the importance of studying general profiles of differences across several brain regions and disorders, rather than focusing heavily on specific phenomena within individual areas or regions in a single developmental disorder. In general, claims about specific neural deficits underlying a developmental disorder need to be treated with caution until other brain areas, and other developmental disorders, are examined in equal depth.

With regard to gross measures of brain structure, overall brain volume can be reduced (microcephaly) or increased (macrocephaly) relative to typical development. Differences in overall volume can be due to changes in the gray (neurons and their local connectivity) or white (fiber bundles and long-range connectivity) matter. An interesting consequence of several major developmental disorders is that microcephaly or macrocephaly are principally due to deviations in the extent of white matter. For example, a consistent finding from structural imaging of autism is larger cerebral volumes (see Filipek, 1999, for review), particularly in temporal, parietal, and occipital regions. Interestingly, however, this increased volume is due to white matter rather than gray matter (Filipek, Kennedy, & Caviness, 1992). In other words, the fiber bundles connecting regions and mediating inter-regional interaction were affected more than the regions themselves. Preliminary MRI studies of Williams syndrome have shown that, unlike autism, overall brain and cerebral volume is smaller than age-matched controls (Reiss et al., 2000). Assessment of tissue composition indicates that, compared to controls, individuals with WS have relative preservation of cerebral gray matter volume and disproportionate reduction in cerebral white matter volume. This pattern is restricted to the cerebral hemispheres, and is not found in the cerebellum (Galaburda & Bellugi, 2000; Reiss et al., 2000). Thus, in at least two major developmental disorders of genetic origin, differences in overall cerebral volume appear to be related to the extent of connectivity (white matter) between regions (gray matter).

The most common type of brain account of developmental disorders focuses on neural systems or pathways that are hypothesized to be impaired or malfunctioning, despite intact and typical circuitry elsewhere in the brain. For such accounts to be credible, they need to demonstrate typical functioning in systems or tasks that are hypothesized not to be affected. Examples of such accounts can be found in the further reading below, and in earlier chapters of this book.

The most detailed level of neuroanatomy considered to account for developmental disorders concerns microcircuitry, dendrites, and synapses. Proponents of the neuro-constructivist approach to developmental disorders have argued that changes at this level, perhaps induced by small differences in neurochemistry, may be associated with developmental disorders (Oliver et al., 2000; Johnson et al., 2002). For example, in cortical matrix models, a lack of pruning of synapses was characteristic of a number of deviant developmental trajectories (Oliver et al., 2000; see also chapter 10).

Further reading on developmental disorders

Skuse, D. (2003). *Child Psychology and Psychiatry: An Introduction*. Abingdon: The Medicine Publishing Company.

Spreen, O., Risser, A., & Edgell, D. (1995). *Developmental Neuropsychology*. Oxford University Press.

Tager-Flusberg, H. (Ed.). (1999). *Neurodevelopmental Disorders*. Cambridge, MA: MIT Press.

Wenar, C., & Kerig, P. (2000). *Developmental Psychopathology* (4th ed.). New York: McGraw-Hill.

Disorder	Genetic basis	Brain atypicality	Behavioral phenotype
Phenylketonuria	Single gene (mutated PAH)	Low dopamine levels in prefrontal cortex	Deficits in executive function, working memory
Fragile-X	Single gene (silenced FMRI gene)	Relative decrease in volume of cerebellum; atypical dendritic spine morphology through neocortex	Retardation, hyperactivity, attention problems, autistic symptoms
Down's syndrome	Chromosomal (extra chromosome 21 or mosaic)	Microcephaly	General retardation, but relative strengths in visuo-spatial cognition and weak verbal and spatial abilities
Turner syndrome	Chromosomal (absence of X in females)		Deficits in motor skills, low non-verbal IQ, social problems
Prader–Willi syndrome	Microdeletion/duplication (SNRPN, NDN)	Hypothalamus	Moderate retardation, but sociable; deficits in motor skills
Williams syndrome	Microdeletion (chromosome 7, 24–30 genes)	Microcephaly but with increased proportional volume of cerebellum; cerebellar abnormalities	Relatively poor at spatial and number tasks, and proficient face processing and language
Autism	Polygenic (unknown)	Macrocephaly	Impaired social function, impaired language, restricted repertoire of interests
Dyslexia/SLI	Polygenic (unknown)	Widespread increased cerebral white matter volume in SLI	Deficits in language and/or reading
ADHD	Polygenic (unknown)	Atypical functioning of frontostriatal and limbic circuitry	Deficits in attention; particularly response inhibition and delay avoidance

A thumbnail sketch of some of the major developmental disorders. For the sake of comparison, the table focuses on contrastive aspects of different disorders. For more detailed accounts of some of these individual disorders see main text, or the sources listed in the further reading.

REFERENCES

Acerra, F., Burnod, Y., & de Schonen, S. (2002). Modelling aspects of face processing in early infancy. *Developmental Science, 5*(1), 98–117.

Adolphs, R. (2002). Recognizing emotion from facial expressions: Psychological and neurological mechanisms. *Behavioral and Cognitive Neuroscience Reviews, 1*(1), 21–62.

Adolphs, R. (2003). Cognitive neuroscience of human social behaviour. *Nature Reviews Neuroscience, 4*(3), 165–178.

Akhtar, N., & Enns, J. T. (1989). Relations between covert orienting and filtering in the development of visual attention. *Journal of Experimental Child Psychology, 48*(2), 315–334.

Akshoomoff, N.-A., & Courchesne, E. (1994). ERP evidence for a shifting attention deficit in patients with damage to the cerebellum. *Journal of Cognitive Neuroscience, 6*(4), 388–399.

Alexander, G. E., DeLong, M. R., & Strick, P. L. (1986). Parallel organization of functionally segregated circuits linking basal ganglia and cortex. *Annual Review of Neuroscience, 9*, 357–382.

Andersen, R. A., Batista, A. P., Snyder, L. H., Buneo, C. A., & Cohen, Y. E. (2000). Programming to look and reach in the posterior parietal cortex. In M. S. Gazzaniga (Ed.), *The New Cognitive Neurosciences* (2nd ed., pp. 515–524). Cambridge, MA: MIT Press.

Andersen, R. A., & Zipser, D. (1988). The role of the posterior parietal cortex in coordinate transformations for visual-motor integration. *Canadian Journal of Physiology & Pharmacology, 66*, 488–501.

Annett, M. (1985). *Left, right, hand and brain: The right shift theory.* Hillsdale, NJ: Erlbaum.

Ansari, D., & Karmilof-Smith, A. (2002). Atypical trajectories of number development. *Trends in Cognitive Sciences, 6*(12), 511–516.

Aslin, R. N. (1981). Development of smooth pursuit in human infants. In D. F. Fisher, R. A. Monty, & J. W. Senders (Eds.), *Eye movements: Cognition and visual perception* (pp. 31–51). Hillsdale, NJ: Erlbaum.

Aslin, R. N., & Hunt, R. H. (2001). Development, plasticity and learning in the auditory system. In C. A. Nelson & M. Luciana (Eds.), *The Handbook of Developmental Cognitive Neuroscience* (pp. 205–220). Cambridge, MA: MIT Press.

Atkinson, J. (1984). Human visual development over the first six months of life: A review and a hypothesis. *Human Neurobiology, 3,* 61–74.

Atkinson, J. (1998). The "where and what" or "who and how" of visual development. In F. Simion & G. Butterworth (Eds.), *The Development of Sensory, Motor and Cognitive Capacities in Early Infancy: From Perception to Cognition* (pp. 3–20). Hove: Psychology Press.

Atkinson, J., & Braddick, O. (2003). Neurobiological models of normal and abnormal visual development. In M. de Haan & M. H. Johnson (Eds.), *The Cognitive Neuroscience of Development* (pp. 43–71). Hove: Psychology Press.

Bachevalier, J. (2001). Neural bases of memory development: Insights from neuropsychological studies in primates. In C. A. Nelson & M. Luciana (Eds.), *The Handbook of Developmental Cognitive Neuroscience* (pp. 365–380). Cambridge, MA: MIT Press.

Bachevalier, J., Brickson, M., & Hagger, C. (1993). Limbic-dependent recognition memory in monkeys develops early in infancy. *Neuroreport, 4,* 77–80.

Bachevalier, J., & Mishkin, M. (1984). An early and a late developing system for learning and retention in infant monkeys. *Behavioral Neuroscience, 98,* 770–778.

Baillargeon, R. (1993). The object concept revisited: New directions in the investigation of infants' physical knowledge. In C. E. Granrud (Ed.), *Visual Perception and Cognition in Infancy* (pp. 265–315). Hillsdale, NJ: Lawrence Erlbaum.

Baird, A. A., Kagan, J., Gaudette, T., Walz, K. A., Hershlag, N., & Boas, D. A. (2002). Frontal lobe activation during object permanence: Data from near-infrared spectroscopy. *NeuroImage, 16,* 1120–1126.

Balaban, C. D., & Weinstein, J. M. (1985). The human pre-saccadic spike potential: Influences of a visual target, saccade direction, electrode laterality and instruction to perform saccades. *Brain Research, 347,* 49–57.

Banks, M. S., & Shannon, E. (1993). Spatial and chromatic visual efficiency in human neonates. In C. E. Granrud (Ed.), *Visual Perception and Cognition in Infancy* (pp. 1–46). Hillsdale, NJ: Lawrence Erlbaum.

Baron-Cohen, S. (1995). *Mindblindness: An Essay on Autism and Theory of Mind.* Cambridge, MA: MIT Press.

Baron-Cohen, S., Leslie, A. M., & Frith, U. (1985). Does the autistic child have a "theory of mind"? *Cognition, 21,* 37–46.

Baron-Cohen, S., Leslie, A. M., & Frith, U. (1986). Mechanical, behavioural and intentional understanding of picture stories in autistic children. *British Journal of Developmental Psychology, 4,* 113–125.

Barth, H., Kanwisher, N., & Spelke, E. (2003). The construction of large number representations in adults. *Cognition, 86*(3), 201–221.

Barto, A. G., Sutton, R. S., & Anderson, C. W. (1983). Neuronlike adaptive elements that can solve difficult learning control problems. *Institute of Electrical Engineers Transactions on System, Man and Cybernetics, 15,* 835–846.

Bates, E. A., & Elman, J. L. (2002). Connectionism and the study of change. In M. H. Johnson, Y. Munakata, & R. Gilmore (Eds.), *Brain Development and Cognition: A Reader* (2nd ed., pp. 420–440). Oxford: Blackwell.

Bates, E. A., & Roe, K. (2001). Language development in children with unilateral brain injury. In C. A. Nelson & M. Luciana (Eds.), *The Handbook of Developmental Cognitive Neuroscience* (pp. 281–307). Cambridge: MA: MIT Press.

Bates, E. A., Thal, D., & Janowsky, J. S. (1992). Early Language Development and its Neural Correlates. In I. Rapin & S. Segalowitz (Eds.), *Handbook of Neuropsychology* (Vol. 7). Amsterdam: Elsevier.

Bateson, P., & Horn, G. (1994). Imprinting and recognition memory: A neural net model. *Animal Behaviour, 48*, 695–715.

Batki, A., Baron-Cohen, S., Wheelwright, S., Connellan, J., & Ahluwalia, J. (2001). How important are the eyes in neonatal face perception? *Infant Behavior and Development, 23*, 223–229.

Bear, M. F., & Singer, W. (1986). Modulation of visual cortical plasticity by acetycholine and noradrenaline. *Nature, 320*, 172–176.

Becker, L. E., Armstrong, D. L., Chan, F., & Wood, M. M. (1984). Dendritic development on human occipital cortex neurones. *Brain Research, 315*, 117–124.

Bednar, J. A., & Miikkulainen, R. (2003). Learning innate face preferences. *Neural Computation, 15*, 1525–1557.

Bell, M. A. (1992a). *A not B task performance is related to frontal EEG asymmetry regardless of locomotor experience.* Paper presented at the Proceedings of the VIIIth International Conference on Infant Studies, Miami Beach, FL.

Bell, M. A. (1992b). *Electrophysiological correlates of object search performance during infancy.* Paper presented at the Proceedings of the VIIIth International Conference on Infant Studies, Miami Beach, FL.

Bell, M. A., & Fox, N. A. (1992). The relations between frontal brain electrical activity and cognitive development during infancy. *Child Development, 63*(5), 1142–1163.

Bellugi, U., Bihrle, A., Neville, H., Jernigan, T., & Doherty, S. (1992). Language, cognition and brain organization in a neurodevelopmental disorder. In M. Gunnar & C. Nelson (Eds.), *Developmental Behavioral Neuroscience* (pp. 201–232). Hillsdale, NJ: Lawrence Erlbaum.

Bellugi, U., Poizner, H., & Klima, E. S. (1989). Language, modality and the brain. *Trends in the Neurosciences, 12*, 380–388.

Benasich, A. A., & Tallal, P. (2002). Infant discrimination of rapid auditory cues predicts later language impairment. *Behavioral and Brain Research, 136*, 31–49.

Benasich, A. A., Thomas, J. J., Choudhury, N., & Leppaenen, P. H. T. (2002). The importance of rapid auditory processing abilities to early language development: Evidence from converging methodologies. *Developmental Psychobiology, 40*, 278–292.

Benes, F. M. (1994). Development of the corticolimbic system. In G. Dawson & K. W. Fischer (Eds.), *Human Behavior and the Developing Brain* (pp. 176–206). New York: Guilford Press.

Benes, F. M. (2001). The development of prefrontal cortex: The maturation of neurotransmitter systems and their interactions. In C. A. Nelson & M. Luciana (Eds.), *The Handbook of Developmental Cognitive Neuroscience* (pp. 79–92). Cambridge, MA: MIT Press.

Berenbaum, S. A., Moffat, S., Wisniewski, A., & Resnick, S. (2003). Neuroendocrinology: Cognitive effects of sex hormones. In M. de Haan & M. H. Johnson (Eds.), *The Cognitive Neuroscience of Development* (pp. 207–236). Hove: Psychology Press.

Berman, S., & Friedman, D. (1995). The development of selective attention as reflected by event-related brain potentials. *Journal of Experimental Child Psychology, 59*, 1–31.

Bishop, D. V. M. (1983). Linguistic impairment after hemidecortication for infantile hemiplegia? A reappraisal. *Quarterly Journal of Experimental Psychology, 35A*, 199–207.

Bishop, D. V. M. (1997). *Uncommon Understanding: Development and Disorders of Language Comprehension in Children.* Hove: Psychology Press.

Bishop, D. V. M., Canning, E., Elgar, K., Morris, E., Jacobs, P., & Skuse, D. (2000). Distinctive patterns of memory function in subgroups of females with Turnes syndrome: Evidence for imprinted loci on the X-chromosome affecting neurodevelopment. *Neuropsychologica, 38*, 712–721.

Blass, E. (1992). Linking developmental and psychobiological research. *Society for Research in Child Development Newsletter*, January, pp. 3–10.

Bolhuis, J. J. (1991). Mechanisms of avian imprinting: A review. *Biological Reviews, 66*, 303–345.

Bolhuis, J. J., McCabe, B. J., & Horn, G. (1986). Androgens and imprinting: Differential effects of testosterone on filial preferences in the domestic chick. *Behavioral Neuroscience, 100*, 51–56.

Born, P., Rostrup, E., Leth, H., Peitersen, B., & Lou, H. C. (1996). Change of visually induced cortical activation patterns during development. *Lancet, 347*(9000), 543.

Born, P., Rostrup, E., Miranda, M. J., Larsson, H. B. W., & Lou, H. C. (2002). Visual cortex reactivity in sedated children examined with perfusion MRI (FAIR). *Magnetic Resonance Imaging, 20*(2), 199–205.

Bourgeois, J. P. (2001). Synaptogenesis in the necortex of the newborn: The ultimate frontier for individuation? In C. A. Nelson & M. Luciana (Eds.), *The Handbook of Developmental Cognitive Neuroscience* (pp. 23–34). Cambridge, MA: MIT Press.

Braddick, O. J., Atkinson, J., Hood, B., Harkness, W., Jackson, G., & Vargha-Khadem, F. (1992). Possible blindsight in infants lacking one cerebral hemisphere. *Nature, 360*, 461–463.

Brannon, E. M., & Terrace, H. S. (2000). Representation of numerosities 1–9 by rhesus maceques (Macaca mulatta). *Journal of Experimental Psychology – Animal Behaviour Processes, 26*, 31–49.

Brodal, A. (1981). *Neurological Anatomy in Relation to Clinical Medicine*. Oxford: Oxford University Press.

Brodeur, D. A., & Boden, C. (2000). The effects of spatial uncertainty and cue predictability on visual orienting in children. *Cognitive Development, 15*, 367–382.

Brodmann, K. (1909). *Vergleichende Lokalisationslehre der Grosshirnrinde in ihren Prinzipien dargestellt auf Grund des Zellenbaues*. Leipzig: Barth.

Brodmann, K. (1912). Neue Ergebnisse über die vergleichende histologische Lokalisation der Grosshirnrinde mit besonderer Berücksichtigung des Stirnhirns. *Anatomischer Anzeiger (Suppl.), 41*, 157–216.

Bronson, G. W. (1974). The postnatal growth of visual capacity. *Child Development, 45*, 873–890.

Bronson, G. W. (1982). *The scanning patterns of human infants: Implications for visual learning*. Norwood, NJ: Ablex.

Brooksbank, B. W. L., Atkinson, D. J., & Balasz, R. (1981). Biochemical development of the human brain: II. Some parameters of the GABAergic system. *Developmental Neuroscience, 1*, 267–284.

Bruinink, A., Lichtensteinger, W., & Schlumpf, M. (1983). Pre- and postnatal ontogeny and characterization of dopaminergic D2, serotonergic S2, and spirodecan one binding sites in rat forebrain. *Journal of Neurochemistry, 40*, 1227–1237.

Bruyer, R., Laterre, C., Serron, X., Feyereisn, P., Strypstein, E., Pierrand, E., et al. (1983). A case of prosopagnosia with some preserved covert remembrance of familiar faces. *Brain and Cognition, 2*, 157–281.

Bullock, D., Liederman, J., & Todorovic, D. (1987). Reconciling stable asymmetry with recovery of function: An adaptive systems perspective on functional plasticity. *Child Development, 58*, 689–697.

Butterworth, G., & Jarrett, N. (1991). What minds have in common is space: Spatial mechanisms serving joint visual attention in infancy. *British Journal of Developmental Psychology, 9*, 55–72.

Cameron, J. L. (2001). Effects of sex hormones on brain development. In C. A. Nelson & M. Luciana (Eds.), *The Handbook of Developmental Cognitive Neuroscience* (pp. 59–78). Cambridge, MA: MIT Press.

Canfield, R. L., & Haith, M. M. (1991). Young infants' visual expectations for symmetric and asymmetric stimulus sequences. *Developmental Psychology, 27*, 198–208.

Canfield, R. L., Smith, E. G., Brezsnyak, M. P., & Snow, K. L. (1997). Information processing through the first year of life: A longitudinal study using the Visual Expectation Paradigm. *Monographs of the Society for Research in Child Development, 62*(2), 1–145.

Carey, S. (2001). Bridging the gap between cognition and developmental neuroscience: The example of number presentation. In C. A. Nelson & M. Luciana (Eds.), *The Handbook of Developmental Cognitive Neuroscience* (pp. 415–432). Cambridge, MA: MIT Press.

Carey, S., & Spelke, E. (in press). On the very possibility of conceptual change: The integer-list representation of number. In *Conceptual Development – A Reappraisal*. Cambridge, MA: MIT Press.

Carpenter, P. A., Just, M. A., Keller, T., Cherkassky, V., Roth, J. K., & Minshew, N. (2001). Dynamic cortical systems subserving cognition: fMRI studies with typical and atypical individuals. In J. L. McClelland & R. S. Siegler (Eds.), *Mechanisms of Cognitive Development* (pp. 353–386). Mahwah, NJ: Lawrence Erlbaum.

Case, R. (1992). The role of the frontal lobes in the regulation of human development. *Brain and Cognition, 20*, 51–73.

Casey, B. J., Thomas, K. M., & McCandliss, B. (2001). Applications of magnetic resonance imaging to the study of development. In C. A. Nelson & M. Luciana (Eds.), *The Handbook of Developmental Cognitive Neuroscience* (pp. 137–148). Cambridge, MA: MIT Press.

Cesaroni, L., & Garber, M. (1991). Exploring the experience of autism through firsthand accounts. *Journal of Autism and Developmental Disorders, 21*, 303–313.

Changeux, J.-P. (1985). *Neuronal Man: The Biology of Mind*. New York: Pantheon Books.

Changeux, J.-P., Courrege, P., & Danchin, A. (1973). A theory of the epigenisis of neuronal networks by selective stabilization of synapses. *Proceedings of the National Academy of Sciences of the United States of America, 70*, 2974–2978.

Changeux, J.-P., & Dehaene, S. (1989). Neuronal models of cognitive functions. *Cognition, 33*, 63–109.

Chapman, M. (1981). Dimensional separability or flexibility of attention? Age trends in perceiving configural stimuli. *Journal of Experimental Child Psychology, 31*, 332–349.

Chi, J. G., Gooling, E., & Gilles, F. H. (1977). Gyral development of the human brain. *Annals of Neurology, 1*, 86.

Chiang, W.-C., & Wynn, K. (2000). Infants' representation and tracking of multiple objects. *Cognition, 77*, 169–195.

Chugani, D. C. (2000). Autism. In M. Ernst & J. M. Rumsey (Eds.), *Functional Neuroimaging in Child Psychiatry* (pp. 171–188). Cambridge: Cambridge University Press.

Chugani, H. T. (1994). Development of regional brain glucose metabolism in relation to behavior and plasticity. In G. Dawson & K. W. Fischer (Eds.), *Human Behavior and the Developing Brain* (pp. 153–175). New York: Guilford Press.

Chugani, H. T., Hovda, D. A., Villablanca, J. R., Phelps, M. E. & Xu, W. F. (1991). Metabolic maturation of the brain: A study of local cerebral glucose utilization in the developing cat. *Journal of Cerebral Blood Flow and Metabolism, 11*(1), 35–47.

Chugani, H. T., & Phelps, M. E. (1986). Maturational changes in cerebral function in infants determined by [18] FDG positron emission tomography. *Science, 231*, 840–843.

Chugani, H. T., Phelps, M. E., & Mazziotta, J. C. (2002). Positron emission tomography study of human brain functional development. In M. H. Johnson, Y. Munakata, & R. Gilmore (Eds.), *Brain Development and Cognition: A Reader* (2nd ed., pp. 101–116). Oxford: Blackwell.

Cicchetti, D., & Cohen, D. J. (Eds.). (1995). *Developmental Psychopathology, Vol. 1: Theory and Methods*. New York: Wiley.

Clancy, B., Darlington, R. B., & Finlay, B. L. (2000). The course of human events: Predicting the timing of primate neural development. *Developmental Science, 3*(1), 57–66.

Clarke, P. G. H. (1985). Neuronal death in the development of the vertebrate nervous system. *Trends in the Neurosciences, 8*, 345–349.

Clohessy, A. B., Posner, M. I., Rothbart, M. K., & Vecera, S. P. (1991). The development of inhibition of return in early infancy. *Journal of Cognitive Neuroscience, 3*(4), 345–350.

Cohen, L. B., & Marks, K. S. (2002). How infants process addition and subtraction events. *Developmental Science, 5*(2), 186–201.

Condry, K. F., Smith, W. C., & Spelke, E. S. (2001). Development of perceptual organization. In F. Lacerda, C. v. Hofsten, & M. Heimann (Eds.), *Emerging Cognitive Abilities in Early Infancy* (pp. 1–28). Hillsdale, NJ: Erlbaum.

Conel, J. L. (1939–1967). *The Postnatal Development of the Human Cerebral Cortex, Vols. I–VI*. Cambridge, MA: Harvard University Press.

Cooper, N. G. F., & Steindler, D. A. (1986). Lectins demarcate the barrel subfield in the somatosensory cortex of the early postnatal mouse. *Journal of Comparative Neurology, 249*, 157–169.

Courchesne, E. (1991). *The theory of mind deficit in autism: Possible biological bases.* Paper presented at the Society for Research in Child Development, Seattle, WA.

Courchesne, E., Hesselink, J. R., Jernigan, T. L., & Yeung-Courchesne, R. (1987). Abnormal neuroanatomy in a non-retarded person with autism: Unusual findings with magnetic resonance imaging. *Archives of Neurology, 44*, 335–341.

Courchesne, E., Yeung-Courchesne, R., Press, G. A., Hesselink, J. R., & Jernigan, T. L. (1988). Hypoplasia of cerebellar vermal lobules VI and VII in autism. *The New England Journal of Medicine, 318*, 1349–1354.

Cowan, M. W., Fawcett, J. W., O'Leary, D. M., & Stanfield, B. B. (1984). Regressive events in neurogenesis. *Science, 225*, 1258–1265.

Coyle, J. T., & Molliver, M. (1977). Major innervation of newborn rat cortex by monoaminergic neurons. *Science, 196*, 444–447.

Craft, S., White, D. A., Park, T. S., & Figiel, G. (1994). Visual attention in children with perinatal brain injury: Asymmetric effects of bilateral lesions. *Journal of Cognitive Neuroscience, 6*, 165–173.

Crick, F. (1989). Neural Edelmanism. *Trends in the Neurosciences, 12*, 240–248.

Cromer, R. E. (1992). A case study of dissociation between language and cognition. In H. Tager-Flusberg (Ed.), *Constraints on Language Acquisiton: Studies of Atypical Children* (pp. 141–153). Hillsdale, NJ: Lawrence Erlbaum.

Csibra, G. (2003). Teleological and referential understanding of action in infancy. *Philosophical Transactions of the Royal Society of London, Series B, Biological Sciences, 358*, 447–458.

Csibra, G., Davis, G., Spratling, M. W., & Johnson, M. H. (2000). Gamma oscillations and object processing in the infant brain. *Science, 290*, 1582–1585.

Csibra, G., Johnson, M. H., & Tucker, L. A. (1997). Attention and oculomotor control: A high-density ERP study of the gap effect. *Neuropsychologia, 35*(6), 855–865.

Csibra, G., Tucker, L. A., & Johnson, M. H. (1998). Neural correlates of saccade planning in infants: A high-density ERP study. *International Journal of Psychophysiology, 29*, 201–215.

Csibra, G., Tucker, L. A., & Johnson, M. H. (2001). Differential frontal cortex activation before anticipatory and reactive saccades in infants. *Infancy, 2*(2), 159–174.

Damasio, A. R., & Maurer, R. G. (1978). A neurological model for childhood autism. *Archives of Neurology, 35*, 777–786.

Dannemiller, J. L. (2001). Brain–behavior relationships in early visual development. In C. A. Nelson & M. Luciana (Eds.), *The Handbook of Developmental Cognitive Neuroscience* (pp. 221–236). Cambridge, MA: MIT Press.

Davies, D. C., Horn, G., & McCabe, B. J. (1985). Noradrenaline and learning: The effects of noradrenergic neurotoxin DSP4 on imprinting in the domestic chick. *Behavioral Neuroscience, 99*, 652–660.

Dawson, G., Carver, L. J., Meltzoff, A. N., Panagiotides, H., McPartland, J., & Webb, S. J. (2002). Neural correlates of face and object recognition in young children with autism spectrum disorder, developmental delay, and typical development. *Child Development, 73*, 700–717.

Deb, S., & Thompson, B. (1998). Neuroimaging in autism. *British Journal of Psychiatry, 173*, 299–302.

de Boysson-Bardies, B., de Schonen, S., Jusczyck, P., McNeilage, P., & Morton, J. (Eds.). (1993). *Developmental Neurocognition: Speech and Face Processing in the First Year of Life.* Dordrecht: Kluwer.

de Haan, M. (2001). The neuropsychology of face processing during infancy and childhood. In C. A. Nelson & M. Luciana (Eds.), *The Handbook of Developmental Cognitive Neuroscience* (pp. 381–398). Cambridge, MA: MIT Press.

de Haan, M., & Johnson, M. H. (Eds.). (2003). *The Cognitive Neuroscience of Development.* Hove: Psychology Press.

de Haan, M., Johnson, M. H., & Halit, H. (2003). Development of face-sensitive event-related potential components during infancy. *International Journal of Psychophysiology, 51*, 45–58.

de Haan, M., Pascalis, O., & Johnson, M. H. (2002). Specialization of neural mechanisms underlying face recognition in human infants. *Journal of Cognitive Neuroscience, 14*, 199–209.

Dehaene, S. (1997). *The Number Sense: How the Mind Creates Mathematics.* New York: Oxford University Press.

Dehaene, S., Spelke, E., Pinel, P., Stanescu, R., & Tsivkin, S. (1999). Sources of mathematical thinking: Behavioural and brain-imaging evidence. *Science, 284*, 970–974.

Dehaene-Lambertz, G., & Dehaene, S. (1994). Speed and cerebral correlates of syllable discrimination in infants. *Nature, 370*, 292–295.

Dehaene-Lambertz, G., Dehaene, S., & Hertz-Pannier, L. (2002). Functional neuroimaging of speech perception in infants. *Science, 298*(5600), 2013–2015.

Dehay, C., Bullier, J., & Kennedy, H. (1984). Transient projections from the frontoparietal and temporal cortex to areas 17, 18, and 19 in the kitten. *Experimental Brain Research, 57*, 208–212.

Dehay, C., Horsburgh, G., Berland, M., Killackey, H., & Kennedy, H. (1989). Maturation and connectivity of the visual cortex in monkey is altered by prenatal removal of retinal input. *Nature, 337*, 265–267.

Dehay, C., Kennedy, H., & Bullier, J. (1988). Characterization of transient cortical projections from auditory somatosensory and motor cortices to visual areas 17, 18, and 19 in the kitten. *Journal of Comparative Neurology, 272,* 68–89.

Dennis, M., & Whitaker, H. (1976). Language acquisition following hemidecortication: Linguistic superiority of the left over the right hemisphere. *Brain and Language, 3,* 404–433.

de Schonen, S., & Mancini, J. (1995). *About functional brain specialization: the development of face recognition.* (Developmental Cognitive Neuroscience Technical Report No. no.95.1.)

de Schonen, S., & Mathivet, E. (1989). First come, first served: A scenario about the development of hemispheric specialization in face recognition during infancy. *Current Psychology of Cognition, 9*(1), 3–44.

Developmental Science. (2003). In M. H. Johnson (Ed.), *Special Issue: Connectionist and Dynamic Systems Approaches to Development* (Vol. 6, pp. 375–447).

Diamond, A. (1985). Development of the ability to use recall to guide action, as indicated by infants' performance on AB. *Child Development, 56,* 868–883.

Diamond, A. (1991). Neuropsychological insights into the meaning of object concept development. In S. Carey & R. Gelman (Eds.), *The Epigenesis of Mind: Essays on Biology and Cognition* (pp. 67–110). Hillsdale, NJ: Lawrence Erlbaum.

Diamond, A. (2001). A model system for studying the role of dopamine in the prefrontal cortex during early development in humans: Early and continuously treated phenylketonuria. In C. A. Nelson & M. Luciana (Eds.), *The Handbook of Developmental Cognitive Neuroscience* (pp. 433–472). Cambridge, MA: MIT Press.

Diamond, A. (2002). A model system for studying the role of dopamine in prefrontal cortex during early development in humans. In M. H. Johnson, Y. Munakata, & R. Gilmore (Eds.), *Brain Development and Cognition: A Reader* (2nd ed., pp. 441–493). Oxford: Blackwell.

Diamond, A., & Doar, B. (1989). The performance of human infants on a measure of frontal cortex function, the delayed response task. *Developmental Psychobiology, 22*(3), 271–294.

Diamond, A., & Goldman-Rakic, P. S. (1986). Comparative development of human infants and infant rhesus monkeys of cognitive functions that depend on prefrontal cortex. *Neuroscience Abstracts, 12,* 274.

Diamond, A., & Goldman-Rakic, P. S. (1989). Comparison of human infants and infant rhesus monkeys on Piaget's AB task: Evidence for dependence on dorsolateral prefrontal cortex. *Experimental Brain Research, 74,* 24–40.

Diamond, A., Werker, J. F., & Lalonde, C. (1994). Toward understanding commonalities in the development of object search, detour navigation, categorization and speech perception. In G. Dawson & K. W. Fisher (Eds.), *Human Behavior and the Developing Brain* (pp. 380–426). New York: Guilford Press.

Diamond, A., Zola-Morgan, S., & Squire, L. R. (1989). Successful performance by monkeys with lesions of the hippocampal formation on AB and object retrieval, two tasks that mark developmental changes in human infants. *Behavioral Neuroscience, 103*(3), 526–537.

Diebler, M. F., Farkas-Bargeton, E., & Wehrle, R. (1979). Developmental changes of enzymes associated with energy metabolism and synthesis of some neurotransmitters in discrete areas of human neocortex. *Journal of Neurochemistry, 32,* 429–435.

Dobkins, K. R., & Anderson, C. M. (2002). Color-based motion processing is stronger in infants than in adults. *Psychological Science, 13*(1), 75–79.

Driver, J., Davis, G., Ricciardelli, P., Kidd, P., Maxwell, E., & Baron-Cohen, S. (1999). Gaze perception triggers reflexive visuo-spatial orienting. *Visual Cognition, 6,* 509–540.

Drummey, A. B., & Newcombe, N. S. (2002). Developmental changes in source memory. *Developmental Science, 5,* 502–513.

Duffy, C. J., & Rakic, P. (1983). Differentiation of granule cell dendrites in the dentate gyrus of the rhesus monkey: A quantitative Golgi study. *Journal of Comparative Neurology, 214,* 224–237.

Duncan, J. (2001). An adaptive coding model of neural function in prefrontal cortex. *Nature Reviews Neuroscience, 2,* 820–829.

Durston, S., Thomas, K., Yang, Y., Ulug, A., Zimmerman, R., & Casey, B. J. (2002). A neural basis for the development of inhibitory control. *Developmental Science, 5*(4), F9–F16.

Dziurawiec, S. (1996). Blink reflex modification in neonates and its relationship to maturational indices. *Infant Behavior & Development, 19,* 67.

Ebbesson, S. O. (1980). The parcellation theory and its relation to interspecific variability in brain organization, evolutionary and ontogenetic development, and neuronal plasticity. *Cell and Tissue Research, 213,* 179–212.

Ebbesson, S. O. (1984). Evolution and ontogeny of neural circuits. *Behavioral and Brain Sciences, 7,* 321–366.

Ebbesson, S. O. (1988). Ontogenetic parcellation: Dual processes. *Behavioral and Brain Sciences, 11,* 548–549.

Edelman, G. M. (1987). *Neural Darwinism: The Theory of Neuronal Group Selection.* New York: Basic Books.

Elbert, T., Heim, S., & Rockstroh, B. (2001). Neural plasticity and development. In C. A. Nelson & M. Luciana (Eds.), *The Handbook of Developmental Cognitive Neuroscience* (pp. 191–202). Cambridge, MA: MIT Press.

Elman, J., Bates, E., Johnson, M. H., Karmiloff-Smith, A., Parisi, D., & Plunkett, K. (1996). *Rethinking Innateness: A Connectionist Perspective on Development.* Cambridge, MA: MIT Press.

Enns, J. T., & Brodeur, D. A. (1989). A developmental study of covert orienting to peripheral visual cues. *Journal of Experimental Child Psychology, 48,* 171–189.

Enns, J. T., & Girgus, J. S. (1985). Developmental changes in selective and integrative visual attention. *Jounral of Experimental Child Psychology, 48,* 315–334.

Ewert, J.-P. (1987). Neuroethology of releasing mechanisms: Prey-catching in toads. *Behavioral and Brain Sciences, 10*(3), 337–405.

Fabiani, M., & Wee, E. (2001). Age-related changes in working memory function: A review. In C. Nelson & M. Luciana (Eds.), *The Handbook of Developmental Cognitive Neuroscience* (pp. 473–488). Cambridge, MA: MIT Press.

Fan, J., Fossella, J., Sommer, T., Wu, Y., & Posner, M. I. (2003). Mapping the genetic variation of executive attention onto brain activity. *Proceedings of the National Academy of Sciences of the United States of America, 100,* 7406–7411.

Fantz, R. L. (1964). Visual experience in infants: Decreased attention to familiar patterns relative to novel ones. *Science, 46,* 668–670.

Farah, M. J. (1990). *Visual Agnosia.* Cambridge, MA: MIT Press.

Farroni, T., Csibra, G., Simion, F., & Johnson, M. H. (2002). Eye contact detection in humans from birth. *Proceedings of the National Academy of Sciences of the United States of America, 99,* 9602–9605.

Farroni, T., Johnson, M. H., Brockbank, M., & Simion, F. (2000). Infants' use of gaze direction to cue attention: The importance of perceived motion. *Visual Cognition, 7*(6), 705–718.

Feigenson, L., Carey, S., & Spelke, E. S. (2002). Infants' discrimination of number vs. continuous extent. *Cognitive Psychology, 44,* 33–66.

Filipek, P. A. (1999). Neuroimaging in the developmental disorders: The state of the science. *Journal of Child Psychology and Psychiatry, 40*(1), 113–128.

Filipek, P. A., Kennedy, D. N., & Caviness, V. S. J. (1992). Neuroimaging in child neuropsychology. In I. Rapin & S. J. Segalowitz (Eds.), *Handbook of Neuropsychology, Vol. 6: Handbook of Neuropsychology* (pp. 301–309). New York: Elsevier Science.

Finlay, B. L., & Darlington, R. B. (1995). Linked regularities in the development and evolution of mammalian brains. *Science, 268*(5217), 1578–1584.

Fischer, B., & Breitmeyer, B. (1987). Mechanisms of visual attention revealed by saccadic eye movements. *Neuropsychologia, 25,* 73–83.

Fodor, J. A. (1983). *The Modularity of Mind.* Cambridge, MA: MIT Press.

Foldiak, P. (1996). Learning constancies for object perception. In V. Walsh & J. Kulikovski (Eds.), *Perceptual Constancy: Why Things Look As They Do* (pp. 144–172). Cambridge: Cambridge University Press.

Fosse, V. M., Heggelund, P., & Fonnum, F. (1989). Postnatal development of glutamatergic, GABAergic and cholinergic neurotransmitter phenotypes in the visual cortex, lateral geniculate nucleus pulvinar and superior colliculus in cats. *Journal of Neuroscience, 9,* 426–435.

Fox, N. A., & Bell, M. A. (1990). Electrophysiological indices of frontal lobe development. In A. Diamond (Ed.), *The Development and Neural Bases of Higher Cognitive Functions* (Vol. 608, pp. 677–698). New York: New York Academy of Sciences.

Fray, P. J., Robbins, T. W., & Sahakian, B. J. (1996). Neuropsychiatric applications of CANTAB. *International Journal of Geriatric Psychiatry, 11,* 329–336.

Friesen, C. K., & Kingstone, A. (1998). The eyes have it! Reflexive orienting is triggered by nonpredictive gaze. *Psychonomic Bulletin and Review, 5,* 490–495.

Friston, K. J., & Price, C. J. (2001). Dynamic representation and generative models of brain function. *Brain Research Bulletin, 54*(3), 275–285.

Frith, U. (2003). *Autism: Explaining the Enigma* (2nd ed.). Oxford: Blackwell.

Frith, U., & Frith, C. D. (2003). Development and neurophysiology of mentalising. *Philosophical Transactions of the Royal Society of London, Series B, Biological Sciences, 358,* 459–473.

Frost, D. O. (1990). Sensory processing by novel, experimentally induced crossmodal circuits. *Annals of the New York Academy of Sciences, 608,* 92–109.

Fulford, J., Vadeyar, S. H., Dodampahala, S. H., Moore, R. J., Young, P., Baker, P. N., et al. (2003). Fetal brain activity in response to visual stimulus. *Human Brain Mapping, 20,* 239–245.

Funahashi, S., Bruce, C. J., & Goldman-Rakic, P. S. (1989). Mnemonic coding of visual space in the monkey's dorsolateral prefrontal cortex. *Journal of Neurophysiology, 61*(2), 331–349.

Funahashi, S., Bruce, C. J., & Goldman-Rakic, P. S. (1990). Visuospatial coding in primate prefrontal neurons revealed by oculomotor paradigms. *Journal of Neurophysiology, 63*(4), 814–831.

Gadian, D. G., Aicardi, J., Watkins, K. E., Porter, D. A., Mishkin, M., & Vargha-Khadem, F. (2000). Developmental amnesia associated with early hypoxic-ischaemic injury. *Brain, 123,* 499–507.

Galaburda, A. M., & Bellugi, U. (2000). Multi-level Analysis of Cortical Neuroanatomy in Williams Syndrome. *Journals of Cognitive Neuroscience, 12*(Supplement), 74–88.

Galaburda, A. M., & Pandya, D. N. (1983). The intrinsic architectonic and connectional organization of the superior temporal region of the rhesus monkey. *Journal of Comparative Neurology, 221,* 169–184.

Galaburda, A. M., Sherman, G. F., Rosen, G. D., Aboitiz, F., & Geschwind, N. (1985). Development dyslexia: Four consecutive patients with cortical anomalies. *Annals of Neurology, 18,* 222–232.

Galaburda, A. M., Wang, P. P., Bellugi, U., & Rosen, M. (1994). Cytoarchitectonic anomalies in a genetically based disorder: Williams syndrome. *Cognitive Neuroscience and Neuropsychology, Neuroreport 5,* 753–757.

Gallistel, C. R. (1990). *The Organization of Learning.* Cambridge, MA: MIT Press.

Gauthier, I., & Nelson, C. (2001). The development of face expertise. *Current Opinion in Neurobiology, 11,* 219–224.

Gauthier, I., Tarr, M. J., Anderson, A. W., Skudlarski, P., & Gore, J. C. (1999). Activation of the middle fusiform "face area" increases with expertise in recognizing novel objects. *Nature Neuroscience, 2,* 568–573.

Gazzaniga, M. (1983). Right-hemisphere damage following brain bisection. *American Psychologist, 25,* 549.

Geschwind, N., & Behan, P. (1982). Left-handedness: Association with immune disease, migraine and developmental learning disorder. *Proceedings of the National Academy of Sciences of the United States of America, 79,* 5097–5100.

Geschwind, N., & Galaburda, A. (1987). *Cerebral Lateralization: Biological Mechanisms, Associations, and Pathology.* Cambridge, MA: MIT Press.

Geschwind, N., & Levitsky, W. (1968). Human brain: Left–right asymmetries in temporal speech region. *Science, 161*(837), 186–187.

Gibson, J. J. (1979). *The Ecological Approach to Visual Perception.* Boston: Houghton Mifflin.

Giedd, J. N., Blumenthal, J., Jeffries, N. O., Castellanos, F. X., Lui, H. Z., A., Paus, T., et al. (1999). Brain development during childhood and adolescence: A longitudinal MRI study. *Nature Neuroscience, 2,* 861–863.

Gilles, F. H., Shankle, W., & Dooling, E. C. (1983). Myelinated tracts: Growth patterns. In F. H. Gilles, A. Leviton, & E. C. Dooling (Eds.), *The Developing Human Brain: Growth and Epidemiological Neuropathology* (pp.117–183). Boston: John Wright-PSG.

Gilmore, R. O., & Johnson, M. H. (1995). Working memory in infancy: Six-month-olds' performance on two versions of the oculomotor delayed response task. *Journal of Experimental Child Psychology, 59,* 397–418.

Gilmore, R. O., & Johnson, M. H. (1997). Egocentric action in early infancy: Spatial frames of reference for saccades. *Psychological Science, 8,* 224–230.

Goldman-Rakic, P. S. (1971). Functional development of the prefrontal cortex in early life and the problem of neuronal plasticity. *Experimental Neurology, 32,* 366–387.

Goldman-Rakic, P. S. (1987). Development of cortical circuitry and cognitive function. *Child Development, 58,* 601–622.

Goldman-Rakic, P. S. (1994). Introduction. In G. Dawson & K. W. Fischer (Eds.), *Human Behavior and the Developing Brain* (pp. 1–2). New York: Guilford Press.

Goldman-Rakic, P. S., & Brown, R. M. (1982). Postnatal development of monoamine content and synthesis in the cerebral cortex of rhesus monkeys. *Brain Research, 256,* 339–349.

Goodale, M. A., Meenan, J. P., Bulthoff, H. H., Nicolle, D. A., Murphy, K. S., & Racicot, C. I. (1994). Separate neural pathways for the visual analysis of object shape in perception and prehension. *Current Biology, 4,* 604–610.

Gopnik, M. (1990). Feature-blind grammar and dysphasia. *Nature, 344,* 715.

Goren, C. C., Sarty, M., & Wu, P. Y. K. (1975). Visual following and pattern discrimination of face-like stimuli by newborn infants. *Pediatrics, 56,* 544–549.

Gottlieb, G. (1992). *Individual Development and Evolution.* New York: Oxford University Press.

Greenberg, F. (1990). Introduction to special issue on Williams syndrome. *American Journal of Medical Genetics Supplement, 6,* 85–88.

Greenough, W. T., Black, J. E., & Wallace, C. S. (2002). Experience and brain development. In M. H. Johnson, Y. Munakata & R. Gilmore (Eds.), *Brain Development and Cognition: A Reader* (2nd ed., pp. 186–216). Oxford: Blackwell.

Grice, S. J., Halit, H., Farroni, T., Baron-Cohen, S., Bolton, P., & Johnson, M. H. (in press). Neural correlates of eye-gaze detection in young children with autism. *Cortex.*

Grill-Spector, K., Kushnir, T., Edelman, S., Avidan, G., Itzchak, Y., & Malach, R. (1998). Differential processing of objects under various viewing conditions in the human lateral occipital complex. *Neuron, 24*(1), 187–203.

Guitton, H. A., Buchtel, H. A., & Douglas, R. M. (1985). Frontal lobe lesions in man cause difficulties in suppressing reflexive glances and in generating goal-directed saccades. *Experimental Brain Research, 58,* 455–472.

Gunnar, M. (2001). Effects of early deprivation: Findings from orphanage-reared infants and children. In C. A. Nelson & M. Luciana (Eds.), *The Handbook of Developmental Cognitive Neuroscience* (pp. 617–630). Cambridge, MA: MIT Press.

Haith, M. M., & Benson, J. B. (1998). Infant cognition. In D. Kuhn & R. Siegler (Eds.), *Handbook of Child Psychology: Cognition, Perception, and Language* (5th ed., Vol. 2, pp. 199–254). New York: Wiley.

Haith, M. M., Hazan, C., & Goodman, G. S. (1988). Expectation and anticipation of dynamic visual events by 3.5-month-old babies. *Child Development, 59,* 467–479.

Halit, H., Csibra, G., Volein, Á., & Johnson, M. H. (2004). Face-sensitive cortical processing in early infancy. *Journal of Child Psychology and Psychiatry, 45*(7), 1228–1234.

Halit, H., de Haan, M., & Johnson, M. H. (2003). Cortical specialisation for face processing: Face-sensitive event-related potential components in 3- and 12-month-old infants. *NeuroImage, 19,* 1180–1193.

Hallett, P. E. (1978). Primary and secondary saccades to goals defined by instructions. *Vision Research, 18,* 1270–1296.

Happé, F. (1994). *Autism: An Introduction to Psychological Theory.* London: UCL Press.

Happé, F., & Frith, U. (1996). The neuropsychology of autism. *Brain, 119,* 1377–1400.

Hauser, M. D., MacNeilage, P., & Ware, M. (1996). Numerical representations in primates. *Proceedings of the National Academy of Sciences of the United States of America, 93,* 1514–1517.

Haxby, J. V., Gobbini, M. I., Furey, M. L., Ishai, A., Schouten, J. L., & Pietrini, P. (2001). Distributed and overlapping representations of faces and objects in ventral temporal cortex. *Science, 293,* 2425–2430.

Held, R. (1985). Binocular vision: Behavioral and neuronal development. In J. Mehler & R. Fox (Eds.), *Neonate Cognition: Beyond the Blooming, Buzzing Confusion* (pp. 37–44) Hillsdale, NJ: Lawrence Erlbaum.

Held, R. (1993). Development of binocular vision revisited. In M. H. Johnson (Ed.), *Brain Development and Cognition: A Reader.* (pp. 159–166). Oxford: Blackwell.

Hellige, J. B. (1993). *Hemispheric Asymmetry: What's Right and What's Left.* Cambridge, MA: Harvard University Press.

Herbert, M. R., Ziegler, D. A., Makris, N. B., Dakardjiev, A., Hodgson, J., Adrien, K. T., et al. (2003). Larger brain and white matter volumes in children with developmental language disorder. *Developmental Science, 6*(4), F11–F22.

Hillyard, S. A., Mangun, G. R., Woldorff, M. G., & Luck, S. J. (1995). Neural systems mediating selective attention. In M. S. Gazzaniga (Ed.), *The Cognitive Neurosciences* (pp. 665–681). Cambridge, MA: MIT Press.

Hinde, R. A. (1961). The establishment of parent–offspring relations in birds, with some mammalian analogies. In W. H. Thorpe & O. L. Zangwill (Eds.), *Current Problems in Animal Behaviour* (pp. 175–193). Cambridge: Cambridge University Press.

Hinde, R. A. (1974). *Biological Bases of Human Social Behaviour.* New York: McGraw-Hill.

Hinshelwood, J. (1907). Four cases of cogenital word-blindness occurring in the same family. *British Medical Journal, 2*, 1229–1232.

Hobson, R. P. (1993). Understanding persons: The role of affect. In S. Baron-Cohen, H. Tager-Flusberg, & D. J. Cohen (Eds.), *Understanding Other Minds* (pp. 204–227). Oxford: Oxford University Press.

Hood, B. M. (1993). Inhibition of return produced by covert shifts of visual attention in 6-month-old infants. *Infant Behavior and Development, 16*, 245–254.

Hood, B. M. (1995). Shifts of visual attention in the human infant: A neuroscientific approach. In C. Rovee-Collier & L. Lipsitt (Eds.), *Advances in Infancy Research* (Vol. 9, pp. 163–216). Norwood, NJ: Ablex.

Hood, B. M., & Atkinson, J. (1991). *Shifting covert attention in infants.* Paper presented at the Abstracts of the Society for Research in Child Development, Seattle, WA.

Hood, B. M., Willen, J. D., & Driver, J. (1998). Adult's eyes trigger shifts of visual attention in human infants. *Psychological Science, 9*, 131–134.

Hopkins, B., & Rönnqvist, L. (1998). Human handedness: Developmental and evolutionary perspectives. In F. Simmion & G. Butterworth (Eds.), *The development of sensory, motor, and cognitive capacities in early infancy: From perception to cognition* (pp. 191–236). Hove: Psychology Press.

Hopkins, B., Lems, W., Janssen, B., & Butterworth, G. (1987). Postural and motor asymmetries in newlyborns. *Human Neurobiology, 6*, 153–156.

Hopkins, B., Lems, Y. L., van Wulfften Palthe, T., Hoeksma, J. B., Kardound, O., & Butterworth, G. (1990). Development of head position preference during early infancy: A longitudinal study in the daily life situation. *Developmental Psychobiology, 23*, 39–53.

Hopkins, W. G., & Brown, M. C. (1984). *Development of Nerve Cells and Their Connections.* Cambridge: Cambridge University Press.

Horn, G. (1985). *Memory, Imprinting, and the Brain: An Inquiry into Mechanisms.* Oxford: Clarendon Press.

Horn, G., & Johnson, M. H. (1989). Memory systems in the chick: Dissociations and Neuronal Analysis. *Neuropsychologia, 27*(Special Issue: Memory), 1–22.

Horn, G., & McCabe, B. J. (1984). Predispositions and preferences: Effects on imprinting of lesions to the chick brain. *Brain Research, 168*, 361–373.

Huffman, K. J., Molnár, Z., Van Dellen, A., Kahn, D. M., Blakemore, C., & Krubitzer, L. (1999). Formation of cortical fields on a reduced cortical sheet. *The Journal of Neuroscience, 19*(22), 9939–9952.

Huttenlocher, P. R. (1990). Morphometric study of human cerebral cortex development. *Neuropsychologia, 28*, 517–527.

Huttenlocher, P. R. (1994). Synaptogenesis, synapse elimination, and neural plasticity in human cerebral cortex: Threats to optimal development. In C. A. Nelson (Ed.), *The*

Minnesota Symposia on Child Psychology (Vol. 27, pp. 35–54). Hillsdale, NJ: Lawrence Erlbaum.

Huttenlocher, P. R. (2002). Morphometric study of human cerebral cortex development. In M. H. Johnson, Y. Munakata, & R. Gilmore (Eds.), *Brain Development and Cognition: A Reader* (2nd ed., pp. 117–128). Oxford: Blackwell.

Huttenlocher, P. R., & Dabholkar, J. C. (1997). Developmental anatomy of prefrontal cortex. In N. A. Krasnegor, G. R. Lyon, & P. S. Goldman-Rakic (Eds.), *Development of the Prefrontal Cortex: Evolution, Neurobiology, and Behavior* (pp. 69–84). Baltimore, MD: Paul. H. Brookes.

Huttenlocher, P. R., de Courten, C., Garey, L. G., & Van der Loos, H. (1982). Synaptogenesis in human visual cortex – evidence for synapse elimination during normal development. *Neuroscience Letter, 33*, 247–252.

Hykin, J., Moore, R., Duncan, K., Clare, S., Baker, P., Johnson, I., et al. (1999). Fetal brain activity demonstrated by functional magnetic resonance imaging. *The Lancet, 354*, 645–646.

Ishai, A., Ungerleider, L. G., Martin, A., Schouten, J. L., & Haxby, J. V. (1999). Distributed representation of objects in the human ventral visual pathway. *Proceedings of the National Academy of Sciences of the United States of America, 96*(16), 9379–9384.

Jacobs, R. A. (2002). What determines visual cue reliability? *Trends in Cognitive Sciences, 6*, 345–350.

Jacobs, R. A., Jordan, M. I., & Barto, A. G. (1991). Task decomposition through competition in a modular connectionist architecture: The what and where vision tasks. *Cognitive Science, 15*, 219–250.

Jaffe, J., Stern, D. N., & Perry, J. C. (1973). "Conversational" coupling of gaze behavior in prelinguistic human development. *Journal of Psycholinguistic Research, 2*, 321–329.

Janowsky, J. S., & Findlay, B. L. (1986). The outcome of perinatal brain damage: The role of normal neuron loss and axon retraction. *Developmental Medicine and Child Neurology, 28*, 375–389.

Jernigan, T. L., & Bellugi, U. (1994). Neuroanatomical distinctions between Williams and Down syndromes. In S. Broman & J. Grafman (Eds.), *Atypical Cognitive Deficits in Developmental Disorder: Implications for Brain Function* (pp. 57–66). Hillsdale, NJ: Lawrence Erlbaum.

Jernigan, T. L., Press, G. A., & Hesselink, J. R. (1990). Methods for measuring brain morphological features on magnetic resonance images: Validation and normal aging. *Archives of Neurology, 47*, 27–32.

Johnson, M. H. (1990). Cortical maturation and the development of visual attention in early infancy. *Journal of Cognitive Neuroscience, 2*, 81–95.

Johnson, M. H. (1991). Information processing and storage during filial imprinting. In P. G. Hepper (Ed.), *Kin Recognition* (pp. 335–357). Cambridge: Cambridge University Press.

Johnson, M. H. (1994). Visual attention and the control of eye movements in early infancy. In C. Umilta & M. Moscovitch (Eds.), *Attention and Perfomance XV: Conscious and Nonconscious Information Processing* (pp. 291–310). Cambridge, MA: MIT Press.

Johnson, M. H. (1995). The inhibition of automatic saccades in early infancy. *Developmental Psychobiology, 28*, 281–291.

Johnson, M. H. (2001). Functional brain development in humans. *Nature Reviews Neuroscience, 2*, 475–483.

Johnson, M. H. (2002). The development of visual attention: A cognitive neuroscience perspective. In M. H. Johnson, Y. Munakata, & R. Gilmore (Eds.), *Brain Development and Cognition: A Reader* (pp. 134–150). Oxford: Blackwell.

Johnson, M. H., & Bolhuis, J. J. (1991). Imprinting, predispositions and filial preference in the chick. In R. J. Andrew (Ed.), *Neural and Behavioral Plasticity* (pp. 133–156). Oxford: Oxford University Press.

Johnson, M. H., Bolhuis, J. J., & Horn, G. (1985). Interaction between acquired preferences and developing predispositions during imprinting. *Animal Behaviour, 33*, 1000–1006.

Johnson, M. H., de Haan, M., Oliver, A., Smith, W., Hatzakis, H., Tucker, L. A., et al. (2001). Recording and analyzing high-density event-related potentials with infants using the Geodesic Sensor Net. *Developmental Neuropsychology, 19*(3), 295–323.

Johnson, M. H., Dziurawiec, S., Bartrip, J., & Morton, J. (1992). The effects of movement of internal features on infants' preferences for face-like stimuli. *Infant Behavior and Development, 15*, 129–136.

Johnson, M. H., Dziurawiec, S., Ellis, H. D., & Morton, J. (1991). Newborns' preferential tracking of face-like stimuli and its subsequent decline. *Cognition, 40*, 1–19.

Johnson, M. H., Gilmore, R. O., Tucker, L. A., & Minister, S. L. (1995). *Cortical development and saccadic control: Vector summation in young infants* (Developmental Cognitive Neuroscience Technical Report No. 95–3). London: MRC Cognitive Development Unit.

Johnson, M. H., Halit, H., Grice, S., & Karmiloff-Smith, A. (2002). Neuroimaging of typical and atypical development: A perspective from multiple levels of analysis. *Development and Psychopathology, 14*, 521–536.

Johnson, M. H., & Horn, G. (1986). Is a restricted brain region of domestic chicks involved in the recognition of individual conspecifics? *Behavioural Brain Research, 20*, 109–110.

Johnson, M. H., & Horn, G. (1987). The role of a restricted region of the chick forebrain in the recognition of individual conspecifics. *Behavioural Brain Research, 23*, 269–275.

Johnson, M. H., & Horn, G. (1988). The development of filial preferences in the dark-reared chick. *Animal Behaviour, 36*, 675–683.

Johnson, M. H., & Karmiloff-Smith, A. (1992). Can neural selectionism be applied to cognitive development and its disorders? *New Ideas in Psychology, 10*, 35–46.

Johnson, M. H., & Morton, J. (1991). *Biology and Cognitive Development: The Case of Face Recognition*. Oxford: Blackwell.

Johnson, M. H., Munakata, Y., & Gilmore, R. (Eds.). (2002). *Brain Development and Cognition: A Reader* (2nd ed.). Oxford: Blackwell.

Johnson, M. H., Posner, M. I., & Rothbart, M. K. (1991). Components of visual orienting in early infancy: Contingency learning, anticipatory looking, and disengaging. *Journal of Cognitive Neuroscience, 3*(4), 335–344.

Johnson, M. H., & Tucker, L. A. (1996). The development and temporal dynamics of spatial orienting in infants. *Journal of Experimental Child Psychology, 63*, 171–188.

Johnson, M. H., Tucker, L. A., Stiles, J., & Trauner, D. (1998). Visual attention in infants with perinatal brain damage: Evidence of the importance of anterior lesions. *Developmental Science, 1*, 53–58.

Johnson, M. H., & Vecera, S. P. (1996). Cortical differentiation and neurocognitive development: The parcellation conjecture. *Behavioural Processes, 36*, 195–212.

Johnson, M. K., Hashtroudi, S., & Lindsay, D. S. (1993). Source monitoring. *Psychological Bulletin, 114*(1), 3–28.

Johnson, S. P., & Aslin, R. N. (1995). Perception of object unity in 2-month-old infants. *Developmental Psychology, 31*, 739–745.

Johnson, S. P., & Aslin, R. N. (1996). Perception of object unity in young infants: The roles of motion, depth and orientation. *Cognitive Development, 11*, 161–180.

Johnson, S. P., & Nanez, J. (1995). Young infants' perception of object unity in two-dimensional displays. *Infant Behavior & Development, 18*, 133–143.

Johnston, M. V., McKinney, M., & Coyle, J. T. (1979). Evidence for a cholinergic projection to neocortex from neurons in basal forebrain. *Proceedings of the National Academy of Sciences of the United States of America, 76*, 5392–5396.

Johnston, T. D. (1988). Developmental explanation and the ontogeny of birdsong: Nature/nurture redux. *Behavioral and Brain Sciences, 11*, 617–663.

Jonides, J., Smith, E. E., Koeppe, R. A., Awh, E., Minoshima, S., & Mintun, M. A. (1993). Spatial working memory in humans as revealed by PET. *Nature, 363*, 623–625.

Kalsbeek, A., Voorn, P., Buijs, R. M., Pool, C. W., & Uylings, H. B. (1988). Development of the dopaminergic innervation in the prefrontal cortex of rat. *Journal of Comparative Neurology, 269*, 58–72.

Kanwisher, N., McDermott, J., & Chun, M. M. (1997). The fusiform face area: A module in human extrastriate cortex specialized for face perception. *The Journal of Neuroscience, 17*(11), 4302–4311.

Karatekin, C. (2001). Developmental disorders of attention. In C. A. Nelson & M. Luciana (Eds.), *The Handbook of Developmental Cognitive Neuroscience* (pp. 561–576). Cambridge, MA: MIT Press.

Karmiloff-Smith, A. (1985). Language and cognitive processes from a developmental perspective. *Language and Cognitive Processes, 1*, 61–85.

Karmiloff-Smith, A. (1992). *Beyond Modularity: A Developmental Perspective on Cognitive Science*. Cambridge, MA: MIT Press/Bradford Books.

Karmiloff-Smith, A. (2002). Development Itself is the key to understanding developmental disorders. In M. H. Johnson, Y. Munakata, & R. Gilmore (Eds.), *Brain Development and Cognition: A Reader* (pp. 336–374). Oxford: Blackwell.

Karmiloff-Smith, A., Grant, J., Ewing, S., Carette, M. J., Metcalfe, K., Donnai, D., et al. (2003). Using case study comparisons to explore genotype/phenotype correlations in Williams syndrome. *Journal of Medical Genetics, 40*, 136–140.

Karmiloff-Smith, A., & Johnson, M. H. (1994). Thinking on one's feet (review of *A Dynamic Systems Approach to the Development of Cognition and Action*, by Esther Thelan and Linda Smith). *Nature, 372*, 53–54.

Karmiloff-Smith, A., Klima, E., Bellugi, U., Grant, J., & Baron-Cohen, S. (1995). Is there a social module? Language, face processing and theory of mind in individuals with Williams syndrome. *Journal of Cognitive Neuroscience, 7*, 196–208.

Kasamatsu, T., & Pettigrew, J. W. (1976). Depletion of brain catecholamines: Failure of monocular dominance shift after monocular conclusion in kittens. *Science, 194*, 206–209.

Kaufman, J., Csibra, G., & Johnson, M. H. (2003). Representing occluded objects in the human infant brain. *Proceedings of the Royal Society B: Biology Letters, DOI 10.1098/rsbl.2003.0067.*

Kaufman, J., Mareschal, D., & Johnson, M. H. (2003). Graspability and object processing in infants. *Infant Behavior and Development, 26*(4), 516–528.

Kavsek, M. J. (2002). The perception of static subjective contours in infancy. *Child Development, 73*(2), 331–344.

Kawabata, H., Gyoba, J., Inoue, H., & Ohtsubo, H. (1999). Visual completion of partly occluded grating in infants under one month of age. *Vision Research, 39*, 3586–3591.

Kellman, P. J., & Spelke, E. S. (1983). Perception of partly occluded objects in infancy. *Cognitive Psychology, 15*(4), 483–524.

Kennedy, H., & Dehay, C. (1993). The importance of developmental timing in cortical specification. *Perspectives on Developmental Neurobiology, 1*(2), 93–99.

Kerszberg, M., Dehaene, S., & Changeux, J.-P. (1992). Stabilization of complex input-output functions in neural clusters formed by synapse selection. *Neural Networks, 5,* 403–413.

Killackey, H. P. (1990). Neocortical expansion: An attempt toward relating phylogeny and ontongeny. *Journal of Cognitive Neuroscience, 2,* 1–17.

Kingsbury, M. A., & Finlay, B. L. (2001). The cortex in multidimensional space: Where do cortical areas come from? *Developmental Science, 4,* 125–142.

Kinsbourne, M., & Hiscock, M. (1983). The normal and deviant development of functional lateralization of the brain. In M. Haith & J. Campos (Eds.), *Handbook of Child Psychology* (pp. 157–280). New York: Wiley.

Kleiner, K. A. (1993). Specific vs non-specific face recognition device. In B. de Boysson-Bardies, S. de Schonen, P. Jusczyk, P. MacNeilage, & J. Morton (Eds.), *Developmental Neurocognition: Speech and Face Processing in the First Year of Life* (pp. 103–108). Dordrecht: Kluwer.

Kleinke, C. L. (1986). Gaze and eye contact; A research review. *Psychological Bullatin, 100,* 78–100.

Klima, E., & Bellugi, U. (1979). *The Signs of Language.* Cambridge, MA: Harvard University Press.

Kolb, B., & Gibb, R. (2001). Early brain injury, plasticity, and behavior. In C. A. Nelson & M. Luciana (Eds.), *The Handbook of Developmental Cognitive Neuroscience* (pp. 175–190). Cambridge, MA: MIT Press.

Kostovic, I., Petanjek, Z., & Judas, M. (1993). Early areal differentiation of the human cerebral cortex: Entorhinal area. *Hippocampus, 3*(4), 447–458.

Krubitzer, L. A. (1998). What can monotremes tell us about brain evolution? *Philosophical Transactions of the Royal Society of London, Series B, Biological Sciences, 353,* 1127–1146.

Lai, C. S. L., Fisher, S. E., Hurst, J. A., Vargha-Khadem, F., & Monaco, A. P. (2001). A forkhead-domain gene is mutated in a severe speech and language disorder. *Nature, 413,* 519–523.

Langton, S. R. H., & Bruce, V. (1999). Reflexive visual orienting in response to the social attention of others. *Visual Cognition, 6,* 541–567.

Lecuyer, R., Abgueguen, I., & Lemarie, C. (1992). *9- and 5-month-olds do not make the AB error if not required to manipulate objects.* Paper presented at the Proceedings of the VIIIth International Conference on Infant Studies, Miami, FL.

Le Grand, R., Mondloch, C. J., Maurer, D., & Brent, H. P. (2001). Early visual experience and face processing. *Nature, 410,* 890.

Lenneberg, E. (1967). *Biological foundations of language.* New York: Wiley.

Leonard, C. M. (2003). Neural substrate of speech and language development. In M. de Haan & M. H. Johnson (Eds.), *The Cognitive Neuroscience of Development* (pp. 127–155). Hove: Psychology Press.

Lewis, T. L., Maurer, D., & Milewski, A. (1979). The development of nasal detection in young infants. *Investigative Opthalmology and Visual Science Supplement, 271.*

Lewkowicz, D. J. (1991). Development of intersensory functions in human infancy: Auditory/visual interactions. In M. J. Salomon Weiss & P. Zelazo (Eds.), *Newborn Attention: Biological Constraints and the Influence of Experience* (pp. 308–338). Norwood, NJ: Ablex.

Lewkowicz, D. J., & Turkewitz, G. (1981). Intersensory interaction in newborns: Modification of visual preferences following exposure to sound. *Child Development, 52,* 827–832.

Liégeois, F., Baldeweg, T., Connelly, A., Gadian, D. G., Mishkin, M., & Vargha-Khadem, F.
(2003). Language fMRI abnormalities associated with FOXP2 gene mutation. *Nature
Neuroscience, 6*(11), 1230–1237.

Lipsitt, L. P. (1990). Learning processes in the human newborn: Sensitization, habituation,
and classical conditioning. *Annals of the New York Academy of Sciences, 608,* 113–127.

Lipton, J. S., & Spelke, E. (2003). Origins of number sense: Large-number discrimination in
human infants. *Psychological Science, 14*(5), 396–401.

Livingstone, M. S., Rosen, G. D., Drislane, F. W., & Galaburda, A. M. (1991). Physiological and
anatomical evidence for a magnocellular defect in developmental dyslexia. *Proceedings
of the National Academy of Sciences of the United States of America, 88,* 7943–7947.

Lorenz, K. (1965). *Evolution and the Modification of Behavior.* Chicago: University of
Chicago Press.

Luciana, M. (2003). The neural and functional development of human prefrontal cortex. In
M. de Haan & M. H. Johnson (Eds.), *The Cognitive Neuroscience of Development* (pp. 157–
174). Hove, UK: Psychology Press.

Luciana, M., & Nelson, C. A. (1998). The functional emergence of prefrontally-guided
working memory systems in four-to-eight year-old children. *Neuropsychologia, 36*(3),
273–293.

Luciana, M., & Nelson, C. A. (2000). Neurodevelopmental assessment of cognitive function
using the Cambridge Neuropsychological Testing Automated Battery (CANTAB): Validation and future goals. In M. Ernst & J. M. Rumsey (Eds.), *Functional neuroimaging in
child psychiatry* (pp. 379–397). Cambridge: Cambridge Universtiy Press.

Luna, B., Thulborn, K. R., Munoz, D. P., Merriam, E. P., Garver, K. E., Minshew, N. J., et al.
(2001). Maturation of widely distributed brain function subserves cognitive development.
NeuroImage, 13(5), 786–793.

Lutchmaya, S., Baron-Cohen, S., & Raggatt, P. (2002a). Foetal testosterone and eye contact
in 12-month-old human infants. *Infant Behavior and Development, 25*(3), 327–335.

Lutchmaya, S., Baron-Cohen, S., & Raggatt, P. (2002b). Foetal testosterone and vocabulary
size in 18- and 24-month-old infants. *Infant Behavior and Development, 24*(4), 418–424.

McCabe, B. J., Cipolla-Neto, J., Horn, G., & Bateson, P. P. G. (1982). Amnesic effects of
bilateral lesions placed in the hyperstriatum ventrale of the chick after imprinting.
Experimental Brain Research, 48, 13–21.

McManus, I. C., & Bryden, M. P. (1991). Geschwind's theory of cerebral lateralization:
Developing a formal, causal model. *Psychological Bulletin, 110,* 237–253.

McManus, I. C., & Bryden, M. P. (1993). The neurobiology of handedness, language and
cerebral dominance: A model for the molecular genetics of behavior. In M. H. Johnson
(Ed.), *Brain Development and Cognition: A Reader.* Oxford: Blackwell.

MacPhail, E. M. (1982). *Brain and Intelligence in Vertebrates.* Oxford: Clarendon Press.

Maguire, E. A., Vargha-Khadem, F., & Mishkin, M. (2001). The effects of bilateral hippocampal
damage on fMRI regional activations and interactions during memory retrieval. *Brain,
124,* 1156–1170.

Maier, V., & Scheich, H. (1983). Acoustic imprinting leads to differential 2-deoxy-D-
glucose uptake in the chick forebrain. *Proceedings of the National Academy of Sciences
of the United States of America, 80,* 3860–3864.

Mallamaci, A., Muzio, L., Chan, C. H., Parnavelas, J., & Boncinelli, E. (2000). Area identity shifts
in the early cerebral cortex of Emx2 -/- mutant mice. *Nature Neuroscience, 3,* 679–686.

Mancini, J., Casse-Perrot, C., Giusiano, B., Girard, N., Camps, R., Deruelle, C., et al. (1998). Face processing development after a perinatal unilateral brain lesion. *Human Frontiers Science Foundation Developmental Cognitive Neuroscience Technical Report Series* (98.6).

Marcus, G. F., & Fisher, S. E. (2003). FOXP2 in focus: What can genes tell us about speech and language? *Trends in Cognitive Sciences, 7*(6), 257–262.

Marcusson, J. O., Morgan, D. G., Winblad, B., & Finch, C. E. (1984). Serotonin-2 binding sites in human frontal cortex and hippocampus: Selective loss of S-2 A sites with age. *Brain Research, 311*, 51–56.

Mareschal, D., & Johnson, M. H. (2003). The "what" and "where" of infant object representations. *Cognition, 88*, 259–276.

Mareschal, D., Johnson, M. H., Sirois, S., Spratling, M., Thomas, M., & Westermann, G. (in press). *Neuroconstuctivism: How the Brain Constructs Cognition.* Oxford: Oxford University Press.

Mareschal, D., Plunkett, K., & Harris, P. (1999). A computational and neuropsychological account of object-oriented behaviours in infancy. *Developmental Science, 2*, 306–317.

Marin-Padilla, M. (1990). The pyramidal cell and its local-circuit interneurons: A hypothetical unit of the mammalian cerebral cortex. *Journal of Cognitive Neuroscience, 2*, 180–194.

Marler, P. (2002). The instinct to learn. In M. H. Johnson, Y. Munakata, & R. Gilmore (Eds.), *Brain Development and Cognition: A Reader* (2nd ed., pp. 305–330). Oxford: Blackwell.

Matsuzawa, J. (1985). Colour naming and classification in a chimpanzee (Pan troglodytes). *Journal of Human Evolution, 14*, 283–291.

Matsuzawa, T. (1991). Nesting cups and metatools in chimpanzees. *Behavioral and Brain Sciences, 14*, 570–571.

Maurer, D. (1985). Infants' perception of facedness. In T. N. Field & N. Fox (Eds.), *Social Perception in Infants* (pp. 73–100). Hillsdale, NJ: Ablex.

Maurer, D. (1993). Neonatal synesthesia: Implications for the processing of speech and faces. In B. de Boysson-Bardies, S. de Schonen, P. Jusczyk, P. McNeilage, & J. Morton (Eds.), *Developmental Neurocognition: Speech and Face Processing in the First Year of Life* (pp. 109–124). Dordrecht: Kluwer.

Maurer, D., & Barrera, M. (1981). Infants' perception of natural and distorted arrangements of a schematic face. *Child Development, 47*, 523–527.

Maurer, D., & Lewis, T. L. (2001). Visual acuity and spatial contrast sensitivity: Normal development and underlying mechanisms. In C. A. Nelson & M. Luciana (Eds.), *The Handbook of Developmental Cognitive Neuroscience* (pp. 237–252). Cambridge, MA: MIT Press.

Maylor, E. A. (1985). Facilitory and inhibitory components of orienting in visual space. In M. I. Posner & O. M. Marin (Eds.), *Attention and Performance XI* (pp. 189–204). Hillsdale, NJ: Erlbaum.

Meek, J. H. (2002). Basic principles of optical imaging and application to the study of infant development. *Developmental Science, 5*(3), 371–380.

Meek, J. H., Firbank, M., Elwell, C. E., Atkinson, J., Braddick, O., & Wyatt, J. S. (1998). Regional hemodynamic responses to visual stimulation in awake infants. *Paediatric Research, 43*, 840–843.

Meltzoff, A. N., & Borton, R. W. (1979). Intermodal matching by human neonates. *Nature, 282*, 403–404.

Meltzoff, A. N., & Moore, M. K. (1977). Imitation of facial and manual gestures by human neonates. *Science, 198*, 74–78.

Merigan, W., & Maunsell, J. (1993). How parallel are the primate visual pathways? *Annual Review of Neuroscience, 16,* 369–402.

Merzenich, M. M., Wright, B. A., Jaenkins, W., Xerri, C., Byl, N., Miller, S. L., et al. (2002). Cortical plasticity underlying perceptual, motor, and cognitive skill development: Implications for neurorehabilitation. In M. H. Johnson, Y. Munakata, & R. Gilmore (Eds.), *Brain Development and Cognition: A Reader* (2nd ed., pp. 292–304). Oxford: Blackwell.

Michel, G. F. (1981). Right-handedness: A consequence of infant supine head orientation preference? *Science, 212,* 685–687.

Miller, K. D. (1990). Correlation-based models of neural development. In M. A. Gluck & D. E. Rumelhart (Eds.), *Neuroscience and Connectionist Theory* (pp. 267–353). Hillsdale, NJ: Lawrence Erlbaum.

Miller, K. D., Keller, J. B., & Stryker, M. P. (1989). Ocular dominance column development: Analysis and simulation. *Science, 245,* 605–615.

Milner, A. D., & Goodale, M. A. (1995). *The Visual Brain in Action.* Oxford: Oxford University Press.

Milner, B. (1982). Some cognitive effects of frontal-lobe lesions in man. *Philosophical Transactions of the Royal Society of London, Series B, Biological* Sciences, 298, 211–226.

Miyashita-Lin, E. M., Hevner, R., Wassarman, K. M., Martinez, S., & Rubenstein, J. L. (1999). Early neocortial regionalization in the absence of thalamic innervation. *Science, 285,* 906–909.

Molnar, Z., & Blakemore, C. (1991). Lack of regional specificity for connections formed between thalamus and cortex in coculture. *Nature, 351,* 475–477.

Moore, R. J., Vadeyar, S. H., Fulford, J., Tyler, D. J., Gribben, C., Baker, P. N., et al. (2001). Antenatal determination of fetal brain activity in response to an acoustic stimulus using functional magnetic resonance imaging. *Human Brain Mapping, 12,* 94–99.

Morton, J., Mehler, J., & Jusczyk, P. W. (1984). On reducing language to biology. *Cognitive Neuropsychology, 1,* 83–116.

Munakata, Y., McClelland, J. L., Johnson, M. H., & Siegler, R. S. (1994). *Now you see it, now you don't: A gradualistic framework for understanding infants' successes and failures in object permanence tasks* (Technical Report No. PDP.CNS.94.2). Carnegie Mellon University.

Munakata, Y., & Stedron, J. M. (2001). Neural network models of cognitive development. In C. A. Nelson & M. Luciana (Eds.), *The Handbook of Developmental Cognitive Neuroscience* (pp. 159–172). Cambridge, MA: MIT Press.

Murray, E. A. (2000). Memory for objects in nonhuman primates. In M. Gazzaniga (Ed.), *The New Cognitive Neurosciences* (2nd ed., pp. 753–764). Cambridge, MA: MIT Press.

Nelson, C. A. (1994). Neural correlates of recognition memory in the first postnatal year. In G. Dawson & K. Fischer (Eds.), *Human Behavior and the Developing Brain* (pp. 269–313). New York: Guilford Press.

Nelson, C. A. (2002). The ontogeny of human memory: A cognitive neuroscience perspective. In M. H. Johnson, Y. Munakata, & R. Gilmore (Eds.), *Brain Development and Cognition: A Reader* (2nd ed., pp. 151–178). Oxford: Blackwell.

Nelson, C. A. (2003). The development of face recognition reflects an exerience-expectant and activity-dependent process. In O. Pascalis & A. Slater (Eds.), *The Development of Face Processing in Infancy and Early Childhood: Current Perspectives* (pp. 79–98). New York: Nova Science Publishers.

Nelson, C. A., & Collins, P. F. (1992). Neural and behavioural correlates of recognition memory in 4- and 8-month old infants. *Brain and Cognition, 19,* 105–121.

Nelson, C. A., & Luciana, M. (Eds.). (2001). *The Handbook of Developmental Cognitive Neuroscience.* Cambridge, MA: MIT Press.

Nelson, C. A., & Ludemann, P. M. (1989). Past, current and future trends in infant face perception research. *Canadian Journal of Psychology, 43,* 183–198.

Nelson, C. A., & Monk, C. S. (2001). The use of event-related potentials in the study of cognitive development. In C. A. Nelson & M. Luciana (Eds.), *The Handbook of Developmental Cognitive Neuroscience* (pp. 125–136). Cambridge, MA: MIT Press.

Nelson, C. A., Thomas, K., de Haan, M., & Wewerka, S. (1998). Delayed recognition memory in infants and adults as revealed by event-related potentials. *International Journal of Psychophysiology, 29,* 145–165.

Nelson, C. A., & Webb, S. J. (2003). A cognitive neuroscience perspective on early memory development. In M. de Haan & M. H. Johnson (Eds.), *The Cognitive Neuroscience of Development* (pp. 99–126). Hove: Psychology Press.

Neville, H. J. (1991). Whence the specialization of the language hemisphere? In I. G. Mattingly & M. Studdert-Kennedy (Eds.), *Modularity and the Motor Theory of Speech Perception* (pp. 269–294). Hillsdale, NJ: Erlbaum.

Neville, H. J., & Bavelier, D. (2002). Specificity and plasticity in neurocognitive development in humans. In M. H. Johnson, Y. Munakata, & R. Gilmore (Eds.), *Brain Development and Cognition: A Reader* (2nd ed., pp. 251–270). Oxford: Blackwell.

Neville, H. J., Bavelier, D., Corina, D., Rauschecker, J. P., Karni, A., Lalwani, A., et al. (1998). Cerebral organization for language in deaf and hearing subjects: Biological constrains and effects of experience. *Proceedings of the National Academy of Sciences of the United States of America, 95,* 922–929.

Newsome, W. T., Wurtz, R. H., & Komatsu, H. (1988). Relation of cortical areas MT and MST to pursuit eye movements. II. Differentiation of retinal from extraretinal inputs. *Journal of Neurophysiology, 60*(2), 604–620.

Nowakowski, R. S. (1987). Basic concepts of CNS development. *Child Development, 58,* 568–595.

Nowakowski, R. S., & Hayes, N. L. (2002). General principles of CNS development. In M. H. Johnson, Y. Munakata, & R. Gilmore (Eds.), *Brain Development and Cognition: A Reader* (2nd ed., pp. 57–82). Oxford: Blackwell.

O'Leary, D. D. M. (2002). Do cortical areas emerge from a protocortex? In M. H. Johnson, Y. Munakata, & R. O. Gilmore (Eds.), *Brain Development and Cognition: A Reader* (pp. 217–230). Oxford: Blackwell.

O'Leary, D. D. M., & Nakagawa, Y. (2002). Patterning centers, regulatory genes and extrinsic mechanisms controlling arealization of the neocortex. *Current Opinion in Neurobiology, 12,* 14–25.

O'Leary, D. D. M., & Stanfield, B. B. (1985). Occipital cortical neurons with transient pyramidal tract axons extend and maintain collaterals to subcortical but not intracortical targets. *Brain Research, 336,* 326–333.

O'Leary, D. D. M., & Stanfield, B. B. (1989). Selective elimination of axons extended by developing cortical neurons is dependent on regional locale: Experiments utilizing fetal cortical transplants. *Journal of Neuroscience, 9,* 2230–2246.

Oliver, A., Johnson, M. H., Karmiloff-Smith, A., & Pennington, B. (2000). Deviations in the emergence of representations: A neuroconstructivist framework for analysing developmental disorders. *Developmental Science, 3,* 1–23.

O'Reilly, R. C. (1998). Six principles for biologically-based computational models of cortical cognition. *Trends in Cognitive Sciences, 2,* 455–462.

O'Reilly, R., & Johnson, M. H. (2002). Object recognition and sensitive periods: A computational analysis of visual imprinting. In M. H. Johnson, Y. Munakata, & R. Gilmore (Eds.), *Brain Development and Cognition: A Reader* (2nd ed., pp. 392–414). Oxford: Blackwell.

Overman, W. H., & Bachevalier, J. (2001). Inferences about the functional development of neural systems in children via the application of animal tests of cognition. In C. A. Nelson & M. Luciana (Eds.), *The Handbook of Developmental Cognitive Neuroscience* (pp. 109–124). Cambridge, MA: MIT Press.

Overman, W., Bachevalier, J., Turner, M., & Peuster, A. (1992). Object recognition versus object discrimination: Comparison between human infants and infant. *Behavioral Neuroscience, 106*, 15–29.

Owen, A. M. (1997). Tuning into the temporal dynamics of brain activation using functional magnetic resonance imaging (fMRI). *Trends in Cognitive Sciences, 1*(4), 123–125.

Oyama, S. (2000). *The Ontogeny of Information: Developmental Systems and Evolution* (2nd rev. ed.). Durham, NC: Duke University Press.

Ozonoff, S. (2001). Advances in the cognitive neuroscience of autism. In C. A. Nelson & M. Luciana (Eds.), *The Handbook of Developmental Cognitive Neuroscience* (pp. 537–548). Cambridge, MA: MIT Press.

Ozonoff, S., Pennington, B. F., & Rogers, S. J. (1991). Executive function deficits in high-functioning autistic individuals: Relationship to theory of mind. *Journal of Child Psychology and Psychiatry, 32*, 1081–1105.

Pallas, S. L. (2001). Intrinsic and extrinsic factors shaping cortical identity. *Neurosciences, 24*, 417–423.

Pandya, D. N., & Yeterian, E. H. (1990). Architecture and connections of cerebral cortex: Implications for brain evolution and function. In A. B. Scheibel & A. F. Weschsler (Eds.), *Neurobiology of Higher Cognitive Function* (pp. 53–84). New York: Guilford Press.

Parmelee, A. H., & Sigman, M. D. (1983). Perinatal brain development and behavior. In M. M. Haith & J. Campos (Eds.), *Infancy and Biological Development: Volume II of Mussen's Manual of Child Psychology* (pp. 95–155). New York: Wiley.

Pascalis, O., de Haan, M., & Nelson, C. A. (2002). Is face processing species-specific during the first year of life? *Science, 14*, 199–209.

Pascalis, O., de Haan, M., Nelson, C. A., & de Schonen, S. (1998). Long-term recognition memory for faces assessed by visual paired comparison in 3- and 6-month-old infants. *Journal of Experimental Psychology: Learning, Memory and Cognition, 24*, 249–260.

Pascalis, O., de Schonen, S., Morton, J., Deruelle, C., & Fabre-Grenet, M. (1995). Mother's face recognition by neonates: A replication and an extension. *Infant Behavior and Development, 18*, 79–85.

Passarotti, A. M., Paul, B. M., Bussiere, J. R., Buxton, R. B., Wong, E. C., & Stiles, J. (2003). The development of face and location processing: An fMRI study. *Developmental Science, 6*(1), 100–117.

Paulesu, E., Frith, U., Snowling, M., Gallagher, A., Morton, J., Frackowiak, R. S. J., et al. (1996). Is developmental dyslexia a disconnection syndrome? Evidence from PET scanning. *Brain, 119*, 143–157.

Pearson, D. A., & Lane, D. M. (1990). Visual attention movements: A developmental study. *Child Development, 61*, 1779–1795.

Peña, M., Maki, A., Kovacic, D., Dehaene-Lambertz, G., Koizumi, H., Bouquet, F., & Mehler, J. (2003). Sounds and silence: An optical topography study of language recognition at birth. *Proceedings of the National Academy of Sciences of the United States of America, 100*, 11702–11705.

Pennington, B. (2001). Genetic methods. In C. A. Nelson & M. Luciana (Eds.), *The Handbook of Developmental Cognitive Neuroscience* (pp. 149–158). Cambridge, MA: MIT Press.

Pennington, B. (2002). Genes and brain: Individual differences and human universals. In M. H. Johnson, Y. Munakata, & R. Gilmore (Eds.), *Brain Development and Cognition: A Reader* (2nd ed., pp. 494–508). Oxford: Blackwell.

Pennington, B., & Welsh, M. (1995). Neuropsychology and developmental psychopathology. In D. Cicchetti & D. J. Cohen (Ed.), *Developmental Psychopathology, Vol. 1: Theory and Methods* (pp. 254–290). New York: Wiley.

Pepperberg, I. M. (1987). Acquisition of the same–different concept by an African Gray Parrot (Psittacus Erthacus) – learning with respect to categories of colour, shape and material. *Animal Learning and Behaviour, 15*, 423–432.

Petersen, S., Fox, P., Posner, M. I., Mintun, M., & Raichle, M. (1988). Positron emission tomographic studies of the cortical anatomy of single-word prossing. *Nature, 331*, 585–589.

Piaget, J. (1954). *The Construction of Reality in the Child* (M. Cook, Trans.). New York: Basic Books.

Piaget, J. (2002). The epigenetic system and the development of cognitive functions. In M. H. Johnson, Y. Munakata, & R. Gilmore (Eds.), *Brain Development and Cognition: A Reader* (2nd ed., pp. 29–35). Oxford: Blackwell.

Piven, J., Berthier, M. L., Starkstein, S. E., Nehme, E., Pearlson, G., & Folstein, S. (1990). Magnetic resonance imaging evidence for a deficit of cerebral cortical development in autism. *American Journal of Psychiatry, 147*, 734–739.

Posner, M. I. (1988). Structures and functions of selective attention. In T. Boll & B. Bryant (Eds.), *Clinical Neuropsychology and Brain Function: Research, Measurement, and Practice* (pp. 171–202). Washington, DC: American Psychological Association.

Posner, M. I., & Cohen, Y. (1980). Attention and the control of movements. In G. E. Stelmach & J. Roguiro (Eds.), *Tutorials in Motor Behavior* (pp. 243–258). Amsterdam: North Holland.

Posner, M. I., & Cohen, Y. (1984). Components of visual orienting. In H. Bouma & D. G. Bouwhis (Eds.), *Attention and Performance* (pp. 531–556). Hillsdale, NJ: Lawrence Erlbaum.

Posner, M. I., & Petersen, S. E. (1990). The attention system of the human brain. *Annual Review of Neuroscience, 13*, 25–42.

Posner, M. I., Rafal, R. D., Choate, L., & Vaughan, J. (1985). Inhibition of return: Neural basis and function. *Cognitive Neuropsychology, 2*, 211–228.

Posner, M. I., & Rothbart, M. K. (1981). The development of attentional mechanisms. In J. H. Flower (Ed.), *Nebraska Symposium on Motivation* (pp. 1–51). Lincoln, NE: University of Nebraska Press.

Previc, F. H. (1994). Assessing the GBG model. *Brain & Cognition, 26*, 174–180.

Puce, A., Allison, T., Bentin, S., Gore, J. C., & McCarthy, G. (1998). Temporal cortex activation in human viewing eye and mouth movements. *Journal of Neuroscience, 18*, 2188–2199.

Purpura, D. P. (1975). Normal and aberrant neuronal development in the cerebral cortex of human fetus and young infant. In N. A. Buchwald & M. A. B. Brazier (Eds.), *Brain Mechanisms of Mental Retardation* (pp. 141–169). New York: Academic Press.

Purves, D. (1994). *Neural Activity and the Growth of the Brain*. Accademia Nazionale Dei Lincei: Cambridge University Press.

Purves, D., & Lichtman, J. W. (1985). *Principles of Neural Development*. Sunderland, MA: Sinauer Associates.

Pylyshyn, Z. W., & Storm, R. W. (1988). Tracking multiple independent targets: Evidence for a parallel tracking mechanism. *Spatial Vision, 3*, 179–197.

Quartz, S. R., & Sejnowski, T. J. (1997). The neural basis of cognitive development: A constructivist manifesto. *Behavioral and Brain Sciences, 20*, 537–556.

Rabinowicz, T. (1979). The differential maturation of the human cerebral cortex. In F. Falkner & J. M. Tanner (Eds.), *Human Growth, Vol. 3: Neurobiology and Nutrition* (pp. 141–169). New York: Plenum Press.

Rafal, R., Smith, J., Krantz, J., Cohen, A., & Brennan, C. (1990). Extrageniculate vision in hemianopic humans: Saccade inhibition by signals in the blind field. *Science, 250*, 1507–1518.

Ragsdale, C. W., & Grove, E. A. (2001). Patterning in the mammalian cerebral cortex. *Current Opinions in Neurobiology, 11*, 50–58.

Rakic, P. (1988). Specification of cerebral cortical areas. *Science, 241*, 170–176.

Rakic, P. (1995). Corticogenesis in human and nonhuman primates. In M. S. Gazzaniga (Ed.), *The Cognitive Neurosciences* (pp. 127–145). Cambridge, MA: MIT Press.

Rakic, P. (2002). Intrinsic and extrinsic determinants of neocortical parcellation: A radial unit model. In M. H. Johnson, Y. Munakata, & R. Gilmore (Eds.), *Brain Development and Cognition: A Reader* (2nd ed., pp. 57–82). Oxford: Blackwell.

Rakic, P., Bourgeois, J.-P., Eckenhoff, M. F., Zecevic, N., & Goldman-Rakic, P. S. (1986). Concurrent overproduction of synapses in diverse regions of primate cerebral cortex. *Science, 232*, 153–157.

Rauschecker, J. P., & Singer, W. (1981). The effects of early visual experience on the cat's visual cortex and their possible explanation by Hebb synapses. *Journal of Psychology (London), 310*, 215–239.

Ravikumar, B. V., & Sastary, P. I. (1985). Muscarinic cholinergic receptors in human foetal brain: Characterization and ontogeny of [3H] quinuclidinyl benzilate bind sites in frontal cortex. *Journal of Neurochemistry, 44*, 240–246.

Reilly, J., Bates, E., & Marchman, V. (1998). Narrative discourse in children with early focal brain injury. *Brain and Language, 61*, 335–375.

Reiss, A. L., Eliez, J., Schmitt, E., Straus, E., Lai, Z., Jones, W., et al. (2000). Neuratomy of Williams Syndrome: A high resolution MRI study. *Journal of Cognitive Neuroscience, 12*(Supplement), 65–73.

Richards, J. E. (1991). Infant eye movements during peripheral visual stimulus localization as a function of central stimulus attention status. *Psychophysiology, 28*, S4.

Richards, J. E. (2001). Attention in young infants: A developmental psychophysiological perspective. In C. A. Nelson & M. Luciana (Eds.), *The Handbook of Developmental Cognitive Neuroscience* (pp. 321–338). Cambridge, MA: MIT Press.

Richards, J. E. (2003). The development of visual attention and the brain. In M. de Haan & M. H. Johnson (Eds.), *The Cognitive Neuroscience of Development* (pp. 73–93). Hove: Psychology Press.

Rodman, H. R., Skelly, J. P., & Bross, C. G. (1991). Stimulus selectivity and state dependence of activity in inferior temporal cortex in infant monkeys. *Proceedings of the National Academy of Sciences of the United States of America, 88*, 7572–7575.

Roe, A. W., Pallas, S. L., Hahm, J. O., & Sur, M. (1990). A map of visual space induced in primary auditory cortex. *Science, 250*, 818–820.

Rogers, S. J., & Pennington, B. F. (1991). A theoretical approach to deficits in infantile autism. *Development and Psychopathology, 3*, 137–162.

Rovee-Collier, C. K. (1993). The capacity for long-term memory in infancy. *Current Directions in Psychological Science*, *2*(4), 130–135.

Rumsey, J. M., & Ernst, M. (2000). Functional neuroimaging of autistic disorders. *Mental Retardation and Developmental Disabilities Research Reviews*, 6, 171–179.

Rutter, M. (1998). Developmental catch-up, and deficit, following adoption after severe global early privation. *Journal of Child Psychology and Psychiatry and Allies Disciplines*, *39*, 465–476.

Rutter, M., Andersen-Wood, L., Beckett, C., Bredenkamp, D., Castle, J., Groothues, C., et al. (1999). Quasi-autistic patterns following severe early global privation. *Journal of Child Psychology and Psychiatry and Allied Disciplines*, *40*(4), 537–549.

Saffran, J. R., Johnson, E. K., Aslin, R. N., & Newport, E. L. (1999). Statistical learning of tone sequences by adults and infants. *Cognition*, *70*, 27–52.

Sampaio, R. C., & Truwit, C. L. (2001). Myelination in the developing human brain. In C. A. Nelson & M. Luciana (Eds.), *The Handbook of Developmental Cognitive Neuroscience* (pp. 35–45). Cambridge, MA: MIT Press.

Schacter, D., & Moscovitch, M. (1984). Infants' amnesia and dissociable memory systems. In M. Moscovitch (Ed.), *Infant Memory* (pp. 173–216). New York: Plenum Press.

Schatz, J., Craft, S., Koby, M., & DeBaun, M. (2000). A lesion analysis of visual orienting performance in children with cerebral vascular injury. *Developmental Neuropsychology*, *17*, 49–61.

Schatz, J., Craft, S., White, D., Park, T. S., & Figiel, G. (2001). Inhibition of return in children with perinatal brain injury. *Journal of the International Neuropsychological Society*, *7*, 275–284.

Schiller, P. H. (1985). A model for the generation of visually guided saccadic eye movements. In D. Rose & V. G. Dobson (Eds.), *Models of the visual cortex* (pp. 62–70). Chichester: Wiley.

Schlaggar, B. L., & O'Leary, D. D. M. (1991). Potential of visual cortex to develop an array of functional units unique to somatosensory cortex. *Science*, *252*, 1556–1560.

Schlaggar, B. L., & O'Leary, D. D. M. (1993). Patterning of the barrel field in somatosensory cortex with implications for the specification of neocortical areas. *Perspectives on Developmental Neurobiology*, *1*(2), 81–91.

Schliebs, R., Kullman, E., & Bigl, V. (1986). Development of glutamate binding sites in the visual structures of the rat brain: Effect of visual pattern deprivation. *Biomedica Biochemica Acta*, *45*, 495–506.

Schneider, W., Noll, D., & Cohen, J. D. (1993). Functional topographic mapping of the cortical ribbon in human vision with conventional MRI scanners. *Nature*, *365*, 150–153.

Schoppik, D., Gadian, D.G., Connelly, A., Mishkin, M., Varga-Khadem, F., & Saunders, R. C. (2001). Volumetric measurement of the subhippocampal cortices in patients with developmental amnesia. *Society for Neuroscience Abstracts*, *27*, 1400.

Scoville, W. B., & Milner, B. (1957). Loss of recent memory after bilateral hippocampal lesions. *Journal of Neurology, Neurosurgery, and Psychiatry*, *20*, 11–21.

Seress, L. (2001). Morphological changes of the human hippocampal formation from midgestation to early childhood. In C. A. Nelson & M. Luciana (Eds.), *The Handbook of Developmental Cognitive Neuroscience* (pp. 45–58). Cambridge, MA: MIT Press.

Shankle, W. R., Kimball, R. A., Landing, B. H., & Hara, J. (1998). Developmental patterns in the cytoarchitecture of the human cerebral cortex from birth to 6 years examined by correspondence analysis. *Proceedings of the National Academy of Sciences of the United States of America*, *95*, 4023–4028.

Shatz, C. J. (2002). Emergence of order in visual system development. In M. H. Johnson, Y. Munakata, & R. Gilmore (Eds.), *Brain Development and Cognition: A Reader* (2nd ed., pp. 231–244). Oxford: Blackwell.

Shepherd, G. M. (1972). The neuron doctrine: A revision of functional concepts. *Yale Journal of Biology and Medicine, 45,* 584–599.

Shimojo, S., Birch, E., & Held, R. (1983). Development of vernier acuity assessed by preferential looking. *Supplement: Investigative Ophthalmology & Visual Science, 24,* 93.

Shrager, J., & Johnson, M. H. (1995). Waves of growth in the development of cortical function: A computational model. In I. Kovacs & B. Julesz (Eds.), *Maturational Windows and Adult Cortical Plasticity* (pp. 31–44). Reading, MA: Addison-Wesley.

Shultz, T. R. (2003). *Computational Developmental Psychology.* Cambridge, MA: MIT Press.

Siegel, M., Körding, K. P., & König, P. (2000). Integrating top-down and bottom-up sensory processing by somato-dendritic interactions. *Journal of Computational Neuroscience, 8,* 161–173.

Silva, A. J., Paylor, R., Wehner, J. M., & Tonegawa, S. (1992). Impaired spatial learning in alpha-calcium-calmodulin kinase II mutant mice. *Science, 257,* 206–211.

Silva, A. J., Stevens, C. F., Tonegawa, S., & Wang, Y. (1992). Deficient hippocampal long-term potentiation in a-calcium-calmodulin kinase II mutant mice. *Science, 257,* 201–206.

Simion, F., Macchi Cassia, V., Turati, C., & Valenza, E. (2003). Non-specific perceptual biases at the origins of face processing. In O. Pascalis & A. Slater (Eds.), *The Development of Face Processing in Infancy and Early Childhood: Current Perspectives* (pp. 13–26). New York: Nova Science Publishers.

Simion, F., Valenza, E., Umilta, C., & Dalla Barba, B. (1995). Inhibition of return in newborns is temporo-nasal asymmetrical. *Infant Behavior and Development, 18,* 189–194.

Simion, F., Valenza, E., Umilta, C., & Dalla Barba, B. (1998). Preferential orienting to faces in newborns: A temporal-nasal asymmetry. *Journal of Experimental Psychology – Human Perception and Performance, 24*(5), 1399–1405.

Singer, W., & Gray, C. M. (1995). Visual feature integration and the temporal correlation hypothesis. *Annual Review of Neuroscience, 18,* 555–586.

Slater, A. M., Mattock, A., & Brown, E. (1990). Size constancy at birth: Newborn infants' responses to retinal and real size. *Journal of Experimental Child Psychology, 49,* 314–322.

Slater, A. M., Morison, V., & Rose, D. (1982). Perception of shape by the new-born baby. *British Journal of Developmental Psychology, 1,* 135–142.

Spelke, E. S., Breinlinger, K., Macomber, J., & Jacobsen, K. (1992). Origins of knowledge. *Psychological Review, 99*(4), 605–632.

Spiridon, M., & Kanwisher, N. (2002). How distributed is visual category information in human occipital-temporal cortex? An fMRI study. *Neuron, 35*(6), 1157–1165.

Spratling, M., & Johnson, M. H. (2004). A feedback model of visual attention. *Journal of Cognitive Neuroscience, 16,* 219–237.

Spreen, O., Risser, A. T., & Edgell, D. (1995). *Developmental Neuropsychology.* New York: Oxford University Press.

Squire, L. R. (1986). Mechanisms of memory. *Science, 232,* 1612–1619.

Squire, L. R., & Knowlton, B. J. (2000). The medial temporal lobe, the hippocampus, and the memory systems of the brian. In M. Gazzaniga (Ed.), *The New Cognitive Neurosciences* (2nd ed., pp. 765–780). Cambridge, MA: MIT Press.

Starkey, P., & Cooper, R. G. (1980). Perception of number by human infants. *Science, 200,* 1033–1035.

Starkey, P., Spelke, E. S., & Gelman, R. (1983). Detection of intermodal correspondences by human infants. *Science, 222*, 179–181.

Starkey, P., Spelke, E. S., & Gelman, R. (1990). Numerical abstraction by human infants. *Cognition, 36*, 97–127.

Stechler, G., & Latz, E. (1966). Some observations on attention and arousal in the human infant. *Journal of the American Academy of Child and Adolescent Psychiatry, 5*, 517–525.

Stein, B. E. (1984). Multimodal representation in the superior colliculus and optic tectum. In H. Vanegas (Ed.), *Comparative Neurology of the Optic Tectum* (pp. 819–841). New York: Plenum.

Stern, J. A. (1977). *The first relationship: Infant and mother.* Cambridge, MA: Harvard University Press.

Stern, J. A., Bremer, D. A., & McClure, J. (1974). Analysis of eye movements and blinks during reading: Effects of valium. *Psychopharmacologia, 40*, 171–175.

Stiles, J., Bates, E., Thal, D., Trauner, D., & Reilly, J. (2002). Linguistic and spatial cognitive development in children with pre- and perinatal focal brain injury: A ten-year overview from the San Diego Longitudinal Project. In M. H. Johnson, Y. Munakata, & R. Gilmore (Eds.), *Brain Development and Cognition: A Reader* (2nd ed., pp. 272–291). Oxford: Blackwell.

Stiles, J., & Thal, D. (1993). Linguistic and spatial cognitive development following early focal brain injury: Patterns of deficit and recovery. In M. H. Johnson (Ed.), *Brain Development and Cognition: A Reader* (pp. 643–664). Oxford: Blackwell.

Streit, P. (1984). Glutamate and aspartate as transmitter candidates for systems of the cerebral cortex. In E. G. Jones & A. Peters (Eds.), *Cerebral Cortex: Functional Properties of Cortical Cells* (Vol. 2, pp. 119–143). New York: Plenum Press.

Streri, A. (1987). Tactile discrimination of shape and intermodal transfer in 2- to 3-month old infants. *British Journal of Developmental Psychology, 5*, 213–220.

Streri, A., & Pecheux, M.-G. (1986). Vision-to-touch and touch-to-vision transfer of form in 5-month-old infants. *British Journal of Developmental Psychology, 4*, 161–167.

Stryker, M. P., & Harris, W. (1986). Binocular impulse blockade prevents the formation of ocular dominance columns in cat visual cortex. *Journal of Neuroscience, 6*, 2117–2133.

Stuss, D. T. (1992). Biological and psychological development of executive functions. *Brain and Cognition, 20*, 8–23.

Sur, M., Garraghty, P. E., & Roe, A. W. (1988). Experimentally induced visual projections into auditory thalamus and cortex. *Science, 242*, 1437–1441.

Sur, M., Pallas, S. L., & Roe, A. W. (1990). Cross-modal plasticity in cortical development: Differentiation and specification of sensory neocortex. *Trends in Neuroscience, 13*, 227–233.

Symons, L. A., Hains, S. M. J., & Muir, D. W. (1998). Look at me: Five-months-old infants' sensitivity to very small deviations in eye-gaze during social interactions. *Infant Behavior and Development, 21*, 531–536.

Taga, G., Asakawa, K., Maki, A., Konishi, Y., & Koizumi, H. (2003). Brain imaging in awake infants by near-infrared optical topography. *Proceedings of the Natonal Academy of Sciences of the United States of America, 100*, 10722–10727.

Tager-Flusberg, H. (2003). Developmental disorders of genetic origin. In M. de Haan & M. H. Johnson (Eds.), *The Cognitive Neuroscience of Development* (pp. 237–261). Hove: Psychology Press.

Takahashi, K., Nowakowski, R. S., & Caviness, V. S. (2001). Neocortical neuronogenesis: Regulation, control points and a strategy of structural variation. In C. A. Nelson &

M. Luciana (Eds.), *The Handbook of Developmental Cognitive Neuroscience* (pp. 3–22). Cambridge, MA: MIT Press.

Tallal, P., Miller, S. L., Bedi, G., Byma, G., Wang, X., Nagarajan, S. J., et al. (1996). Language comprehension in language-learning impaired children improved with acoustically modified speech. *Science, 271*, 81–84.

Tallal, P., & Stark, R. E. (1980). Speech perception of language-delayed children. In G. H. Yeni-Komshian, J. F. Kavanagh, & C. A. Ferguson (Eds.), *Child phonology: Perception* (Vol. 2, pp. 155–171). New York: Academic Press.

Tallal, P., Stark, R. E., Clayton, K., & Mellits, D. (1980). Developmental dysphasia: Relation between acoustic processing deficits and verbal processing. *Neuropsychologia, 18*(3), 273–284.

Tallon-Baudry, C., Bertrand, O., Peronnet, F., & Pernier, J. (1998). Induced-band activity during the delay of a visual short-term memory task in humans. *Journal of Neuroscience, 18*, 4244–4254.

Tanapat, P., Hastings, N. B., & Gould, E. (2001). Adult neurogenesis in the hippocampal formation. In C. A. Nelson & M. Luciana (Eds.), *The Handbook of Developmental Cognitive Neuroscience* (pp. 93–106). Cambridge, MA: MIT Press.

Teszner, D., Tzavaras, A., Gruner, J., & Hecaen, H. (1972). L'asymetrie droite–gauche du planum temporale: À propos de l'étude anatomique de 100 cerveaux. *Revue Neurologique, 126*, 444.

Thatcher, R. W. (1992). Cyclic cortical reorganization during early childhood. Special Issue: The role of frontal lobe maturation in cognitive and social development. *Brain and Cognition, 20*, 24–50.

Thatcher, R. W., Walker, R. A., & Giudice, S. (1987). Human cerebral hemispheres develop at different rates and ages. *Science, 236*, 1110–1113.

Thelen, E., & Smith, L. B. (1994). *A Dynamic Systems Approach to the Development of Cognition and Action.* Cambridge, MA: MIT Press.

Thomas, M., & Karmiloff-Smith, A. (2003). Modeling language acquisition in atypical phenotypes *1. *Psychological Review, 110*, 647–682.

Thompson, D. W. (1917). *On Growth and Form.* Cambridge: Cambridge University Press.

Tinbergen, N. (1951). *The Study of Instinct.* New York: Oxford University Press.

Tipper, S. P., Bourque, T. A., Anderson, S. H., & Brehaut, J. C. (1989). Mechanisms of attention: A developmental study. *Journal of Experimental Child Psychology, 48*, 353–378.

Tole, S., Goudreau, G., Assimacopoulos, S., & Grove, E. A. (2000). Emx2 Is required for growth of the hippocampus but not for hippocampal field specification. *The Journal of Neuroscience, 20*(7), 2618–2625.

Townsend, J., & Courchesne, E. (1994). Parietal damage and narrow "spotlight" spatial attention. *Journal of Cognitive Neuroscience, 6*(3), 220–232.

Tramo, M. J., Loftus, W. C., Thomas, C. E., Green, R. L., Mott, L. A., & Gazzaniga, M. S. (1994). *The surface area of human cerebral cortex and its gross morphological subdivisions.* Unpublished manuscript, University of California, Davis.

Tranel, D., & Damasio, A. R. (1985). Knowledge without awareness: An autonomic index of facial recognition by prosopagnosics. *Science, 228*, 1453–1454.

Trick, L. M., & Pylyshyn, Z. W. (1994). Why are small and large numbers enumerated differently? A limited-capacity preattentive stage in vision. *Psychological Review, 101*, 80–102.

Tulving, E. (1983). *Elements of Episodic Memory.* Oxford: Clarendon Press.

Turkewitz, G., & Kenny, P. A. (1982). Limitations on input as a basis for neural organization and perceptual development: A preliminary theoretical statement. *Developmental Psychobiology, 15,* 357–368.

Tzourio-Mazoyer, N., de Schonen, S., Crivello, F., Reutter, B., Aujard, Y., & Mazoyer, B. (2002). Neural correlates of woman face processing by 2-month-old infants. *Neuroimage, 15,* 454–461.

Udwin, O., & Yule, W. (1991). A cognitive and behavioural phenotype in Williams syndrome. *Journal of Clinical and Experimental Neuropsychology, 13,* 232–244.

van Essen, D. C., Anderson, C. H., & Felleman, D. J. (1992). Information processing in the primate visual system: An integrated systems perspective. *Science, 255,* 419–423.

Vargha-Khadem, F., Gadian, D., & Mishkin, M. (2001). Dissociations in cognitive memory: The syndrome of developmental amnesia. *Philosophical Transactions of the Royal Society of London, Series B, Biological Sciences, 356,* 1–6.

Vargha-Khadem, F., Gadian, D. G., Watkins, K. E., Connelly, A., van Paesschen, W., & Mishkin, M. (1997). Differential effects of early hippocampal pathology on episodic and semantic memory. *Science, 277,* 376–380.

Vargha-Khadem, F., Issacs, E., & Muter, V. (1994). A review of cognitive outcome after unilateral lesions sustained during childhood. *Child Neurology, 9*(supplement), 2S67–62S73.

Vargha-Khadem, F., Watkins, K., Alcock, K. J., Fletcher, P., & Passingham, R. E. (1995). Praxic and nonverbal cognitive deficits in a large family with a genetically transmitted speech and language disorder. *Proceedings of the Natonal Academy of Sciences of the United States of America, 92,* 930–933.

Vaughan, H. G., & Kurtzberg, D. (1989). Electrophysiological indices of normal and aberrant cortical maturation. In P. Kellaway & J. Noebels (Eds.), *Problems and Concepts of Developmental Neurophysiology* (pp. 263–287). Baltimore, MD: Johns Hopkins University Press.

Vecera, S. P., & Johnson, M. H. (1995). Eye gaze detection and the cortical processing of faces: Evidence from infants and adults. *Visual Cognition, 2,* 101–129.

Ververs, I. A. P., de Vries, J. I. P., van Geijn, H. P., & Hopkins, B. (1994). Prenatal head position from 12–38 weeks. I. Developmental aspects. *Early Human Development, 39,* 83–91.

Volpe, J. J. (1987). *Neurology of the Newborn* (2nd ed.). Philadelphia: Saunders.

von Melchner, L., Pallas, S. L., & Sur, M. (2000). Visual behaviour mediated by retinal projections directed to the auditory pathway. *Nature, 404,* 871–876.

Vuilleumier, P. (2000). Faces call for attention: Evidence from patients with visual extinction. *Neuropsychologia, 38*(5), 693–700.

Vuilleumier, P., Sagiv, N., Hazeltine, E., Poldrack, R. A., Swick, D., Rafal, R. D., et al. (2001). Neural fate of seen and unseen faces in visuospatial neglect: A combined event-related functional MRI and event-related potential study. *Proceedings of the National Academy of Sciences of the United States of America, 98*(6), 3495–3500.

Wada, J. A., Clark, R., & Hamm, A. (1975). Cerebral hemispheric asymmetry in humans. *Archives of Neurology, 32,* 239.

Waddington, C. H. (1975). *The Evolution of an Evolutionist.* Edinburgh: Edinburgh University Press.

Wainwright, A., & Bryson, S. E. (2002). The development of exogenous orienting: Mechanisms of control. *Journal of Experimental Child Psychology, 82,* 141–155.

Wallace, R. B., Kaplan, R., & Werboff, J. (1977). Hippocampus and behavioral maturation. *International Journal of Neuroscience, 7,* 185.

Wattam-Bell, J. (1990). The development of maximum velocity limits for direction discrimination in infancy. *Perception, 19*, 369.

Wattam-Bell, J. (1991). Development of motion-specific cortical responses in infants. *Vision Research, 31*, 287–297.

Webb, S. J., & Nelson, C. A. (2001). Perceptual priming for upright and inverted faces in infants and adults. *Journal of Experimental Child Psychology, 79*(1), 1–22.

Welsh, M. C., Pennington, B. F., Ozonoff, S., Rouse, B., & McCabe, E. R. B. (1990). Neuropsychology of early-treated phenylketonuria: Specific executive function deficits. *Child Development, 61*, 1697–1713.

Werker, J. F., & Polka, L. (1993). Developmental changes in speech perception: New challenges and new directions. *Journal of Phonetics, 21*, 83–101.

Werker, J. F., & Vouloumanos, A. (2001). Speech and language processing in infancy: A neurocognitive approach. In C. A. Nelson & M. Luciana (Eds.), *The Handbook of Developmental Cognitive Neuroscience* (2nd ed., pp. 269–280). Cambridge, MA: MIT Press.

Whalen, J., Gallistel, C. R., & Gelman, R. (1999). Nonverbal counting in humans: The psychophysics of number representation. *Psychological Science, 10*, 130–137.

Wiesel, T. N., & Hubel, D. H. (1965). Comparison of the effects of unilateral and bilateral eye closure on cortical unit responses in kittens. *Journal of Neurophysiology, 28*, 1029–1040.

Wimmer, H., & Perner, J. (1983). Beliefs about beliefs: Representation and constraining function of wrong beliefs in young children's understanding of deception. *Cognition, 13*, 103–128.

Witelson, S. F. (1987). Neurobiological aspects of language in children. *Child Development, 58*(3), 653–688.

Witelson, S. F., & Pallie, W. (1973). Left hemisphere specialization for language in the newborn: Neuroanatomical evidence of asymmetry. *Brain, 94*, 641.

Wolff, P. H., Matsumiya, Y., Abroms, I. F., Van Velzar, C., & Lombroso, C. T. (1974). The effect of white noise on the somatosensory evoked response in sleeping newborn infants. *Electroencephalography and Clinical Neurophysiology, 37*, 269–274.

Wood, F., Flowers, L., Buchsbaum, M., & Tallal, P. (1991). Investigation of abnormal left temporal functioning in dyslexia through rCBF, auditory evoked potentials, and positron emission tomography. *Reading and Writing: An Interdisciplinary Journal, 3*, 379–393.

Wynn, K. (1992). Addition and subtraction by human infants. *Nature, 358*, 749–750.

Wynn, K. (1998). Psychological foundations of number: Numerical competence in human infants. *Trends in Cognitive Sciences, 2*, 296–303.

Xu, F., & Spelke, S. (2000). Large number discrimination in 6-month-old infants. *Cognition, 74*, B1–B11.

Yakovlev, P. I., & Lecours, A. (1967). The myelogenetic cycles of regional maturation of the brain. In A. Minokowski (Ed.), *Regional Development of the Brain in Early Life* (pp. 3–70). Philadelphia: Davis.

Yamada, H., Sadato, N., Konishi, Y., Kimura, K., Tanaka, M., Yonekura, Y., et al. (1997). A rapid brain metabolic change in infants detected by fMRI. *Neuroreport, 8*, 3775–3778.

Yamada, H., Sadato, N., Konishi, M., Muramoto, S., Kimura, K., Tanaka, M., et al. (2000). A milestone for normal development of the infantile brain detected by functional MRI. *Neurology, 55*, 218–223.

Zipser, D., & Andersen, R. A. (1988). A back-propagation programmed network that simulates response properties of a subset of posterior parietal neurons. *Nature, 331*, 679–684.

INDEX

Abroms, I. F. 173
Acerra, F. 96
acetylcholine 50
alexia 139
amnesia
  developmental 128–129
  source of 126
amygdala 48
Andersen, R. A. 70
Anderson, S. H. 75
animal studies 12, 85
  see also types of animals
Annett, M. 159
aphasias 133
architectural constraints 9, 17, 156, 163,
    165
architecture
  innate 33, 160
  neural 103
Aslin, R. N. 126
Asperger's syndrome 113
Atkinson, J. 73, 81
attention 53–77
  ability to disengage 75
  auditory 75
  covert shifts of 72–75, 77
  field of 74
  joint 109–112
  load 128
  mechanisms of engaging 110–112
  obligatory 64

overt shifts of 72–73
speed of shift of 74, 75
sustained 73–74
termination of 74
visual 72–77
attention deficit/hyperactivity disorder
    (ADHD) 76, 185–186, 188
autism 17, 76, 113–115, 162, 174, 179,
    185–186, 188
  brain structures & pathways damaged
    115
  and cognitive deficits 17
axons 25
  geniculate 57

Bachevalier, J. 121–123
Banks, M. S. 54
Baron-Cohen, S. 115
barrel fields 38, 44
Barrera, M. 97
Bartrip, J. 97
Bates, E. 141
Bates, E. A. 133–134
Bednar, J. A. 96–97
Behan, P. 160
behavioral psychology 4
behaviorism 4
Bellugi, U. 116, 135
biased brain models 159–160
biased gene models 159
biased head position 162

biased head/uterus models 159, 162
binocular vision 77
  development of 54–60
  stereoacuity 57
  timing of development 57
biology 9, 10
birds 87, 89
  song learning in passerine 12
Black, J. E. 7
Blakemore, C. 36
blastocyst 20
blindsight 64
Borton, R. W. 174
Bourque, T. A. 75
brain
  atypical 41
  computer models 4
  evolution model 23
  function 181–182
  generalised systems impairment 144
  interaction between regions 166
  metabolism 46, 142
    rates of 29–30
  relations with mind 1–2
  representations 43
  self organising 179
  social nature 92–94, 109
    regions of functionality 93–94
  system models 182
  volume 27, 51, 116, 186
  see also social brain
brain damage 9, 13, 18, 76, 105, 133–134
brain development 19–52, 98, 103–109
  architectural constraints 84
  atypical 183, 185–188
  and cognitive development 9–13
  critical periods 12, 13
  functional 164–167
    consequences of 54
    viewpoints on 15–17, 164–167
  inside out pattern of growth 45,
    50–52
  postnatal 48–49
  time course of 23, 51, 52
brain imaging 9, 10–11
brain structure 8–9, 181–182
  and function 9–13, 17–18
  genes-environment interaction 2–9

hierarchical and parallel systems 13
  origins of 2
Brehaut, J. C. 75
Brennan, C. 64
Broca's area 140, 142
Brodeur, D. A. 75
Bronson, G. W. 61
Bruce, C. J. 67
Bryden, M. P. 159, 160–162
Buchsbaum, M. 140
Bullock, D. 163
Burnod, Y. 96

Cambridge Neuropsychological Testing
    Automated Battery (CANTAB) 151
Canfield, R. L. 65, 69
Carey, S. 89
Carpenter, P. A. 166
Case, R. 153–154
Casey, B. J. 151
cats 23, 30
causal epigenesis see maturational view
cell displacement active/passive 22
cell growth pattern of 36, 45, 50–51
cell migration 22, 34, 113–114
  atypical 114
cell type determination 36
  timing of 36–37
cellular-molecular interactions 36
cerebellum 20, 48, 116–117, 127, 129
  developmental damage 76
  layers of 49
cerebral cortex 20, 23–26
  architecture of 118
  areas for language aquisition 132–137
  areas of 32–40
  atypicalities 139
  bilateral parietal damage 76
  changes in characteristic features 42
  changes in size 40–41
  differential development of 45–48
  equipotential of 44
  extent of folding 160
  face specific regions 104
  functional area bias 141
  functions 17, 18
  growth, inside-out pattern 63
  hemispheric bias 163

hemispheric damage 133–134
internal organisation of 32, 44
laminar structure 26, 32–40, 41
localization 107, 167–168, 176
middle temporal area (MT) 62
no innate representations in 9, 17
perinatal damage 76, 105
postnatal development 103
prespecification 41
regionalisation of 37–38
sensory input 41
somatosensory 39–40
specialization of 26, 141, 167–168, 176
surface area 34
cerebral lateralization 158–163
  see also handedness
Changeux, J. P. 169–170
Chi, J. G. 160
chicks (domestic) 104–105
  beak formation in embryo 6
  imprinting 12, 98–103
  intermediate & medial hyperstriatum
    ventrale (IMHV) 99–103
chinchillas 137
chreods 14, 18, 184
chromosomal structure 185
Chugani, H. T. 185
cingulate gyrus 48
clones 22
cognitive development 179–180
  and brain development 9–13
cognitive neuroscience 9
  developmental approach 6–13
Cohen, A. 64
color processing 172
computer models 4
Conel, J. L. 45
connectionist models 181
  chick, IMHV 99–100
  object processing 83–85
  vision 70
  see also neural networks
connectivity 37
  changes in 166, 181
  models of 168
  patterns of 33, 170
conspecifics 100
constructivism 5–6, 13, 15, 183, 187

cortical functioning onset of 61
cortical matrix models 175–176, 183–184
cortical processing 68
  increased localization of 107
cortical reorganization cycles of 154,
  156–157
cortical visual processing development of
  105
Courchesne, E. 76–77, 113–114
Craft, S. 76
Csibra, G. 68, 152
CT scanning 140

Darlington, R. B. 34–35
Darwin, C. 2
Dawson, G. 115
de Haan, M. 106, 109
de Schonen, S. 96, 105, 109, 163
deaf signers 135–137
deafness 135
  congenital 133
Deb, S. 185
Dehaene, S. 138, 169–170
Dehaene-Lambertz, G. 138, 152
Dehay, C. 172–173
dendrites 25–26, 27, 64, 187
  directed growth 171
  selective loss 171
dendritic trees
  branching orders in 45
  size and complexity 27
dentate gyrus 48
development
  analysis of 6–9
  animal models 12, 85
  atypical 17–18, 168, 174
  cause of change 13–15
  differential timing of 157, 163
  genotype-phenotype 179
  inter sensory functions 173
  mosaic cellular 166
  patterns of
    progressive 27–29
    regressive 27–32
    rise and fall 27–32, 50
  perinatal 18
  postnatal 17, 18, 103, 117, 146
  prenatal 18, 23, 34

development (*cont'd*)
  regulatory 166
  timing of human 17
  timing of social-cognitive deficit 115
  viewpoints on 1–6
  see also brain development; cognitive
    development; lifespan development
developmental cognitive neuroscience
  approach 9–13
  characteristics xiii–xiv, 9–13
  integration of 178–184
  issues in 2–9
developmental disorders 113, 145, 147,
    166, 179–180, 183, 185–188
  emergent approach 183, 187
  as responses to constraints 15, 17–18
  shared atypicalities 186
  static approach 183
  see also autism; dyslexia;
    phenylketonuria; Williams syndrome
Diamond, A. 147, 149–150, 157
differentiation 20, 32–40
disparity-selective cells 57
domain specific bias 112, 117
dopamine 51, 149
dorsolateral prefrontal cortex (DLPC)
    66–67, 152
Down's syndrome 117, 185, 188
Drummey, A. B. 125
dynamic inhibition 163
dynamic processing 172
dynamic systems theory 181–182
dyscalculia 90
dyslexia 17, 90, 139–141, 162, 179, 186,
    188
dyspraxia orofacial 142
Dziurawiec, S. 97

Ebbesson, S. O. 170, 171
echolalia 113
ectoderm 20
Edelman, G. M. 170
electroencephalography (EEG) 10, 149,
    153–156
  gamma frequency 85–87
  visual processing 85
electron microscope 27
embodiment 18

embrainment 18
embryonic disk 20
Emx2 gene 41
endoderm 20
Enns, J. T. 75
entorhinal cortex 38, 48
environment 2–9
  external 182–183
  individual-specific 7
  interaction of genes and 2–9
  species-typical or "primal" 7
epigenesis 14–15, 184
epilepsy 64
Ernst, M. 185
ethology 9–10, 98
event related potential (ERP) 10, 68–69,
    168
  auditory attention 75–76
  cortical plasticity 135
  eye contact processing 112
  face processing 106
  habituation 127–128
  high density 10, 115, 138
  N170 106
  P1 validity effect 75–76
  phonetic discrimination 138
  prefrontal cortex 152
  short latency, visual stimulus 57
  spike potential (SP) 68–69
evolution *see* phylogeny
executive function tasks 115
extrinsic factors 5, 37, 41, 77, 165, 170,
    181
eye blink conditioned 126
eye contact 162
  mutual 109–112
eye gaze 97, 110–112
  bias 118
  processing 115
eye movements 13
  anticipatory 64–65
  rapid reflexive 62
  smooth 64
  step-like 6
  see also oculomotor control; saccades
eyes
  acting on information from 109–112
  perception of others 109–112

spontaneous activity, correlation of 59
see also vision

face bias (Conspec) *see* face preference;
    face recognition newborn preference
face preference 104, 112, 118
    neural basis of 105
    three system theory 109
    two system theory 104–105
face processing 117, 144, 163, 168
    covert recognition 104
    emotion 104
    fusiform face area 17, 93, 104
    increasing specialisation of 106–107
    neural basis of 106–107
face recognition 94–99, 103–109, 115,
    159
    domain specific circuits 96
    expressions 94
    of individuals 94, 103–104
    in infants 12
    newborn preference 95–97
        complex face representations 96–97
        face biasing system (Conspec) 97–98
        sensory hypothesis 95–97
    predispostion to 102–103
    recognising behavior 94
    spatial frequency 97
false belief task 114–115
Fantz, R. L. 94
feedback
    positive 100
    top-down 176
ferrets 41–42
Filipek, P. A. 185–186
Finlay, B. L. 34–35, 38
Flowers, L. 140
folding *see* gyral development
FOXP2 gene 142
Fragile-X 179, 185–186, 188
frames of reference
    extra retinal 70–72
    eye centred 70
    head centred 70
Friston, K. J. 166
Frith, C. D. 93
Frith, U. 93, 115
frontal cortex 146–157

frontal eye fields (FEF) 62, 64, 66–67, 69
    pathway 62, 69
Frost, D. O. 42
Funahashi, S. 67
functional magnetic resonance imaging
    (fMRI) 10–11, 54, 70, 135–137, 166,
    168
    face processing 107
    KE family disorder 142
    lateralization 163
    prefrontal cortex 152
    speech perception 138
    working memory 151
functional specialization 13, 33
fusiform face area (FFA) 17, 93, 104

Galaburda, A. M. 116, 139, 160
gamma-aminobutyric acid (GABA) 31,
    50
Gauthier, I. 16–17
GBG hypothesis 160–161
gene behaviour mapping 180
gene expression
    gradients of 38–39, 41
    patterns of 179
    region specific 165
genes 2–9, 179–180
    and environment 2–9
    immediate early 180
    individual 179
    knockout models 12, 37, 179–180
    mutations of 185
    regulator & switching 4
genetic defects 179
genetic deviation 185
Geschwind, N. 160
Gilles, F. H. 160
Gilmore, R. O. 67, 70, 150
Girgu, J. S. 75
glial cells 22, 25–26
glutamate 31, 49–50
Goldman-Rakic, P. S. 46, 67, 147–148
Goodale, M. A. 80
Goodman, G. S. 65
Gooling, E. 160
Goren, C. C. 95
Gottlieb, G. 6, 14
Greenough, W. T. 7

grey matter 46, 186
Grice, S. J. 115
Guitton, H. A. 66
gyral development 48

habituation 11–12, 127–128
 differential 67
Haith, M. M. 65, 124
handedness 32, 159–160, 162
 genetic models of 159–160
Hazan, C. 65
heart rate marker 73
Hebbian associative learning 171, 176
Held, R. 57, 172
hemispheric specialization 163
Hertz-Pannier, L. 138
Heschl's gyrus see primary auditory cortex
Hinshelwood, J. 139
hippocampus 48–49, 120–124, 125,
 128–129, 175
homeorhesis 14
Hood, B. 73, 110
Hopkins, B. 159, 162
hormone levels 160–161
Horn, G. 101–102
Huttenlocher, P. R. 29–30, 45
hydrocephalus 117
hyperdimensional plaid see gene
 expression gradients of
hypothalamus 20

ideal observer analysis 54
infantile hypercalcemia see Williams
 syndrome
information storage experience-dependent/
 expectant 7
innate
 architecture 9, 33, 160
 characteristics 170
 language module 145
 representations 9, 17, 163
 use of term 6–7, 8
 vs aquired components 6
input process see dendrites
interactive specialization (IS) 16, 18,
 59–60, 77, 164–177, 181, 182
 chick imprinting 103
 eye contact 112

face processing 106, 107
face recognition 97
frontal cortex 147
language 145
modelling of 175–176
object processing 82
prefrontal cortex 152–156
social brain 94, 118
vision 62, 69–70
see also neuroconstructivism
interrupted stimulus method 73–74
intrinsic factors 5, 37, 77, 165, 170,
 181

Janowsky, J. S. 141
Johnson, E. K. 126

Karmiloff-Smith, A. 116–117,
 174–175
Kaufman, J. 85
KE family disorder 142
Kingsbury, M. A. 38
Klima, E. S. 135
knockout strains 12, 37, 179–180
Krantz, J. 64

Lane, D. M. 75
language 12, 32, 89, 116, 117, 118,
 130–145, 159, 163
 biologically special 132, 137, 145
 deficits 133–134
 delay 140–141
 grammar burst 142
 predisposition to learn 132
 related skills 141
 requirement of 90
 segmental processing 138–139
 stabilization of 142
language acquisition 174–175
 cortical areas 132–137
 landmarks in 141
 levels of development 134
 typical & atypical 141–144
lateral geniculate nucleus (LGN) 23,
 36–37, 62
 projection pattern 59
laterality 158–163
Le Grand, R. 117

learning 7, 119–129
  & development, boundary between
    119–129
  associative 171, 176
  language specific 90
  and memory 119–129
  retained 127
  rules 8–9
  sensitive periods for 12
  systems, neural basis of 119–129
left planum temporale 160
left temporal lobe 145
Lenneberg, E. 133
lesions 42, 73, 104, 127, 132
Leslie, A. M. 115
Levitsky, W. 160
Lewkowicz, D. J. 173
lexical decision 142
Liederman, J. 163
lifespan development timing of 45
limbic system 48, 120–124
  postnatal development 123
linguistic repair
  discourse-cohesion repairs 174–175
  thematic participant constraint 175
locus coeruleus 50
Lombroso, C. Y. 173
Luciana, M. 151
luminance contrasts 56

McClelland, J. L. 150
McManus, I. C. 159, 160–162
macrocephaly see brain volume
magnetic resonance imaging (MRI) 27,
    32
  selective language impairment (SLI) 144
  Williams syndrome 186
  see also functional MRI; structural MRI
Mancini, J. 109
manual lateralization see handedness
Marchman, V. 134
Mareschal, D. 83–85, 85
Marin-Padilla, M. 36
marker tasks 11, 62–63, 65–72, 150–151
  memory 120
  weaknesses of 11
Mathivet, E. 163
Matsumiya, Y. 173

maturational view 13, 14, 16, 58, 67, 77,
    165–167, 181, 182
  brain, social nature 94
  chick imprinting 103
  face processing 106, 107, 118
  face recognition 95–97
  frontal cortex 147
  object processing 81
  prefrontal cortex 156
  vision 62
Maurer, D. 97, 117, 174
medial geniculate nucleus (MGN) 23
medulla 20
Meltzoff, A. N. 174
memory 83, 119–129, 122
  cognitive 120
  conditioning 124–125
  declarative 120
  delayed-non match to sample (DNMS)
    122–123, 125
  development of 119–129
  developmental tasks 122
  different types 120–129
  episodic 125, 128–129
  explicit 120, 124–125, 126, 129
  graded development of 129
  habit 120, 129
  implicit 120, 124–125, 126, 127
  increasing specialization 129
  and learning 119–129
  neural basis of 119–129
  pathways 128
  planning 151
  pre-explicit 124–125, 128
  procedural 120, 129
  recognition 81
    coordination of information 124–125
  semantic 125, 128–129
  source (autobiographical) 125–126
  visual recognition 123–124
  working 147–181, 151, 154
    protracted development 125
    updating of 128, 138
Merzenich, M. M. 140–141
mesoderm 20
metabolic disorders 149
mice 12, 36, 41
microcephaly see brain volume

migration 160
Miikkulainen, R. 96–97
Miller, K. D. 59–60
Milner, A. D. 80
mind
    relations with body 2
    relations with brain 1–2
    see also "theory of mind"
Mishkin, M. 121–123
modularity
    emergent 171–175
    see also parcellation
molecular biology 179
molecular genetics 12, 13
Molnar, Z. 36
monkeys 121–123, 148
    macaque 41, 46, 67, 70
    rhesus 45, 50
Morton, J. 6, 95, 97–98, 103–105
mosaic quilt see protomap hypothesis
Moscovitch, M. 120
motion processing 172
motor cortex 21
motor output graded view 150–151
Munakata, Y. 150
myelin 27, 46
myelination 29, 64, 116, 127, 146, 149
myelomeningocele 117

nasal visual field 105
nativism 4
nature-nurture 2–9
    historical perspectives 3–6
near infra-red spectroscopy (NIRS) 11, 139
    optical imaging 56
Nelson, C. A. 120, 124–125, 126,
        127–128, 151
neocortex 22
    layers 26
nervous system 20
neural activity spontaneous 38
neural architecture 144
neural atypicality 139–140
neural growth inside out pattern of 45,
        50–51
neural mechanisms activity dependent 58
neural networks 8–9
    innate architecture 9, 33, 160

neural tube 20
neuroanatomical events timing of 45
neuroanatomy 9
neuroconstructivism 182–184
    see also interactive specialization
neurogenesis postnatal 49
neuroimaging 10–11
neuromodulators 49–51
neurons 22, 25–26
neurotoxin DSP4 101
neurotransmitters 30–31, 49–51, 101,
        180
    excitatory effect 49
    extrinsic 49
    graded differences 156
    inhibitory effect 49–50
    intrinsic 49
neurulation 20
Neville, H. J. 135
Newcombe, N. S. 125
Newport, E. L. 126
noradrenaline see norepinephrine
norepinephrine 50, 101
number processing 87–90, 144
    accuracy of discrimination 88
    analog-magnitude representation 87–90
        Weber's Law 87–89
    counting 89
    exact number representations 87–88
    integer-list representation 89
    numeracy deficits 90
    object-file system 90

object 78–91
    active 87
    anticipation of movement 80
    concept 82–83
    detection of 72
        latencies 72
    hidden 82–85
    occlusion 150
    parsing 78
    partial occlusion 78, 82
    perceptual binding 85
    preferred orientation 80
    relative motion 80
    spatial-temporal trajectory 82–83
    tracking motion 80

transformation-invariant representation
    81
view centred representation 80
object file system 87–90
object permanence 146–157
object processing 78–87, 90, 104
    dorsal & ventral pathway development
        81, 83–85
    neural oscillations 85–87
object recognition 13, 78–80, 90
    view invariant 81, 83
occipital cortex 56
ocular dominance columns 56–58, 172
    atypical 58
    neural network model 59–60
oculomotor control 168
    pathways 61–63
    structures involved 65–72
oculomotor delayed response task 67, 150
O'Leary, D. D. M. 43–44
Oliver, A. 183
ontogeny 2, 14, 171
optical imaging 11, 149
orbitofrontal cortex 93
O'Reilly, R. 99–100
orthographic tasks 140
output process see axons
ovists 3
Oyama, S. 4, 5

parahippocampal gyrus 48
parcellation 171–175, 177
    cross modal transfer 174–175
    cross-modal integration 172–174
    prenatal 175
parietal cortex 66, 70
Pascalis, O. 107
Paulesu, E. 140
Pax6 41
Pearson, D. A. 75
Pecheux, M. G. 174
perception development of 54, 78–91
phenylketonuria (PKU) 114, 149, 179,
    185–186, 188
phonemes 137
phonemic discrimination 140–141
phonological processing 139
phylogeny 2, 171

physical world
    acting on 78–91
    perceiving 78–91
Piaget, J. 5, 5–6, 14, 82, 148, 149, 150
planning 146–157
plasticity 13, 30, 99–100, 103, 141, 145,
    167, 170
    cortical 40–44, 135
    synaptic 180
    trauma induced 163
Poizner, H. 135
Polka, L. 137
positron emission tomography (PET) 10,
    27, 29, 30, 46, 49
    dyslexia 140
    face processing 107
    memory 127
    object processing 81
    prefrontal cortex 152
    vision 67, 70
    visual attention 73
Prader-Willi syndrome 185, 188
predetermined epigenesis see maturational
    view
preferential looking 11
preformationism 3, 5
prefrontal cortex 17, 147–181, 152–156,
    156
    development 125
    perinatal damage 153
prepotent responses 149–150
prepotent tendencies 151
Previc, F. H. 160–162
Price, C. J. 166
primary auditory cortex 29, 160
primary sensory cortex 44
primary visual cortex (V1) 38, 56–58, 62,
    64
    layer-4 36–37, 56–58, 172
primates 50, 87, 89
    development of representations 9
priming 127
probablistic epigenesis 14–15, 18, 163
    see also interactive specialization
proliferative zones 22, 34
prosopagnosia 103–104
protocortex hypothesis 38–39, 52
protomap hypothesis 38–39, 51

pruning 50, 174, 176, 187
    selective 169–171, 177
psychology 4, 9
pulvinar 105–106
Purkinje cells 22
putamen 142
pyramidal cells 25–26

Quartz, S. R. 170–171, 175

radial unit model 34
Rafal, R. 64
Rakic, P. 34, 45
raphe nuclei 50
rats 7, 49–50, 50, 51
Ravens Matrices 144
Reilly, J. 134
representations
    acquisition due to spatial location
        43–44
    and cerebral cortex 9
    changes in 18
    development of 9, 43
    graded development of 181
    innate 9, 17, 163
    prerepresentations 169
response inhibition 151
retinal development 54, 77
Richards, J. E. 73–74, 75
right shift theory 159
rodents 42, 48, 87
    knockout models 37, 179–180
Rodman, H. R. 81–82
Rönnqvist, L. 159, 162
Rosen, M. 116
Rovee-Collier, C. K. 124
Rumsey, J. M. 185

saccades 60–77
    anticipatory 62, 69
    involuntary automatic 66–68
    neural basis of 60
    pursuit tracking 63–64
    reactive 69
Saffran, J. R. 126
Schacter, D. 120
Schatz, J. 76
Schiller, P. H. 62

schizophrenia 113
Schlaggar, B. L. 44
Schneider, W. 32
Sejnowski, T. J. 170–171, 175
selectionism 169
selective loss 169
selective stabilization 169
sensorimotor cells 80
sensorimotor pathways 104
sensory cortex 20–21
sensory input integration with motor
        output 60, 62
serotonin 31, 50
Shultz, T. R. 171
Siegler, R. S. 150
sign language 135–137
Simion, F. 105
skill learning view 16–17, 67–69,
        165–167, 181, 182
    brain, social nature 94
    chick imprinting 103
    face processing 106, 107, 117–118
    face recognition 95–96
    frontal cortex 147
    object processing 82
    prefrontal cortex 152–156
    vision 62
Smith, J. 64
social brain 116–117
    atypical 112–118
    atypicalities, location of 113–114
    emergence of 117–118
social cognition 92–118
social deprivation consequences 117–118
social world
    acting on 92–118
    perceiving 92–118
social-cognitive deficit timing of in
        development 115, see also
        developmental disorders; "theory
        of mind"
spatial cognition 159
species differences 23, 34, 45–46
specific language impairment (SLI) 142–144
speech perception 130–145
speech processing 130–145
    bias 139
    infants 137–139

neural basis of 137–139
    selective decrease of sensitivity 137–138
Spelke, E. 89
spermists 3
spike potential (SP) 68–69
Spratling, M. 176
standardised spatial cognition task *see*
    Ravens Matrices
Stanfield, B. B. 43–44
Steri, A. 174
Stiles, J. 76, 133
stimulus onset asynchrony (SOA) 73
structural magnetic resonance imaging 46,
    140
    autism 76
subcortical control 63–64, 105
    collicular pathway 64
subcortical processing shift to cortical 175
subcortical structures 48–49, 129
    functional reorganisation of 48
    interactions of 48
substantia nigra 51
subventricular zone 22
superior colliculus 62, 68–69, 70, 105,
    175
superior temporal sulcus (STS) 93,
    109–112
Sur, M. 42
synapses 27, 180, 187
    density of 27–30, 142, 146
    loss of contacts 169–171, 177
    pruning 50
    selective loss 171

Taga, G. 56
Tallal, P. 140
Tallon-Baudry, C. 85
temporal visual field 105
testosterone 160–161
Thal, D. 141
thalamus 20, 23, 36
    extent of inputs 40
    visual 36, 38
    visual relay 62
Thatcher, R. W. 153–154, 157, 181
"theory of mind" 93–94, 114–117
Thompson, B. 185
Thompson, D. W. 14

Tipper, S. P. 75
Todorovic, D. 163
tonic inhibition 62, 64
Tower of Hanoi planning task 115
Townsend, J. 76–77
Tramo, M. J. 32
Tucker, L. A. 68
Turkewitz, G. 173
Turner syndrome 188
twin studies 32

Van Velzar, C. 173
Vargha-Khadem, F. 128–129, 142
Vecera, S. P. 171, 172–173, 174–175
ventricular zone 22, 38
vision 53–77
    chromatic 54
    detection of motion 62
    development of 53–60
    habituation 60
    selective loss
        information-processing 57
        processes of 57–58
    spatial 54
    spatial cueing 109–110
    see also binocular vision
visual abilities changes in 54
visual attention 72–77
    inhibition of return 72–73
    regions involved in 73
    shifts of 73
visual cortex 27–29, 30, 53
visual expectations 124–125, 126
visual field
    nasal 105
    temporal 62
visual input 23
visual orienting 53–77, 60–72, 168
    behavioral evidence 65
    model of development 67–68
    reasons for study 60
    relation to brain development 60
visual pathways dorsal & ventral 79–82,
    90
visual processing 135
    location of 61
visual stimulation 32
    responses to 56

vitalists 3
Vuilleumier, P. 105

Waddington, C. H. 14–15, 18, 184
Wallace, C. S. 7
Wang, P. P. 116
Webb, S. J. 120, 128
Weber's Law 87–89
Werker, J. F. 137
Wernicke's area 139–140

white matter 46, 47, 144, 168, 186
Williams syndrome 17, 90, 113,
    116–117, 179–180, 185–186,
    188
Wisconsin card sorting task 115
Witelson, S. F. 163
Wolff, P. H. 173
Wood, F. 140

Zipser, D. 70